ANZACS
AND IRELAND

JEFF KILDEA is a barrister in Sydney with a PhD in
history from the University of N   W─l──
where he has lectured in Irish Stud
of *Tearing the Fabric: Sectarianism in*
and has written articles and given
in early twentieth-centur

ANZACS
AND IRELAND

JEFF KILDEA

CORK **CUP** UNIVERSITY PRESS

Published by
Cork University Press
Youngline Industrial Estate
Pouladuff Road, Togher
Cork, Ireland

First published in Australia by UNSW Press
© Jeff Kildea 2007

British Library Cataloguing in Publication Data

A CIP catalogue record for this book is available from the British Library.

ISBN 978-185918-422-6

The author has asserted his moral rights in this work.

Design Joshua Leui'i
Cover 'Off to the lakes', Corporal James Nelson next to his bride Joy on a jaunting cart in Killarney (Photo courtesy of John Gallagher). During the First World War the red ensign was widely associated with Australian soldiers, while the Irish tricolour, adopted as the national flag in 1922, symbolised Irish nationalism, particularly after the 1916 Easter Rising.
Printer Everbest, China

CONTENTS

FOREWORD

Some years past I met Jeff Kildea at a conference at the University of
New South Wales. I became aware that this personable fellow was a
lawyer amongst historians, as I was a novelist amongst historians. But
he was also a historian amongst historians, and this book proves that.

When Australians speak of Gallipoli, they think of two colonial
peoples, the Australians and New Zealanders, rising from the trenches
to show the Old World their fibre. But Kildea reminds us of a long-
colonised people, the Irish, who were also there to prove something. If
they were nationalists, they hoped to prove that their loyalty deserved
home rule. If they were loyalists, they wanted to prove that they were
Britons par excellence, and must not be sold out to the Sinn Féiners.
The same Turkish artillery that cut its awful swathes in the Australians
and New Zealanders, also indiscriminately and without prejudice
ended Irish lives, Green and Orange, in regiments that fought beside
the Anzacs on that terrible peninsula.

This is where Jeff Kildea begins his tale, in the Dardanelles where
Australians, many of them of Celtic derivation, were brothers-in-arms
to the Irish. But that was but the beginning of the association. When

the Australian survivors of Gallipoli, including Private Chapman who had landed in the first wave, reached Britain after the evacuation of Gallipoli, many were inevitably drawn to Ireland as springtime came to Europe. But 1916 was a time of great nationalist and republican unrest, and the part of the Anzacs in all that has never been systematically researched or related.

On the eve of the first anniversary of Gallipoli, the Irish rebels rose in Dublin. Expert Anzac snipers, recalled to arms from their leave, directed accurate fire on rebels from the roof of Trinity College. Despite antipodean rebel traditions, they were not tempted to side with the rebels, Pearse, de Valera and Connolly, any more than were most Dubliners at that time – it would be later, through the folly of British reprisals and the poetry of Yeats, that the Easter Rising would take on its 'terrible beauty'. The above-mentioned Private Chapman fought in the south-west sector of the city and nonchalantly accepted rifle and ammunition and 'nearly got hit several times'. Others were also caught up in one of the Empire's last Irish gasps. But the defeat of the rebels was inevitable and it was Australian arms, amongst others, who guarded the rebels at Arbour Hill. Eyewitness accounts of the brutal behaviour of some Crown troops were published in Australian newspapers, and the severity with which the British treated many of the rebels would shock much Australian opinion, and have an influence on the peace movement and the two failed conscription referenda Billy Hughes introduced in 1916 and 1917.

And what was the reaction of the almost seven thousand Irish-born who served in the Australian forces, let alone that of the far more numerous first-generation Australians whose parents were Irish? Did any Australian soldiers, of whatever background, toy with the idea of deserting, or even actually desert in Ireland? And did Australians on leave experience the increasing hostility of the Irish, as lines between nationalists and the rest hardened. And in the end, when the war was over, how did Australia remember the dead? And how did Ireland, where the question was: which dead?

One last question: are you fascinated yet? By the connections, the ironies, the unpredictabilities of these issues? The most useful history expands the equation we believe we already understand. We think we know about Ireland and Australia, and our own uneasy brands of republicanism and loyalism. But with its rich research, this book helps break that accepted mould. In doing so, it excites and stimulates our imagination, and may even change the way historians deal with a given question in the future.

Tom Keneally

ACKNOWLEDGMENTS

I am grateful to the many people who have assisted me in the research and writing of this book, including Seamus Breslin, Philip Lecane, Jill Mabbott, Paul Maguire, Paudie McGrath, Oliver Murphy, Joe O'Loughlin, Anne Stevens, Robert Thompson and Peter Threlfall, who have given me the benefit of their research; Christine Armstrong, Yvonne Bell, John Gallagher, Jane Keneally, Barrie Kinchington, Christy Mannix, Bill McHugh, Margaret McKenna, Phill McKenna, Frank Quinane and Terry Quinane, who have provided information on their relatives; Geoff Barr, Steven Becker, Paul Brennan, John Connor, Peter Dennis, Bill Gammage, Keith Jeffery, Michael Kildea, Jenny Macleod, Michael McKernan, Cheryl Mongan, Peter Moore, the late Patrick O'Farrell and Richard Reid, who have read chapters or provided leads; Gordon Bickley and Rosemary Kildea, who have assisted with the research; Geoff Graham, who helped me find the graves; and the staff at the Australian War Memorial, the National Archives of Australia, the National Archives (UK), the National Archives of Ireland, the National Library of Ireland, the Irish Military Archives, Trinity College Manuscripts Department and the Mitchell

Library, whose cheery and efficient assistance made the research task a pleasant experience. Thanks also to Phillipa McGuinness of UNSW Press for believing in the project, to Thomas Keneally for generously agreeing to write the foreword and to Scott Forbes for his thorough and sympathetic editing of the manuscript. Research for chapter 2 was carried out with assistance from the Army History Research Grants Scheme. I would especially like to thank my wife Robyn and our children, who have put up with me for the many years during which I have wrestled with this project.

ABBREVIATIONS
AND EXPLANATIONS

AANS	Australian Army Nursing Service
ADB	Australian Dictionary of Biography
ADFA	Australian Defence Force Academy
AIF	Australian Imperial Force
AFC	Australian Flying Corps
AWL	Absent Without Leave
AWM	Australian War Memorial
CWGC	Commonwealth War Graves Commission
NAA	National Archives of Australia
OTC	Officer Training Corps
PRO	Public Record Office (UK)
RAN	Royal Australian Navy
RN	Royal Navy
RNR	Royal Navy Reserve
RSSILA	Returned Sailors' and Soldiers' Imperial League of Australia
TCDLMD	Trinity College Dublin Library Manuscripts Department
TNA	The National Archives (UK)

The word 'Anzac' derives from the acronym for Australia and New Zealand Army Corps, the name of the formation to which the

Australian and New Zealand soldiers were assigned prior to the landing at Gallipoli in April 1915. When referring to persons, it originally applied only to those who served at Gallipoli, but in popular use it has been extended to all who served in the Australian and New Zealand forces during the First World War. In this book 'Anzac' is preferred to 'ANZAC' in recognition of the fact that the acronym has passed into the language as a noun. However, it is acknowledged that for some authors and readers this is a contentious issue.

Australia's currency during the First World War was made up of pounds (£), shillings (s.) and pence (d.). There were 12 pence to a shilling and 20 shillings to a pound. On 14 February 1966, Australia adopted decimal currency, converting each pound to two dollars.

Unless otherwise indicated, soldiers' personal details are taken from their service records in the National Archives of Australia in Canberra (Series: B2455, First Australian Imperial Force Personnel Dossiers, 1914-1920).

All internet references were accessed as at 10 October 2006, unless otherwise stated.

A note on Australian and British military organisation

The following should be used as a general guide only as it is a very approximate description of a complex reality that varied greatly during the First World War, depending on time, place and circumstance.

The main fighting formation during the war was the infantry division. Two or more divisions constituted a corps and two or more corps constituted an army. A division was commanded by a major general and included a headquarters (with a staff of about eighty) and three infantry brigades, each made up of four infantry battalions. The battalion, the chief infantry unit, was commanded by a lieutenant colonel and consisted of a headquarters and four companies, each made up of four platoons of four sections. A battalion's full strength was about 1000, though in the field its normal fighting strength was about 550, after taking into account casualties not yet replaced, the sick and those attending courses or on leave.

An infantry division also included a pioneer battalion (which performed construction tasks in the forward area not requiring the special equipment of engineers), a machine-gun battalion and supporting arms (artillery and engineers) and services (transport, medical and veterinary). At full strength, a division comprised about 18 000 officers and other ranks, though in the field its normal fighting strength was about 10 000.

In the Australian Light Horse, the equivalent of a battalion was a regiment, consisting of three squadrons, each made up of four troops. A light horse regiment's full strength was about 550, though in the field its normal fighting strength was about 340 (or 250 when dismounted, as it was at Gallipoli).

When war broke out, the Australian government did not expand the existing military force but built from the ground up a new army, the Australian Imperial Force (AIF). Each of the six military districts, roughly coextensive with the six states, raised battalions that were organised into brigades as recruiting progressed. In all, five infantry divisions, comprising sixty infantry battalions, were raised. The 1st Division comprised the 1st Brigade (four battalions from New South Wales), the 2nd Brigade (four battalions from Victoria) and the 3rd Brigade (one battalion from each of Queensland, South Australia and Western Australia and a composite fourth battalion that included Tasmanians). A similar pattern followed with the 2nd and 3rd Divisions. In early 1916, the AIF was reorganised and expanded with some existing brigades being split in half to create new brigades whose establishment strength was made up by the addition of new recruits. In this way two new divisions, the 4th and 5th, were formed with a core of experienced soldiers. A sixth division was formed in February 1917 but dissolved in September for lack of recruits. In addition, the AIF included supporting arms and services as well as 15 light horse regiments organised into five brigades.

The AIF was raised and reinforced throughout the war as a voluntary army. Faced with a Senate where a majority of senators were opposed to compulsion, the government in October 1916 held a plebiscite to seek the people's approval of conscription for overseas service in order to apply moral force to persuade the Senate to pass the necessary legislation. After a divisive campaign, the proposal was narrowly defeated. A further plebiscite in December 1917 was also defeated, this time by a larger margin.

The United Kingdom (which during the war included the whole of Ireland) used its existing regimental system to raise what became known as the New Army. Under that system, a regiment was not a combat unit but an administrative organisation that recruited in the local area in which it was based. In Ireland, where there were eight infantry regiments, the Royal Munster Fusiliers, for instance, was based at Tralee, County Kerry, and drew recruits from the south-west of Ireland. In peace time, a regiment comprised two battalions, one of which served overseas in one of Britain's colonies while the other battalion remained at home. Every few years, the battalions would alternate. On the outbreak of war, the regiments were expanded by the raising of additional battalions for active service. However, a regiment's battalions were not grouped into brigades and divisions but were separately assigned, with the result that each division comprised battalions from a number of regiments. Some divisions were raised in a particular region – Ireland, Scotland or the north, east or west of England. In such cases, a division's battalions would be drawn from regiments situated in that region. For example, in 1915, all but one of the 10th (Irish) Division's battalions were drawn from Irish regiments, an English battalion being added to make up the numbers. In other divisions, particularly regular army divisions, battalions were drawn from regiments situated throughout the United Kingdom. For example, the 29th Division included a battalion from each of three Irish regiments – the Royal Dublin Fusiliers, the Royal Munster Fusiliers and the Royal Inniskilling Fusiliers – as well as battalions from English, Scottish and Welsh regiments.

Initially the New Army was raised by voluntary enlistment. However, in March 1916 compulsory military service was introduced in Great Britain. Ireland was excluded in deference to the Irish National Party's opposition to compulsion, based partly on principle but also on the pragmatic concern that it would split the country. In April 1918, following a major German offensive in March, which threatened the Allies with defeat, the government extended conscription to Ireland, but the legislation was never implemented because widespread opposition made it impracticable.

INTRODUCTION

In the small graveyard of Grangegorman, off Blackhorse Avenue near Dublin's Phoenix Park, a cluster of headstones marks the last resting place of seven Australian soldiers of the First World War. Unlike their counterparts in the hundreds of graveyards scattered across Gallipoli, France and Belgium, these men are the forgotten soldiers of a war that has continued to fascinate Australians despite the passing of the years.

For a nation that claims to be the most Irish country in the world outside of Ireland, with more than a quarter of the population professing Irish descent[1], it is surprising that so little is known in Australia of the association between Australian soldiers and Ireland during the First World War. That association began at Gallipoli when Australians and Irishmen fought and died alongside each other in battle. It continued in France and Belgium, where Irishmen of the 16th (Irish) Division and the 36th (Ulster) Division joined with the Australian 3rd and 4th Divisions in June 1917 to defeat the Germans at Messines, and in Palestine, where the Australian Light

Horse served alongside the 10th (Irish) Division against the Turks. But it was mostly in Ireland itself that Australian soldiers forged their relationship with the Irish people.

Apart from the seven soldiers at Grangegorman, a further eighteen Australian servicemen of the First World War are buried in graveyards around Ireland – a total of twenty in the Republic and five in Northern Ireland. Another four Australian servicemen drowned in the seas around Ireland as a result of naval action, their remains never being recovered.[2] Furthermore, many Australian servicemen who died in the war are commemorated on memorials erected in towns throughout Ireland. Mostly, they were local lads who had emigrated to Australia and were killed while serving in the Australian Imperial Force (AIF). In County Tipperary, for instance, three names appear on the war memorial in the town of Cahir, under the word 'Australians', while on memorials in other towns Australians are indicated by designations such as 'AIF' or 'Aust forces'.

In addition, thousands of Australian soldiers visited Ireland, usually on a fourteen-day leave pass that gave them a brief respite from the horrors of the Western Front or the boredom of camp life in England. Some of these men found themselves caught up in the momentous events of the times such as the Easter Rising of 1916. Others stayed on in Ireland to evade further war service, often placing themselves under the protection of Sinn Féin, while after the war some participated in the Irish War of Independence, on one side or the other.[3]

But mostly the diggers spent their precious leave as tourists visiting the sights, in much the same way as Australian tourists do today. Dublin, Belfast and the Lakes of Killarney were the favourite spots. Indeed, it is remarkable how similar the soldiers' itineraries were to those of the packaged holidays now offered by tour operators. The main difference between now and then, however, is that from the time Australian soldiers began arriving in numbers, Ireland was in the process of a revolution that led to the establishment of the Irish Free State in 1922 and, eventually, the Republic of Ireland as it is today. As a result, attitudes to the war in the two countries have been very different.

By the beginning of the twentieth century, nationalist Ireland, then led by a moderate, John Redmond MP, had been using parliamentary methods for decades in an effort to gain Irish home rule, a limited form of self-government within the United Kingdom. In April 1912, the goal seemed within reach when the Liberal government introduced the Home Rule Bill. However, Irish unionists (that is, those who supported continuing the political union of Great Britain and Ireland) were determined to resist establishment of a Dublin parliament dominated by Catholics. In the north-eastern counties of Ulster, where there was a Protestant majority, unionists threatened civil war if the legislation were passed. When the First World War broke out, the legislation was enacted but suspended for the duration of the conflict, with the government promising to address Ulster's concerns once the war was over. Meanwhile, Redmond, wishing to demonstrate Ireland's loyalty and convince unionists they had nothing to fear from home rule, pledged nationalist Ireland to the war effort, with the result that Ireland sent more than 200 000 men to the front, 35 000 of whom were killed. All were volunteers, for, like Australia, Ireland did not have conscription.

Not all nationalists agreed with Redmond's support of the war. So-called advanced nationalists, who were in the minority in 1914, were convinced that England, not Germany, was Ireland's real enemy and that the British government would never willingly relinquish control over their native land. They therefore regarded Irishmen who enlisted in the British Army as degenerates who were prepared to pollute the national ideal in order to take 'the King's shilling'. In April 1916, advanced nationalists took up arms against the British government in what became known as the Easter Rising. Although defeated, their cause was strengthened by British reprisals and growing anti-war sentiment that undermined the constitutional nationalists, with the result that by 1918 the advanced nationalists had assumed leadership of Irish national opinion. From 1919 to

1921, they again took up arms against the British and fought for an independent Ireland. By 1921, when they achieved victory of a sort (Michael Collins' 'freedom to achieve freedom') with the signing of the Anglo-Irish Treaty granting Ireland dominion status, their negative attitude to 'England's war' predominated.

As the years passed, antipathy to the war and the Irishmen who fought and died in it took on the form of institutionalised social amnesia, which is incomprehensible to generations of Australians used to being regularly reminded of Australia's willing participation alongside Britain in wars ranging from Sudan in 1885 to Iraq in 2003. The most relevant comparison might be the frosty attitude which Australians until recently adopted towards veterans of the Vietnam War, though the level of popular antagonism in that case never approached that which Ireland at times reserved for its soldiers of the First World War. The partition of Ireland has been another source of division. In the six counties of Northern Ireland, unionists enthusiastically commemorate Remembrance Day and the anniversary of the Somme, whereas nationalists, even those with relatives who fought and died in the war, have tended to ignore these events.

In recent years, however, attitudes in Ireland have been changing. In the 1980s, writers, both academic and popular, began to show an interest in the role played by the Irish in the First World War. This new attitude received a major boost in 1998 when Ireland's President Mary McAleese stood beside Queen Elizabeth II at Mesen (known during the war by its French name Messines) in Belgium to inaugurate the Irish Peace Park, where an Irish round tower has been constructed in memory of all Irish soldiers who fought and died during the First World War. In 2006, the Irish state for the first time commemorated the anniversary of the Battle of the Somme, with a ceremony in Dublin as well as ministerial representation at commemorations in France. As a result, there is growing common ground between Australia and Ireland in the way the two countries remember those who fought and died in the war.

It is an appropriate time, therefore, to tell the story of the relationship between Australian soldiers and Ireland during the First World War. As well as relying on official records and published accounts, this book draws, in particular, on the experiences of the servicemen themselves, through their letters, diaries and service records, which, in turn, reveal their attitudes to Ireland, its people and its politics during this critical period in the history of both Australia and Ireland.

In chapter 1 the shared experience of Gallipoli is explored, comparing the landings on 25 April 1915 of the Australians at Anzac Cove and the Irish at V Beach and examining a series of battles in which Irishmen and Anzacs fought side by side. Lone Pine has a special place in Australian military history, yet it is not widely known that Irishmen of the 5th Battalion Connaught Rangers fought along-side men of the Australian 1st Division in that momentous battle. Both Australians and Irishmen came away from Gallipoli disappointed at their failures and angry at the way they had been misled and misused by their British commanders. But whereas the Gallipoli experience reinforced Australia's emerging sense of nationhood without rupturing its links with the Empire, for many in Ireland the Dardanelles disaster was a turning point in that country's relations with Britain, one that was to prove explosive during and after the Easter Rising. Chapter 2 looks at the rising from the point of view of Australian soldiers who found themselves caught up in the fighting in Dublin during Easter week 1916.

Chapter 3 tells the stories of some of the thousands of Irish men and women who joined the AIF and fought for Australia – the Irish Anzacs. From the ranks of private soldiers to generals, Irishmen were to be found at all levels of the Australian forces, while many Irish women enlisted as nurses. Most had emigrated to Australia before 1914 and joined up when their new country found itself at war.

Of the thousands of Australian soldiers who took their leave in Ireland, many kept diaries or wrote letters home describing their impressions of the country and its people. Chapter 4 looks at a number of these accounts, while chapter 5 tells the stories of those Australian servicemen who never returned to Australia and lie buried in Ireland. Chapter 6 explores the variable forms of remembrance of the war in Australia and Ireland over the course of the 20th century and the part remembrance has played in the building of each nation.

The story of the Anzacs is the enduring foundation myth of the Australian nation, though in recent years a number of studies have questioned the Anzac tradition.[4] Although it is outside the scope of this book to attempt a further revision of that tradition, it is intended to add to the corpus of information upon which it is based, examining hitherto-unexplored aspects of the digger experience. Hopefully, those who do re-examine the tradition will find this book a valuable addition to that growing body of evidence. In particular, this book examines a variety of experiences, ranging from bitter fighting at the front to languid days of leave in Ireland's far south-west. A few of the servicemen whose stories are told match the popular stereotype of 'hero' and therefore fit comfortably within the Anzac tradition, but much of the book is about ordinary men and women whose experiences are not readily recognisable in the accepted narrative of the tradition. While an organised tour of the Lakes of Killarney might have been the favourite pastime of Australian soldiers in Ireland, it hardly squares with the essential characteristics of the digger of popular representation: 'brash, cocky, resourceful, innovative, a larrikin'.[5]

The people of Australia and Ireland have much in common, based on genealogy and a shared heritage, a fact evidenced both by the thousands of Australians who travel to Ireland each year searching for their roots or simply as tourists, and by the thousands of Irish men and women who travel to Australia to work in or explore the country. Each nationality feels very much at home in the land of the other. By examining various facets of the relationship between Australian soldiers and Ireland, its land and people, its soldiers and civilians, this book aims to fill a gap in our knowledge of the shared experiences of the two peoples at a critical time in the formation of their two nations.

Chapter 1

Shared experience

Gallipoli

In Australia and New Zealand, Gallipoli continues to resonate down the generations. Each year on 25 April, tens of thousands of Australians and New Zealanders turn out in cities, towns and suburbs to attend commemoration services and to march, or watch others march, in honour of those who fell in all the wars in which their countries have participated. In both countries, Gallipoli is widely regarded as 'the dawning of our sense of nationhood'.[1] In Ireland, especially the Republic, the Dardanelles campaign is largely unknown, notwithstanding that about the same number of Irishmen as New Zealanders died there. To the few Irish men and women who have heard of it, Gallipoli was a tragic mistake, something best forgotten.[2]

So strongly do the Anzac nations self-identify with Gallipoli that many of their citizens are unaware that soldiers from other countries took part in the campaign. It is generally known that troops from Britain were involved, but Peter Weir's film *Gallipoli* has reinforced the popular belief that the British contribution was not much – and not much good. There is a scene in the film where an Australian radio operator reports that the British are ashore at Suvla. An Australian officer inquires whether they are meeting heavy opposition. 'None sir,' replies the radio operator, who adds caustically, 'Apparently they're just sitting on the beach drinking cups of tea'.

There is no doubt that the part played by the Anzacs in the campaign was significant and the cost in men killed and wounded was high. In less than eight months, Australia suffered over 28000 casualties including more than 8700 killed, and New Zealand 7500 casualties with 2700 killed – appalling losses for the young nations. But British casualties were about double those of Australia and New Zealand combined, with over 21000 killed and another 52000 wounded, while other participants on the Allied side also lost heavily: the French lost 10000 killed, many of them Africans from the French colonies, while more than 1300 Indian Army soldiers died. The defenders, however, suffered the most, with the Ottoman forces, mostly Turks, incurring over a quarter of a million casualties, 86000 of them killed.[3]

Not many Australians or New Zealanders would be aware that hidden among the statistics of British casualties are thousands of Irishmen – estimated to account for ten percent or more of those killed.[4] But not only were the Irish present at Gallipoli, they actually fought alongside the Anzacs in battles such as Second Krithia, Lone Pine, Chunuk Bair and Hill 60, and at iconic places such as Quinn's Post.[5] In common with the Anzacs, many Irishmen died on the first day of the landings in failed attempts to seize objectives beyond the beachhead. But it is not only antipodeans who have forgotten the part played by their Irish comrades-in-arms; the collective amnesia extends to the Irish themselves. The anniversary of the landing passes almost unmarked in Dublin, except for commemorations organised by Australians and New Zealanders.[6] For, although the Irish were as gallant in battle as the Anzacs, their sacrifice at Gallipoli in the Empire's cause came to be portrayed at home as a betrayal of the Irish nation and its struggle for independence. In the words of the nationalist song *The Foggy Dew*, which commemorates those who died in the Easter Rising: 'Twas better to die 'neath an Irish sky than at Suvla or Sedd-el-Bahr'.

The young Irishmen who fought and died at Gallipoli would have preferred a long life at home with family and friends, but with a similar mix of motives that inspired their cousins down-under, they enlisted in order to serve Ireland, recently granted home rule, as much as the Empire, despite the advanced nationalist taunt that they 'were unthinking slaves and crawlers ... willing to sell their souls as well as their country's independence for an English shilling and an English promise.'[7]

The rows of desiccated headstones at Gallipoli are grim testimony to the tragedy of lost youth, not only of the well-celebrated Anzacs but also the forgotten Irish. This chapter aims to revive the memory of the shared experience of Anzacs and

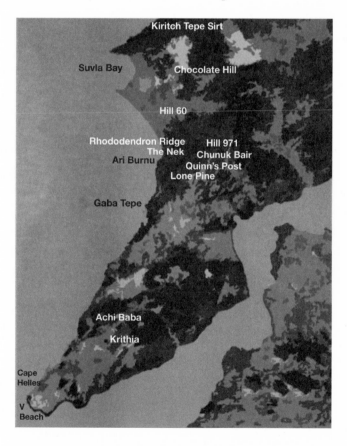

The Gallipoli Peninsula, 1915

Irishmen who fought and died together in the debacle that was Gallipoli. Although they would later fight together in battles on the Western Front and in Palestine, their experience at Gallipoli was exceptional, for there they literally fought shoulder to shoulder in a campaign that was to have a profound effect on both nations.

The landing: Slaughter on V Beach

Australians are familiar with the story of the Anzacs' landing at Ari Burnu. It is a story taught to them at school and reinforced by the media each year on Anzac Day. From an early age, Australian children learn how the Royal Navy landed the Australians in the wrong place, requiring them to scale steep cliffs in order to engage the Turks, who all the while fired down on them as they struggled ashore. Although Denis Winter has cast doubt on the 'wrong beach' theory, arguing that there was a last-minute change of orders, it remains the orthodox view among historians and the public.[8]

Ari Burnu consists of a spur line running down from the heights and jutting out into the Aegean Sea. To its north, the beach runs for 6 kilometres in a long, sweeping arc to Suvla Bay; to its south, a narrow beach extends for about 600 metres to a small promontory known as Hell Spit, lapped by the waters of what is now called Anzac Cove. Behind Ari Burnu the land rises steeply, particularly on its northern side where eroded cliffs of golden clay tower over the beach.

On 25 April 1915, the area around Ari Burnu was lightly defended, for obvious reasons: who in their right mind would attempt to land a military force there? So, although the terrain beyond the shore-line posed a major obstacle to the keen but inexperienced Anzacs, the landing itself was not strongly opposed. It was not until they struggled onto the high ground that the resistance stiffened. The failure of the Anzacs to seize their objectives that day was due less to the strength of the enemy's defences at the landing beaches than to the fact that the attackers had become disorganised and scattered by reason of the confusion that occurred in the initial stages of the landing and of the near-impenetrability of the terrain beyond. As a result, the Anzacs were unable to mount a coordinated attack before Turkish reserves reached the area in sufficient numbers to restrain the invaders. Nevertheless, as so eloquently described by Charles Bean in *The Official History of Australia in the War of 1914–1918*, the raw, young soldiers acquitted themselves creditably that day, in difficult terrain in which the defenders had all the advantages. Some men even made it as far as the Third Ridge, the objective for the first day, and from that elevated position were able to look out over the Dardanelles on the far side of the peninsula, the ultimate goal of the campaign. But they were in small, isolated groups and had to withdraw to avoid being cut off from their units. The main force got no further than the Second Ridge, where they maintained a tenuous hold for the next eight months.

If the gallantry of the Anzacs who stormed the heights above Anzac Cove deserves to be remembered, as it undoubtedly does, then that of the Irish at Cape Helles should never be forgotten either. At 6.25 am, a small flotilla of open boats carrying three companies of the 1st Battalion Royal Dublin Fusiliers, about 700 in total, struggled against the current towards a thin strand of sand near the village of Sedd-el-Bahr, designated in the plan of attack as V Beach. Alongside them, a 2000-ton collier, the *River Clyde*, steamed towards the beach carrying about 2100 men, comprising the 1st Battalion Royal Munster Fusiliers, two companies of the 2nd Battalion Hampshire Regiment, the remaining company of the Dublin Fusiliers and additional support troops.

Unlike the citizen soldiers of the Anzac force, the Dublins and Munsters were regulars. On the outbreak of hostilities, Lord Kitchener, Secretary of State for War, had launched an appeal to the young men of the United Kingdom to enlist, his moustachioed face and beckoning finger appearing on the most famous recruiting poster of the war above the words 'Your Country Needs You'. Existing regiments were expanded to cater for the resulting influx of 'New Army' recruits, by increasing the number of battalions in each regiment. In this way, 59 New Army divisions were raised, three of them in Ireland: the 10th (Irish) Division and the 16th (Irish) Division comprising battalions raised largely in the south and the 36th (Ulster) Division comprising battalions raised largely in the north.[9] While the New Army was being raised and trained, regular battalions in the far reaches of the Empire were recalled for active service, including the 1st Battalion Royal Dublin Fusiliers from Madras and the 1st Battalion Royal Munster Fusiliers from Rangoon. Both were posted to the 86th Brigade of the newly formed 29th Division, a British division comprising the 86th, 87th and 88th Brigades. The 87th Brigade included another Irish regular unit, the 1st Battalion Royal Inniskilling Fusiliers. On 16 March 1915 the division sailed for Alexandria, where it joined other formations of the Mediterranean Expeditionary Force preparing to invade Turkey. Thus, on the morning of 25 April 1915, as the haze lifted to reveal a beautiful spring day, these proud Irish regular battalions, whose history in the British Army dated back hundreds of years, prepared to do battle.

V Beach forms a semicircle, a natural amphitheatre about 300 metres in diameter. It is bounded on the eastern end, or the right as viewed from the sea, by Sedd-el-Bahr fort; on the left, 200 metres of sloping ground rises to cliffs 60 metres above sea level, capped by another fortification, designated in the British plan as Fort No. 1. This fort was a key objective of the landing but, unbeknown to the attackers, it was also a nest for Turkish machine-guns and riflemen. The beach itself, no more than 10 metres wide, was edged on the landward side by a small, perpendicular bank of sand, less than 2 metres high, with a spit or rocky outcrop extending from beneath Sedd-el-Bahr fort into the bay.

This was one of five beaches in the Helles sector assaulted that day. The main attacks in the sector were at V and W beaches, with subsidiary attacks at S beach (Morto Bay) on the eastern side of the peninsula and X and Y beaches on the western side. W Beach would become known as 'Lancashire Landing' in honour of the men of the 1st Battalion Lancashire Fusiliers, who in the course of the morning won six Victoria Crosses, giving rise to the regiment's proud boast that they had won 'six VCs before breakfast'. One of them was won by the 28-year-old Irishman, Private William Keneally of County Wexford, one of six brothers who served in the war from which two would not return, including William himself who was killed in the Gallipoli campaign two months later.[10] At X beach, the third Irish battalion in the 29th Division, the 1st Battalion Royal Inniskilling Fusiliers, which had also been recalled from India, landed without significant opposition, and with the other battalions of the 87th Brigade 'advanced 500 yards, took the cliff line against stiff opposition, beat off a counter-attack and then bivouacked for the night'.[11]

At V Beach it would be a different story. The plan was for the first wave to land from open boats, just as the Anzacs had done two hours before, followed soon after by the main party in the *River Clyde*. The idea was to run the collier aground in the shallow waters off the beach so that a string of lighters, or small barges, that were being towed by the ship would be carried forward to the beach by their momentum and, with the assistance of a smaller support vessel, be held in place to form a bridge between the ship and the shore. The soldiers inside the hold of the *River Clyde*, shielded from Turkish bullets until the last minute, would emerge through access ways cut into the ship's sides and run the short distance across the lighters to the beach, where they would form up and advance to their objectives. But as with so many of the battles of the Gallipoli campaign, what on paper seemed reasonable and achievable failed miserably in its execution.

The open boats were delayed by the current, and some became entangled with the *River Clyde* and its tows. The lighters, instead of going straight ahead, swung wide of the vessel, eventually having to be manhandled back into position by the *River Clyde*'s skipper and crew, under constant fire from the defending Turks.[12] This was an ominous sign, for the defenders were supposed to have been neutralised by the naval bombardment that had pounded the shore defences for over an hour before the landing. With the gangway finally in place, the soldiers filed out of the ship's hull to be met by an intense hail of bullets and shrapnel. Captain GW Geddes, Officer Commanding X Company of the 1st Battalion Royal Munster Fusiliers, described the scene in his report of the landing:

> The River Clyde beached according to plan at 6.30. None
> of us felt it, there was no jar. As she beached 2 Companies
> of the Dublins in 'TOWS' came up on the Port side and
> were met with a terrific rifle and machine gun fire. They
> were literally slaughtered like rats in a trap …
>
> We got it like anything, man after man behind me was
> shot down but they never wavered. Lieut. Watts who was
> wounded in five places and lying on the gangway cheered
> the men on with cries of 'Follow the Captain'.
>
> Captain French of the Dublins told me afterwards that
> he counted the first 48 men to follow me, and they all fell, I
> think no finer episode could be found of the men's bravery
> and discipline than this – of leaving the safety of the RIVER
> CLYDE to go to what was practically certain death.[13]

For the defenders it was easy work. The machine-gunners and
riflemen inside Fort No. 1, at a range of no more than 300 metres,
enfiladed the attacking troops, whose only cover was the sandbank,
where Captain Geddes took shelter with the survivors.

> We all made, Dublins and all, for a sheltered ledge on the shore
> which gave us cover. Here we shook ourselves out and tried
> to appreciate the situation, rather a sorry one. I estimated that
> I had lost about 70 percent of my company …

The losses among the troops in the open boats were also high. In
some cases, the Turks shot the oarsmen so that the boats drifted and
machine-gun fire could be turned on the helpless soldiers. In other
cases, the Turks waited until the men, having tossed their oars,
were within 20 metres of the shore and then swept the boats with
fire. Captain Guy Nightingale of the Munsters wrote in his diary
that, of the first boat-load of 40 men, only 3 reached the shore,
all wounded, while altogether the Dublins in the open boats lost
560 men and 21 officers in 15 minutes.[14] During the landing from
the *River Clyde*, one of the bridges broke away and the men on it
began jumping into the water, now stained scarlet, but it was too
deep to stand up in and many of them drowned after being dragged
under by their heavy equipment. In addition, the narrowness of the

pontoon bridge forced the disembarking soldiers to bunch up near the rocky spit where the enemy's fire was strongest. In all, it is estimated that more than half of the troops were killed or wounded.[15] Lieutenant Colonel HE Tizard, the commanding officer of the Munsters wrote in his report of the landing:

> This fire was so accurate that those in the boats were practically wiped out & very few got ashore. Wounded men jumped from the boats & took cover on the far side but were all eventually shot down & drowned … The fire directed at the exits from the vessel being very accurate & men were hit before they left the vessel.[16]

Their chaplain, Father William Finn, a Tipperary man, was determined to be beside them. According to Myles Dungan:

> He attempted to save a number of drowning and wounded men before being hit himself in the right arm. He managed to get ashore and crawled around the beach offering help or consolation to the wounded and dying Dublins and Munsters. In order to give absolution he had to hold up an injured right arm with his left. While he was blessing one of the men in this fashion, there was a shrapnel burst above him which blew part of his skull away. He was buried on the beach and his grave marked with a cross made out of an ammunition box 'To the Memory of the Revd Capt. Finn'.[17]

More attempts were made during the morning to land the remaining troops until in one such effort Brigadier Napier and members of his staff were killed, whereupon the landing operation was postponed.

Apart from a small party that had managed to get close to the Sedd-el-Bahr fort and had dug itself in, the survivors continued to shelter under the sandbank until nightfall, when the rest of the troops on board the *River Clyde* were landed under cover of darkness. According to Geddes, the two companies of Hampshires who disembarked at night did so without a shot being fired at them. He summed up his feelings on the landing in his report:

V Beach from the *River Clyde*. The dark mass in the centre
of the photo is the men huddling under the sandbank.
(AWM A03076)

I felt we were for it. That the enterprise was unique and would demand all I was possible of giving, and more. That it was no picnic but a desperate venture. I just longed to get on with it and be done with it. I felt I was no hero and that I had not the pluck of a louse. My nerves were tense and strung up, and yet I never doubted that we would not win through, because I knew the splendid fellows at my back, highly trained, strictly disciplined, and they would follow me anywhere.[18]

The memoir of Sir Ian Hamilton, commander in chief of the expedition, in some ways is even more poignant: 'Would that we had left [V Beach] severely alone and landed a big force at Morto Bay, where we could have forced the Sedd-el-Bahr Turks to fall back'.[19] So heavy were the Irish losses, that for three weeks after the landing the Dublins and the Munsters ceased to exist as separate units, being amalgamated into a composite battalion attached to the 87th Brigade and nicknamed the 'Dubsters'.

Second Krithia: 'An unrecognised Balaklava'

In early May, the 2nd Australian Infantry Brigade under Irish-born Colonel James McCay and the New Zealand Infantry Brigade under Colonel FE Johnston were sent to Cape Helles to assist the 29th Division with their planned assault on the town of Krithia and the high ground behind it known as Achi Baba.[20] As they came ashore near the beached *River Clyde*, the Anzacs, looking up at the fort on the cliffs, would immediately have appreciated the brutal reality behind the stories they had heard about the slaughter of the Irish at V Beach. Private John Turnbull of the 8th Battalion wrote in his diary:

When we looked at the 'River Clyde' then up to the semi-circular beach with a ruined light house on the right point; & sheer cliffs honeycombed with concealed machine gun positions, we thanked our lucky stars we were not in the position this Irishman was who told us of his experience.[21]

The new attack, subsequently known as the Second Battle of Krithia, was carried out in daylight because Major General Aylmer Hunter-Weston, commanding the 29th Division, had recommended against a night attack, fearing that his troops would get lost in the dark. Sir Ian Hamilton had acquiesced, though he would have preferred the attack to have commenced an hour before dawn. Instead of the cover of darkness, the plan provided for a preliminary artillery bombardment designed to neutralise the enemy's defences. Hamilton recorded in his diary: '[Hunter-Weston] thinks it best to blaze away freely before closing and to trust our bayonets when we get in'.[22] The problem, however, was that the gunners did not know the location of the well-concealed Turkish defenders, with the result that the bombardment, though terrifying in its intensity, was ineffective and merely served to warn the Turks of the impending attack.

At 11 am on 6 May, troops of the 88th Brigade began the attack, the Anzacs being held in reserve. But it faltered before it really got started. The attacking formations had advanced only a few hundred metres before they ran into heavy fire from hidden machine-guns, which was so effective that it halted their progress for the rest of the day. However, poor communications led the generals to believe that more progress had been made than was in fact the case. Encouraged by the perceived imminence of victory, Sir Ian Hamilton ordered Hunter-Weston to resume the attack the next day, but this time to start an hour earlier. As before, the Turkish machine-gun positions, which were invisible to the artillery observers, had a devastating effect on the lines of advancing infantry. By 2 pm the second attack had also stalled. Hunter-Weston then committed the 87th Brigade, which included two Irish battalions, the 1st Battalion Royal Inniskilling Fusiliers and the survivors of V Beach, the Dubsters. Again the attack failed.

Observing the adage 'If at first you don't succeed, try, try again,' Hamilton ordered another attack on the third day. He considered it imperative to advance his frontline further inland in order to gain sufficient territory to deploy properly and effectively the troops he already had, let alone the reinforcements he would need in order to defend his position from the increasing numbers of Turks, who were daily being reinforced from the north.

The plan of attack for the third day provided for the New Zealanders to replace the 88th Brigade. The Irish of the 87th Brigade would be on their left. As Major CB Brereton of the Canterbury Battalion led his company out of the Dubsters' trench, one of the Irishmen called out, 'It's no good advancing, sir, you'll all be killed. It's no good, sir'.[23] He was not far wrong. By midday the attack was once more brought to a halt, with only a minimal gain of ground. Sustained Turkish machine-gun and rifle fire had inflicted heavy casualties on the New Zealanders, including Major Brereton, who was severely wounded.[24]

Despite four failed attempts, Hamilton was still not ready to admit defeat, even though his force had not yet reached or even sighted the Turkish front line, let alone captured any occupied ground. Notwithstanding the evidence of the previous three days and as if all that stood between success and failure was an act of will, Hamilton determined on one more attempt, this time throwing the Australians into the assault.

At 5.30 pm on 8 May, the attack began after yet another spectacular but ineffective artillery bombardment. In the words of the British official historian, 'The defenders were quite unshaken; and from shore to shore of the peninsula, as soon as the advance started, the Allied troops were lashed and scourged by a hurricane of lead'.[25] The leading battalion of the 87th Brigade was shot down as soon as it left its trenches and not a metre of ground was gained. Meanwhile, the 2nd Australian Brigade, given only a half-hour's notice, ran forward to a trench occupied by British soldiers, which the Australians called the 'Tommies' Trench'. Unclear as to what they were meant to do next, many of the Australians either jumped into the trench or lay down behind it. When Colonel McCay arrived, he climbed onto the parapet and called out, 'Now then, Australians! Which of you men are Australians? Come on, Australians!' With Turkish bullets whizzing into the parapet and raising clouds of dust, the soldiers of the 2nd Brigade, mainly men from Victoria, rallied to the cry of 'On Australians! Come on, Australians!' and scrambling out of the Tommies' Trench, their bayonets glinting in the afternoon sun, advanced towards an unseen enemy, who poured a hail of bullets and shrapnel down on them. A British major later observed:

> The machine guns bellowed and poured on them sheets of flame and of ragged death, buried them alive ... Their pluck was titanic. They were not men, but gods, demons infuriated. We saw them fall by the score. But what of that? Not for one breath did the great line waver or break. On and up it went, up and on, as steady and proud as if on parade. A seasoned staff officer watching choked with his own admiration. Our men tore off their helmets and waved them, and poured cheer after cheer after those wonderful Anzacs.[26]

His report reads more like a commentary on a rugby match than a description of men marching to their death.

All the while McCay prowled up and down the parapet, exposed to fire, urging newly arrived men, exhausted by reason of the rush and their heavy packs, to press on. When the attackers reached a point within 550 metres of the Turkish line they could see for the first time where the enemy was located, but it was a cruel deception – what they couldn't see were Turkish skirmishers hidden by the scrubby undergrowth 100 metres in front of the Turkish trench, who continued to pour a heavy fusillade into the advancing Australians. Not only that, having raced ahead of the New Zealanders on their left and the French on their right, the Australians were now exposed to enfilade fire from the Turkish machine-guns. Indeed, Charles Bean wrote that the advance from the Tommies' Trench had been made 'in the teeth of rifle and machine-gun fire such as Australians seldom again encountered during the war'.[27]

With the Turkish trench still more than 350 metres ahead, the remnants of the 2nd Brigade's front line eventually faltered and became stationary, with the survivors desperately scraping holes in the ground in order to find some respite from the Turkish bullets.

As darkness fell, the sound of gunfire abated, giving way to the cries of the wounded, who littered the battlefield. The British official historian recorded:

> In half an hour the gallant charge of this brigade – an unrecognised Balaklava – had ended with a loss of over a thousand men out of 2,000 engaged, including the brigadier and both staff officers wounded.[28]

There would be no attempt the next day to resume the attack. Hamilton had done his dash; even the grand display of flashing steel had failed to dislodge the Turks. Without effective artillery support and against an unseen and disciplined enemy, it was always going to be a worthless gesture. We can only speculate as to whether Hamilton's original idea of a night attack might have succeeded, but on that final night British troops advancing to link up with the exposed Australian right 'were able to cross, without a casualty, a belt of country as wide as that which had cost the Australians a thousand men to capture'.[29]

Even allowing for the fact that Hamilton felt it essential to extend his beachhead, and for the fact that commanders in all theatres were struggling to adjust to the conditions of modern warfare, the Second Battle of Krithia was conducted in a manner that resulted in a dreadful and avoidable tragedy. To paraphrase Oscar Wilde – another Irishman – to lose a battle once may be regarded as a misfortune, but to lose it five times looks like carelessness – or worse.

Three nights later, the Anzac brigades were withdrawn from the front line and within the week they were back at Anzac Cove. Like the Irish, they were unimpressed by their short period of service alongside and under the command of the regulars of the British army.

The August offensive

Over the next three months, the British and French at Cape Helles continued to push the frontline closer to Achi Baba. But hampered by a lack of artillery support, which time and again left lines of advancing infantry exposed to Turkish shrapnel and bullets, the Allies suffered over 17 000 casualties for a gain of just 500 metres. And still the heights of Achi Baba were in Turkish hands.

In July, Sir Ian Hamilton decided to shift the point of attack to the northern sector, at Anzac Cove. Here the frontline to the east of the cove extended along the Second Ridge running from Chunuk Bair, near the summit of the Sari Bair range, to Lone Pine on the 400 Plateau. The aim was to capture the high points of Chunuk Bair and Hill 971, and to join up with a subsidiary force that would advance from Russell's Top across the Nek to Baby 700, a knoll just south of Chunuk Bair. A series of feints would be made to deceive the Turks as to the direction of the main attack including a 'demonstration' at Lone Pine and attacks on the Turkish trenches from positions along the Second Ridge. At the same time, a force would be landed at Suvla Bay to secure a base of operations for all the forces in the northern sector.

The attacks on Chunuk Bair and Hill 971 were to be carried out by men of the New Zealand and Australian Division, commanded by an Irishman, Major General Alexander Godley.[30] The division comprised the New Zealand 1st Infantry Brigade, a Maori infantry battalion, the New Zealand Mounted Rifles Brigade, the New Zealand Otago Mounted Rifles Regiment, the Australian 4th Infantry Brigade and the bulk of the 1st and 3rd Australian Light Horse Brigades, excluding those left behind in Egypt to look after the horses, plus supporting arms and services. The Anzacs would be reinforced for the attack on Sari Bair by the 29th Indian Brigade, comprising regular battalions of Gurkhas and Sikhs, and by four brigades of the British New Army, including the 29th Brigade of the 10th (Irish) Division, comprising the 6th Battalion Royal Irish Rifles, the 6th Battalion Leinster Regiment and the 5th Battalion Connaught Rangers as well as the 10th Battalion Hampshire Regiment.[31] The Lone Pine feint was assigned to the 1st Australian Division, while the Suvla Bay landing was to be carried out by Britain's IX Army Corps, comprising New Army troops of the

11th (Northern) Division and the two remaining brigades of the 10th (Irish) Division, the 30th and 31st.

Between 2 and 6 August, the New Army reinforcements landed at Anzac Cove at night under cover of darkness. In the early hours of 6 August 1915, the Irishmen of the 29th Brigade found themselves camped alongside Australians and New Zealanders in Shrapnel Gully. Within a short time they learned why it had been so named, when a few of their number were killed or wounded by exploding shells.[32] These men were citizen soldiers like the Anzacs alongside whom they were about to fight. But unlike the Anzacs, they had not been in battle before. Private John Turnbull of the 8th Battalion adopted the patronising tone of a veteran when he described the newcomers in his diary:

> We have now a Battalion of Kitchener's Army, The Leinsters, in our line. To us they seem a doped lot. Put them in a post and send them away for anything [and] they never find their way back, but get lost in the support trenches somewhere stumbling over our fellows trying to sleep, who abuse them unmercifully. You often hear the cry in the front line, 'Has anyone lost a Leinster, we have one here[?]'[33]

Lone Pine

At 4.00 pm on 6 August, the great offensive began, starting with a feint at Helles to divert Turkish attention. An hour and a half later, the Australian 1st Division commenced its assault on Lone Pine. It was to be one of the bloodiest fights of the whole campaign, resulting in more than 2000 Australian and 5000 Turkish casualties over the next four days. Seven Australians would win Victoria Crosses as the Turks fought desperately to retake the trenches seized by the Australians on the first night. Much of it was brutal hand-to-hand fighting whereby men fought each other with bayonet and bomb in the subterranean world of the Turkish trenches, which had been roofed over with pine logs and which soon became clogged with the bodies of the dead and the dying. It was at Lone Pine that the 5th Battalion Connaught Rangers first saw action, supporting the Australians and helping to clear the Turkish trenches of the dead, dragging the bodies to Brown's Dip for burial. It was gruesome work for the young men from the west of Ireland, but as nothing compared to the horror they would soon encounter in the action at Hill 60.

Meanwhile, two companies of the 6th Battalion Leinster Regiment also had an early introduction to modern warfare when they relieved Australians holding Courtney's Post and Quinn's Post, both precarious positions on the Second Ridge, where throughout the night the Turks kept up a stream of rifle and machine-gun fire.[34] General Godley later wrote to the commander of the 29th Brigade that 'the work of the Leinster Regiment at Quinn's Post & Russell's Top has been excellent throughout'.[35] But once again this experience, harrowing though it was for inexperienced troops, was to be as nothing compared to what lay ahead.

For all its heroism and brutality, the action at Lone Pine was nevertheless merely a diversion, whose purpose was to draw Turkish reserves to the south of the Anzac position, while the main Allied force under General Godley stealthily climbed the rugged spurs leading to the coveted prizes of Chunuk Bair and Hill 971, the high points of the Sari Bair range.

The assault on Sari Bair

The initial phase of this operation was completed successfully with the New Zealand Mounted Rifles seizing the foothills that left the way open to Chunuk Bair. Unfortunately, the task of actually getting that far had proved more difficult than the plan had envisaged and the assault on the peak was running behind schedule – enough for the Turks to work out what was afoot and to reinforce their flimsy force on top of the hill. The Anzacs, many of whom were lost in the labyrinth of ravines and all of them fatigued by the ordeal of having to find their way in the dark through a series of steep-sided gullies that had not previously been reconnoitred, halted to rest, thereby giving the Turks even more time to reinforce the heights. The assault on Sari Bair, designed as a surprise attack at night against an undefended position, was thus transformed into what ultimately proved to be a mission impossible.

In the meantime, on Russell's Top, men of the 3rd Light Horse Brigade moved into the front-line trenches in preparation for their attack on the Nek, timed for 4.30 am on 7 August. Lieutenant General William Birdwood, the commander in chief of the Anzac forces, was aware that the New Zealanders, whose role was to take the Turks from the rear and join up with the Australians, had not yet reached Chunuk Bair and that the other assaults on the Turkish trenches on the Second Ridge during the night had failed. Nevertheless, Birdwood ordered the attack to proceed, later claiming he did so in order to put pressure on the Turkish centre so as to help the New Zealanders by diverting the Turks from Chunuk Bair. The tragedy that befell the Australians at the Nek is well known to present generations because of its graphic portrayal in Peter Weir's film *Gallipoli*. The artillery barrage ended seven minutes early, allowing the Turkish machine-gunners and riflemen ample time to prepare for the assault. The first wave of 150 light horsemen was cut down by the Turks' withering fire as soon as it left the trench; so, too, were the second and third waves. Despite the obvious futility of continuing the attack, the action ended only after the fourth and final wave met a similar fate. In the 8th Light Horse Regiment, more than half of those who started the assault were killed, and more than half of the survivors were wounded. The 10th Light Horse Regiment lost nearly half of its men. Charles Bean wrote of the attack:

> The flower of the youth in Victoria and Western Australia
> fell in that attempt. The cost to the smaller population of
> the West was especially severe – hardly a pioneer family but
> mourned its one or more dead.[36]

Meanwhile the New Zealanders continued their slow and difficult ascent to Chunuk Bair. The battalions that reached Rhododendron Ridge, which ran up to the summit, halted to await the rest of the brigade, thus allowing the Turks further opportunity to strengthen their position. As a result, all attempts to seize the summit during the day were beaten back at great expense to the attackers.

In the early hours of the next morning, 8 August, the Wellington Battalion of the New Zealand 1st Infantry Brigade, supported by two New Army battalions of the 13th (Western) Division attacked under cover of darkness. Much to the surprise of the Wellington commander, Lieutenant Colonel William Malone, a London-born New Zealander of Irish descent, the crest at the southern shoulder of Chunuk Bair was found to be unoccupied. During the artillery barrage that had preceded the attack, the Turks had abandoned the position. For the first time since 25 April, men of the Anzac force could look out on the Dardanelles – the ultimate prize of the whole campaign. But theirs was a feeble foothold, for once day broke the Turks began to pour a withering fire onto the position and onto Rhododendron Ridge, forcing the rest of the Allied troops to scatter into the deep gullies on either side of the spur. By 9 am, the companies of the Wellington Battalion clinging to the crest had been wiped out, leaving the support companies holding a trench just below the crest. For a day and a half they held on. On the night of 9–10 August they were relieved by two English battalions. Out of the 760 men of the Wellington Battalion who went into the fight, only 70 were unwounded, with Malone among the dead.[37]

Despite the delays on 7 August, Birdwood still saw the chance to achieve success by bringing up additional troops to attack Chunuk Bair. He had ordered his reserves, including the 6th Battalion Royal Irish Rifles, to join Godley's force. Leaving Anzac Cove at 10 am on 8 August, the reserve force marched north to Chailak Dere, one of the ravines that led inland. But their progress was blocked by a stream of wounded and other traffic coming down the gully from the battlefield above. After a night of scrambling over very rough country, which is difficult enough to cross in daylight, they found themselves many hours after the time appointed for the attack at a small plateau beneath Chunuk Bair called 'the Farm', where British and New Zealand troops occupied trenches around its outer edge. In the *Official History*, Bean wrote that the Farm 'projected from the hillside like a terraced tennis-court or cricket-field ... any attempt to cross the terrace was deadly'. He then described what happened next:

> As they lay there, an order came to a company commander of the [Royal Irish] Rifles to advance over the terrace. 'Surely you won't do it – it can't be done,' said an officer of the Maoris who lay next him. 'I'm going – I've been told to,' was the reply. He led forward the men round him, and, according to the testimony of the Maori officer, none came back.[38]

Captain FE Eastwood, Officer Commanding D Company of the 6th Battalion Royal Irish Rifles, who led one of the platoons attempting to cross the terrace, later wrote:

> There was not a falter, they followed like one man, soon catching me up and we tore forward like driven birds. A mine did not explode at our feet, but shrapnel, machine guns, rifle fire poured into us, a sort of enfilade fire as the man on my left seemed to take my lot. I only got a bit of shrapnel in the neck, not enough to bring me down. I did not see a man rise again. Would the Second Platoon take warning? No! orders must be obeyed. I saw the Platoon Commander, a man of thirty, a Dublin barrister, come forth, his platoon also after him; they would have followed him anywhere. They were just laid low in the same way as No. 1 platoon. Once the volley was over, there was no more firing, as every man was lying flat in the long grass. We had to reinforce the Wiltshires, the order was again shouted down the line.
>
> I shouted, 'GO!' About seven men arose out of the original hundred and I was hit in the wrist. Fortunately or not, as they got it later, the second half of my Company did not [continue the attack]. There I lay, receiving a shrapnel bullet which went through my helmet touching my head and top of my ear, and knowing I had nothing to go on with, I lay flat on my stomach, and pushed myself back into the Rifle-pit I had started from. While sitting here two smart Staff Officers came along, crouching along, moving at a very smart pace, along what they might have

thought was the firing line. They asked me, 'How are you getting on?'

'Not at all,' I said, 'my Company has been knocked out.'[39]

Bean recorded in a footnote to his account that bodies of men of the Royal Irish Rifles were found after the war within 20 metres of the crest of Chunuk Bair.

The 6th Battalion Leinster Regiment was also committed to the fight, arriving on the night of 9 August at the Apex, a knoll on Rhododendron Ridge a few hundred metres from the summit. But by then the Turks, under Mustapha Kemal, were assembling on the far side of Chunuk Bair in readiness for a counterattack that was unleashed the next morning. Waves of Turkish infantry swept over the summit, killing most of the New Army defenders on the crest and driving the remainder back down the western side. So fierce was the fighting that the commander of the Allied force at the Farm, Brigadier General Baldwin, was killed and thereafter nine officers who successively took command were either killed or severely wounded.[40] The 6th Battalion Royal Irish Rifles, fighting desperately to hold the Farm, lost almost all its officers before withdrawing from the position.

On Rhododendron Ridge, the advance position at the Pinnacle, occupied by the Loyal North Lancashires, was overwhelmed and the way was open for the Turks to push the British Empire troops off the ridge. In front of them was the Apex held by the remnants of the Wellington Battalion, the Leinsters and the massed machine-guns of the New Zealand Infantry Brigade. Major Bryan Cooper, an officer with the 10th (Irish) Division, described what happened next:

> On the right the Leinsters stood their ground. At last the moment had arrived to which they had so anxiously looked forward. Turk and Irishman, face to face, and hand to hand, could try which was the better man ... In spite of the odds, the two companies in the front line succeeded in checking the attack, and at the crucial moment they were reinforced by 'B' and 'C' Companies from the support line ... Shouting,

> they flung themselves into the fray, and drove the Turks back
> after a desperate struggle at close quarters.[41]

Holding the Apex was vital as the New Zealand machine-gunners, who had been concentrated there, were able to pour a withering fire into the Turks, stopping their further advance. Chris Pugsley in his account of the fighting mistakenly claims 'Panic spread and the Leinsters at the Pinnacle also fled'. However, it was the Loyal North Lancashire Regiment that was at the Pinnacle. The Leinsters held on at the Apex, as described by Major Cooper, whose account is supported by both the Australian and British official histories. Furthermore, after the battle Major General Godley sent for the commanding officer of the Leinsters and complimented him on the work of the battalion that morning.[42]

The Connaught Rangers, who were brought up to support the New Zealanders, reoccupied the Farm. But with the Turks in command of the high ground, their position was untenable and they were ordered to withdraw. Thus ended the battle of Chunuk Bair, the last best hope of an Allied victory at Gallipoli.

The Australians had also failed to capture Hill 971 after they had become hopelessly lost in the wild country on the northern extremity of the Anzac sector. But the brunt of the fighting had been done at Chunuk Bair by the New Zealanders and the soldiers of the New Army, including the three Irish battalions of the 10th (Irish) Division.

When they had landed at Anzac Cove on 6 August, they had each had a strength of about 25 officers and 750 other ranks. The fighting at Chunuk Bair exacted a heavy toll: the 6th Battalion Royal Irish Rifles lost 21 officers and 354 other ranks; the 6th Battalion Leinster Regiment lost 11 officers and 250 other ranks; and the 5th Battalion Connaught Rangers lost 8 officers and 105 other ranks.[43] So mauled was the Royal Irish Rifles that it was unable to continue to fight as a unit. Instead, on 19 August it sent 200 of its men to reinforce the 8th Australian Infantry Battalion at Lone Pine.[44] The Leinsters were withdrawn from Rhododendron Ridge on the night of 11 August and two days later redeployed for duty with the 9th and 10th Australian Light Horse Regiments in the fire trenches at Russell's Top, before being assigned to road-digging duties a fortnight later.[45]

Suvla Bay

On the morning of 7 August, while the men of the 3rd Light Horse Brigade were being sacrificed at the Nek and the 29th Brigade was waiting at Anzac Cove in support of the main force, the remainder of the 10th (Irish) Division was landing at Suvla Bay. The scandalous failure of Lieutenant General Sir Frederick Stopford, the elderly yet inexperienced commander, to order his corps to advance immediately from the beachhead and seize the high ground when the landing was relatively unopposed is notorious, leading to derisory comments such as that of the radio operator in *Gallipoli* described above. Sir Ian Hamilton wrote to Lord Kitchener on 11 August 1915:

> When I got to Suvla Bay about 5 o'clock, I found most of the troops strolling about as if it was a holiday ... I found it was intended to do nothing that day ... but that any advance was to be made ... at dawn next morning. I was horrified at this and ordered Stopford to get a move on at once ... The men are perfectly splendid and, by the mercy of God, we shall get good value out of them yet. But at present their senior officers seem to have no drive or control over them ...[46]

For Australians, Suvla is considered a bad joke, an irrelevance synonymous with inertia which, thanks mainly to Peter Weir, provokes a smirk or a sneer of inverted colonial snobbery. However, for the Irish, Suvla is no joke. Coming at a sensitive time in the relationship between Britain and Ireland, with the divisive issue of home rule having been tentatively put on hold, it became politicised, symbolising the waste of young Irish lives and English indifference. The 10th (Irish) Division suffered severely during the Suvla campaign, being not only inexperienced, but also ill-equipped and under strength. As we have seen, one of its brigades, the 29th, was deployed at Anzac Cove, while the 30th and 31st Brigades landed at Suvla minus the division's artillery, which was still in Egypt, and the division's engineers, who were delayed. Nevertheless, the 10th had an early success on the first day, when five of its battalions took part in the seizure of Chocolate Hill, after having advanced across open ground under intense Turkish fire in the heat of the day and without adequate supplies of water. A New Zealand officer, Captain Thornhill described the action:

> The Empire can do with a heap more 'freshies' of the Irish brand ... Those that witnessed the advance will never forget it. Bullets and shrapnel rained on them, yet they never wavered ... God! The men were splendid. The way they took that hill (now called Dublin Hill) was the kind of thing that would make you pinch yourself to prove that it was not a cheap wine aftermath. How they got there Heaven only knows. As the land lay, climbing into hell on an aeroplane seemed an easier proposition than taking that hill.[47]

Apart from this success, however, the 'freshies' of the 10th Division had little else to show for their sacrifice. Over the following weeks they suffered heavy casualties, particularly in the assault on the high ridge of Kiritch Tepe Sirt, which had been reinforced by the Turks following Stopford's delay in moving from the beachhead. Their plight was not helped when, in the middle of the battle, their divisional commander, Lieutenant General Bryan Mahon, resigned in a fit of pique, after he was passed over for promotion to corps commander following Sir Ian Hamilton's sacking of General Stopford on 15 August. Six days later, Irish regulars of the 29th Division, brought up from Helles to reinforce the New Army, suffered badly at Scimitar Hill, which had been taken but abandoned on the first day. During the battle, the continuous shelling set the undergrowth ablaze and many of the wounded were burnt alive where they had fallen. Attack after attack failed to dislodge the Turks and when the action was called off more than a third of the attacking force had been killed or wounded.[48]

Major Bryan Cooper, whose 10th (Irish) Division had been formed twelve months before, in the opening days of the war, later wrote, 'The 10th Division had been shattered, the work of a year had been destroyed in a week, and nothing material had been gained'.[49] Private John Turnbull of the 8th Battalion AIF wrote in his diary:

> We do not blame the Kitch Army too much for their failure. Considering they came straight from home here. They were not acclimatised. The heat, no training to rush these hills, and water beat them.[50]

The old hands among the Australians and New Zealanders who fought alongside the Irish at Anzac Cove had no grounds to doubt their courage, an assessment that was confirmed in the last days of the August offensive when the men of the 5th Battalion Connaught Rangers joined in the action at Hill 60.

Hill 60

The low pimple of a knoll, which gloried in the name 'Hill 60', was of tactical importance because it formed a link between the Suvla and Anzac sectors and provided a view north towards Anafarta. When the first attack began at 3.30 pm on 21 August, the Connaught Rangers on the left of the attacking force had the task of seizing Kabak Kuyu, a well which could provide much-needed water for the parched troops fighting in the heat of the Gallipoli summer. This they did with relative ease, as there were few Turks there, though they came under heavy fire from Hill 60 and from snipers concealed in the scattered bushes. Much to the annoyance of Lieutenant Colonel HFN Jourdain, commanding officer of the 5th Battalion Connaught Rangers, Sir Ian Hamilton in his dispatches attributed the victory to the 29th Indian Brigade without mention of the Rangers. This erroneous account was published in *The Times*, fuelling complaints by the Irish that their efforts were not being recognised. After correspondence between Jourdain, Godley and Hamilton, *The Times* eventually acknowledged the Rangers' part in the attack, but not until 1920.[51]

After capturing the well, the Rangers charged Hill 60 in support of the New Zealanders. In the words of Charles Bean:

> They were seen dashing up the seaward end of the hill, the Turks running before them. This fine charge called forth the admiration of all who beheld it, and such a movement, if it had been concerted and delivered along the whole line of attack with the flanks well guarded, would probably have carried Hill 60. As far as it can be ascertained it crossed the first trench on the western face of the hill, but, as it approached the summit, withered under fire poured upon it by the enemy. The losses were heavy, and no ground was gained.[52]

In their wild charge the Rangers lost 12 officers and 248 men, of whom 46 were killed.[53]

By nightfall, the Allies had secured but a foothold on Hill 60, with only the New Zealanders in possession of a small section of the Turkish trenches. The New Zealand commander, Brigadier General Andrew Russell, inspected the troops that night and, realising that his men were too worn out to extend the line, requested fresh reinforcements.

The 18th Battalion of the Australian 2nd Division had landed at Gallipoli just two days before. Compared to the haggard Anzac veterans, these men looked like bright, young giants, but they were inexperienced and General Godley had initially determined not to deploy them prematurely. However, the local commanders persuaded him that the communication trenches leading to the summit of Hill 60 could be carried if fresh troops were used. At their briefing, the battalion's officers were instructed to use bayonets and bombs only. When it was pointed out that they had not been issued with any bombs, they were told they would have to do the best that was possible without them. The battalion, 750 strong, charged the Turkish line, but it was met by a storm of enfilade fire that in a short time reduced its numbers by 11 officers and 372 men, half of whom were killed. Les Carlyon has written that there was 'something contemptible about the way the 18th had been sent out to die'.[54]

In less than two days, the attacking force had lost more than 1300 men – one third of its number. Nevertheless, it had a toehold on Hill 60, and Birdwood ordered another assault on 27 August. Reinforced by men of the 4th Australian Infantry Brigade who had returned from the failed attack on Hill 971, the Australians launched a fresh attack at 4 pm, again suffering severely for little gain as wave after wave was cut down. The New Zealanders and Connaught Rangers, however, managed to gain access to a section of Turkish trench shown on their maps as 'D–C'. From there, as night fell, the battle became one of hand-to-hand fighting with bayonet and bomb in the maze of trenches that crisscrossed the hill. During the night, the attacking force was reinforced by the 9th Light Horse Regiment. The War Diary of the 5th Battalion Connaught Rangers gives some indication of the fierceness of the fighting in which Australians and Irishmen fought literally shoulder to shoulder:

> [A]t 23.55 [11.55 pm] the Light Horse had come into communication with the OC [Officer Commanding] Connaught Rangers & had arranged for retaking the trench from D to C. The Australians progressed some distance but were in their turn driven back to D. A further portion of them took & held the more southern portion of the cross trench about 80 yds in front of & parallel to the old New Zealand line. This was done & measures were taken to consolidate this new line. The men advanced in spite of the galling cross fire & shrapnel, in splendid fashion, & made good their footing little by little. It was found, however, that the trench could not be used to the extent desired on account of the piles of dead & debris, which not only littered the trench from D to C, but simply choked it up.[55]

As dawn broke, the Allied forces held disconnected sections of the Turkish line. During the day both sides deepened and extended their trenches and in between bombing duels tried to rest in preparation for the night to come. But for the Connaught Rangers the fight was over. Reduced to only 164 men, they were relieved and replaced by men of the 10th Light Horse Regiment, one of the regiments that had been mauled at the Nek three weeks before.

The Allies never did capture the summit of Hill 60. Nevertheless, they continued to hold the seaward slopes, securing the Anzac flank and keeping open the link with Suvla. Like so much of what happened at Gallipoli from 25 April onwards, the action at Hill 60 was a half-victory gained at great expense, with the fighting of 27–29 August adding another 1100 names to the casualty list.

'Our work unfinished'

The Irishmen of the 29th Brigade did no more fighting at Anzac. Reduced to under effective strength, they were employed mostly in work parties until 29 September, when they marched down to the shore and, with their compatriots of the 30th and 31st Brigades from Suvla, boarded ships for Lemnos. Moved by the sight of his men filing down to the beach, Major Bryan Cooper wrote:

> We had passed that way less than two months before, but going in the opposite direction full of high hopes. Now we were leaving the Peninsula again, our work unfinished and the Turks still in possession of the Narrows. Nor was it possible to help thinking of the friends lying in narrow graves on the scrub-covered hillside or covered by the debris of filled-in trenches, whom we seemed to be abandoning. Yet though there was sorrow at departing there was no despondency.[56]

Among Anzacs and Irishmen there was a mutual respect. Lieutenant Colonel Jourdain recounted how in November 1915 a party of Australian soldiers who had been evacuated wounded to England met John Redmond MP, leader of the Irish National Party, while visiting the House of Commons and expressed to him their 'highest admiration for the fighting qualities of the Irish soldiers. One charge by the Connaught Rangers was, they said, the finest thing they had seen in the war'.[57] Fifteen years later, Jourdain told the British Official Historian:

> I must say I liked soldiering with the A. & NZ Division,
> they were delightful to serve with – they remember all
> this even now in Australia, and they look back with much
> pleasure to those days in August 1915 – when they were
> with us in Gallipoli.[58]

The 10th (Irish) Division's reprieve was brief, for in December it
was sent to Salonika to fight the Bulgarians who, sensing the way
the war was then going, had allied themselves with Turkey. The
Irishmen's experiences in that theatre would prove no more uplifting
than their brief but tragic sojourn at Gallipoli. In September 1917
the division was transferred to Palestine, where it fought alongside
the Australian Light Horse in battles such as Beersheba and in the
capture of Jerusalem. During its time there, the Irish component
was steadily diluted due to declining enlistments until by the end of
the war it was effectively an Indian division.

For the Anzacs, the Gallipoli campaign ended in December 1915
when they were evacuated in what proved to be the most successful
operation of the whole campaign. Despite Hamilton's fear that up
to one half of the force could be lost during the evacuation, not one
man was killed and only two were slightly wounded. The Suvla and
Helles evacuations were similarly successful. If as much planning
and preparation had gone into some of the battles, the outcome of
the campaign might have been different.

Gallipoli was a severe defeat for the military forces of the British
Empire, and was to have a profound effect on its emerging nations.
Anzacs and Irishmen both came away from the peninsula convinced
they had been mucked about and butchered by the incompetence
of the British generals. Irish nationalist MP John Dillon referred
in the House of Commons to British officers 'who had led our
regiments at Suvla ... and who hurled them to death on the slopes
of those hills which they would have carried, and which would
have enabled them to get to Constantinople had they been decently
led'.[59] Unionist leaders were also critical, with Sir Edward Carson
telling Parliament that Gallipoli 'hung around our necks like a
millstone'.[60]

The Real Irish Spirit, an Irish recruiting poster, c. 1915.
Recruiting in Ireland became more difficult after
the failure of the Dardanelles campaign.
(AWM ARTV00957)

For Australians and New Zealanders, eager to impress the mother country of their worthiness, Gallipoli, despite the cost, had a salutary effect on the nation-building process without rupturing relations with the British Empire. In contrast, nationalist Irishmen, who sought to impress no-one as they wanted to become not a nation so much as 'a nation once again', were not so forgiving. Separatist nationalists, who were opposed to the war, exploited the Dardanelles fiasco to whip up anti-British sentiment, while moderate nationalists began to lose faith in the idea that supporting Britain in the war effort would assure home rule, leading to a decline in recruiting.

For some it was Gallipoli rather than the Easter Rising of 1916 that marked 'the moment their feelings towards the British began to turn'.[61] In her 1919 memoirs, Katharine Tynan, Irish poet and novelist, wrote:

> There was a rather sad visit to Dublin the September of 1915, for Lord and Lady Aberdeen were going to America; and before that there had been Suvla Bay, when blow after blow fell day after day on one's heart. So many of our friends had gone out in the 10th Division to perish at Suvla. For the first time came bitterness, for we felt that their lives had been thrown away and that their heroism had gone unrecognised. Suvla – the burning beach, and the poisoned wells, and the blazing scrub, does not bear thinking on. Dublin was full of mourning, and on the faces one met there was a hard brightness of pain as though the people's hearts burnt in the fire and were not consumed ... One met the mourners everywhere ... At least we started with utter enthusiasm for the war and its purposes. One did not know all that would happen, how it would drag and drag, till weariness of it and longing for it to end overcame all other feelings.[62]

While revolutionaries and politicians calculated the next moves in the propaganda war for the hearts and minds of nationalist

Ireland, families across Australia, New Zealand and Ireland shared the experience of mourning the husbands, sons and brothers who would no longer return to their native lands.

CHAPTER 2

CALLED TO ARMS

AUSTRALIAN SOLDIERS AND THE EASTER RISING OF 1916

As dawn broke across Australia on 25 April 1916, heralding the first Anzac Day, an anniversary that commemorates the defining moment of the Australian nation, Irish rebels who had seized the General Post Office (GPO) in Dublin the day before were fighting to establish a nation of their own. For six days, the insurgents, armed only with rifles and shotguns and numbering fewer than 1000 at the start, maintained their hold on the GPO and other strategically placed buildings throughout the city against the military might of the British Empire, which assembled a force of at least 16 000 men and armaments that included artillery and the armed patrol vessel *Helga*.[1]

The insurgents were members of two paramilitary forces: the Irish Volunteers, an advanced nationalist force opposed to the moderate nationalists' support for the war; and the Irish Citizen Army, a trade union militia formed in 1913 to protect striking workers from the police. Their purpose was to inspire the Irish people to rise up and overthrow British rule in Ireland.

When the Crown was marshalling its forces to strike back, Australian soldiers on leave in Ireland were called to arms to help put down the rising. Thus, while the men of the AIF, newly arrived in Belgium and France, were preparing themselves to do battle with the Germans in the anticipated summer offensive, these Australians found themselves called upon to do their duty, fighting not 'the Hun' but Irishmen with whom they had no quarrel.

Diggers in Dublin

In the voluminous literature on the Easter Rising, only a few writers acknowledge the role of dominion troops. In an article published in *Blackwood's Magazine* in July 1916, the author, using the pseudonym 'One of the Garrison', wrote of 'the Anzacs' and the part they played in defending Trinity College. After describing an incident in which they shot 'a despatch-rider of the enemy', he recounted how he later met the soldiers:

> After being relieved, I joined the Anzacs on the roof. They were undoubtedly men fashioned for the enjoyment of danger. And certainly it would be harder to find nicer comrades. Alas for thousands of these fine soldiers who have left their bones on Gallipoli!

And he gave them even higher praise, claiming: 'There can be no doubt that the accurate fire maintained from the college was an important factor in the salvation of the City'.[2] Another contemporary reference to Anzacs in the Easter Rising is contained in *A History of the Irish Rebellion of 1916*:

> Stray soldiers were summoned from the adjacent streets and from the Central Soldiers' Club hard by the College to reinforce the garrison; these included some 'Anzac' sharpshooters.[3]

Some later accounts of the rising also refer to Anzacs at Trinity College. Max Caulfield in his 1963 work, *The Easter Rebellion*, wrote:

Trinity was put into a state of siege by the University
O.T.C. within an hour of the Rebellion starting. Early in
the afternoon, a handful of Canadian and Anzac soldiers,
in Ireland for a brief furlough, made their way into the
university when they learned it was being held for the
Government. Several more were recruited by Trinity
students who paraded the streets in mufti, looking for
anyone who would help ...[4]

In his book, Caulfield described an encounter between 'an Australian
sergeant' and WJ Brennan-Whitmore, one of the rebels, after the
insurgents had surrendered:

Later an Australian sergeant came to the doorway and
shouted obscenities at them. Then he asked, "Ere, what about
the German sniper?'

'We had no German snipers,' insisted Brennan Whitmore
indignantly. 'By the way, you British had some pretty good
snipers yourselves. We had a cable across Sackville Street
and one of your fellows hit the canister from Trinity.'

The Aussie gave a whoop. 'Do you mean I got it?'

'You mean it was you?' asked Brennan Whitmore
astonished. 'Well, you didn't cut the cable, but you were
within half-an-inch of doing so.'

'Listen,' said the Aussie, suddenly friendly. 'I'll try to
find you something to eat.' Smiling happily he went away.

'You know, that fellow's crazy,' said [Captain Frank]
Thornton [of the Irish Volunteers].

In a short time the Aussie returned carrying a big biscuit
tin and a jug of cold tea.

'I'm sorry, but this is all I could scrounge,' he apologized.
'But anyway, here, take it,' and added, 'for Auld Lang Syne!'

Brennan Whitmore looked at the tin of biscuits—
everyone broken—at the jug of cold tea, and at the eager,
friendly face of the Australian. Then he reached out for
them. 'For Auld Lang Syne,' he said.[5]

Anzacs outside Trinity College during the
Easter Rising (Courtesy of the trustees of the
Imperial War Museum)

Amongst the published literature, only one account identifies the
Empire defenders of Trinity College Dublin by name: the *1916
Rebellion Handbook*, a detailed account of the rising compiled by
the *Weekly Irish Times*.[6] In a section headed 'Colonial Soldiers who
Assisted in Defence of TCD' it names six South Africans, five New
Zealanders, two Canadians and one Australian, the last identified as
'1985 Pte McHugh, 9th Aus. Infantry Force'.[7] This does not square
with Caulfield's reference to an Australian sergeant being at Trinity

College. However, a New Zealand sergeant is among the colonial defenders named in the *1916 Rebellion Handbook*, so it is possible that Brennan-Whitmore mistook the New Zealander for an Australian.

Individual service records and diaries in the personal records collection of the Australian War Memorial (AWM) also help build a picture of the activities of Australian soldiers during the Easter Rising. Other than Private McHugh, who was at Trinity College, the diggers known to be in Dublin included Private George Edward Davis and Private Robert Henry Grant of the 2nd Australian Motor Transport Company and Private John Joseph Chapman of the 9th Battalion.

Private John Joseph Chapman

Chapman was on convalescent leave when he visited Ireland in April 1916. Born in Ballarat in 1888, he enlisted on 15 September 1914 in Brisbane and within a fortnight was on his way to Alexandria on board the *Omrah* with the 9th Battalion. He trained in Egypt and with his battalion was in the first wave that landed at Gallipoli on 25 April 1915. Chapman served there until August and would have seen action in some of the battles to seize the heights during the August offensive, before he fell ill on 14 August 1915 and was evacuated to Malta and from there to England.

On the night of Thursday, 20 April 1916, Chapman and an unnamed companion caught the overnight train and ferry to Dublin, checking in at the Waverley Hotel in Sackville Street (now O'Connell Street). They spent the Friday sightseeing in Dublin before taking a train the next morning to Killarney to visit the lakes. On the journey, Chapman and his mate teamed up with two Australian nurses, members of the Red Cross Voluntary Aid Detachment (VAD) who were staying at Ross's Hotel in Parkgate Street (now rebuilt as the Ashling Hotel).

After a weekend of sightseeing, horse riding and boating on the lakes, the Australians caught the train back to Dublin on Easter Monday, but they only travelled as far as Limerick before it was stopped, no doubt due to events then unfolding in Dublin. After a delay, the train was diverted to the south, but it was again held up at Cork, where Chapman and his fellow travellers were forced to stay on board the train overnight. Leaving Cork the next afternoon at 2.30 pm, the train took six hours, rather than the usual three, to reach Dublin. When it arrived at Kingsbridge (now Heuston) Station, Chapman was escorted to the nearby Royal Barracks (now Collins Barracks) and told to be ready for duty at any time.

At the time of the rising, the Royal Barracks was home to the 10th Battalion of the Royal Dublin Fusiliers, made up of 37 officers and 430 men. The next morning, Wednesday 26 April, Chapman found himself in the thick of the fighting. The insurgents had seized buildings on both sides of the Liffey in the vicinity of the barracks, and a group of about 20 men under 19-year-old Sean Heuston had occupied the Mendicity Institution on the south side, preventing troops from moving along the northern quays towards another insurgent stronghold at the Four Courts. The British needed to capture Heuston's position in order to free up their access along the quays. Chapman was ordered to join in the fight. However, it took more than two days to achieve the objective. Chapman's account of his involvement is brief: 'Given rifle and ammunition and had to fight enemy in the streets. Nearly got hit several times. Only a few casualties on our side'.[8]

Chapman remained on duty throughout 26 April, not returning to the barracks until the following morning. Thereafter, his tour of duty in Dublin consisted mostly of guarding the barracks or the nearby Arbour Hill military prison, which was filling up with captured insurgents. Sir Roger Casement, the renowned Anglo-Irish civil servant turned revolutionary, had been held there briefly the week before on his way to London, and the rebel leader Pádraic Pearse was imprisoned there after he surrendered to the British commander Brigadier William Lowe on the afternoon of Saturday 29 April. Chapman's diary does not record whether he was aware that he was guarding the leader of the rising. What it does indicate, however, is that on the first night of Pearse's captivity Chapman was only a short distance away visiting Ross's Hotel, where he took tea with the Australian VADs and exchanged stories of their experiences during the rising.

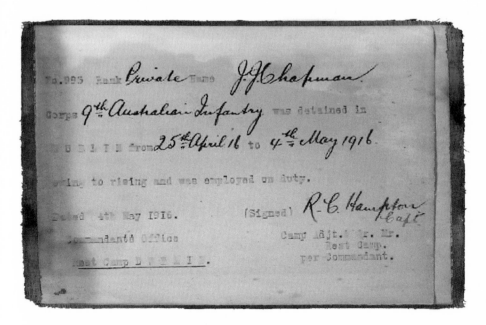

A copy of Private John Chapman's chit
(Jeff Kildea)

On the afternoon of Tuesday 2 May, Chapman was given leave until 9 o'clock the next morning. He took the opportunity to walk into the city centre to view the damage caused during the rising. Two days later, he was on his way back to England carrying a chit explaining his delay in returning from leave.

Following his brief, but action-packed sojourn in Ireland, Chapman remained in England for another three months before crossing the Channel to France, where he rejoined the 9th Battalion on 9 August 1916. Despite being wounded soon thereafter, during the battalion's unsuccessful attack on Mouquet Farm, near Pozières, he survived the war, being commissioned on 2 February 1918.[9]

Privates George Edward Davis and Robert Henry Grant

Private Davis was born in Coromandel, New Zealand, and enlisted on 16 September 1914 at Albert Park in Victoria at the age of 21 years. Three days before Christmas, he embarked for the Middle East on board the *Ceramic*. Although he arrived off Anzac Cove on 28 April 1915, he did not land at Gallipoli until 11 May 1915. In the meantime he was engaged in assisting the transport of stores between Lemnos and Anzac Cove. But being in the Q Store was no guarantee of safety once he landed on the crowded peninsula, and in his diary Davis wrote about a couple of incidents where he survived close calls from sniper fire.[10]

In August, he contracted enteric dysentery and was evacuated to Lemnos, from where he was transferred to England aboard the *Aquitania* in October. He was treated in military hospitals at Hammersmith and then Feltham, and upon discharge was posted to AIF Headquarters in Horseferry Road, London, where he became an ambulance driver. In April 1916, Davis was given leave, and on the evening of Thursday 20 April he left London by train, crossing over to Kingstown (now Dún Laoghaire) by ferry next morning, Good Friday. He was with a mate from the Australian Motor Transport Section, Private Bob Grant. Born at Oakleigh in Victoria, Grant was a mechanic when he enlisted in the 11th Battalion on 10 September 1914, aged 21 years. Like Davis, he was invalided to England after falling ill at Gallipoli in September 1915.

On Easter Saturday, the two men took the train to Killarney to visit the lakes. They spent the weekend seeing the sights before catching the Sunday evening train back to Dublin. Unlike Chapman, who did not leave Killarney until the next day, Davis and Grant were in Dublin when the rising broke out. In fact, they witnessed a group of Volunteers making their way to the GPO, as Davis recorded in his diary:

> A squad of about forty men and boys, all carrying firearms, passed us. There were all makes of deadly weapons and all calibres from pea-rifles to shot-guns. Many of them wore a bluish-grey uniform similar to those worn by German soldiers. They were a motley crew, but the grim look on their faces told us they were not on pleasure bent, and we were not then interested enough to enquire.

A short while later a sergeant in the Royal Dublin Fusiliers approached the two Australians and warned them to leave Dublin as the Sinn Féiners were about to rise and attack the city. At first,

Davis did not take the warning seriously. After hearing rifle fire, they joined a crowd that had gathered on the corner opposite the old Parliament House, near Trinity College, and observed insurgents on the roof of City Hall firing at people in the street below. Onlookers implored the Australians to hide, telling them they would be shot, but they nonchalantly replied that they were tourists and disclaimed any interest in the fight. But their complacency was soon dispelled, as Davis described:

> Walking towards Parliament Street, we were brought to our senses by a rifle bullet which struck the kerb nearby, and was followed by a quick succession of shots. I ducked into the doorway as a bullet struck the concrete pillar close to my head, the chips stinging in my face. My pal dodged around the corner, and knowing discretion to be the better part of valour, I followed.

As they joined the civilians fleeing the scene, a man running along-side them was shot in the back and fell to the ground. They dragged him around the corner and bundled him into a taxi. Davis and his companion crossed over the river to the north side, but upon sighting two insurgents with rifles they took refuge in a second-hand furni-ture shop where they discovered a small family of refugees whose motor car had been confiscated by the rebels. The family lived at Rathmines, one of the better suburbs of Dublin, and offered to take Davis and Grant with them to their home. Covering their uniforms with civilian clothes, the two Australians tagged along with the locals as they walked through the streets to Rathmines, arriving at a large mansion, where Davis was impressed at being waited on by liveried servants. Invited to stay with the family until the rioting had ceased, they decided it would be wiser to report themselves to the military authorities, which they did after dinner.

At Portobello Barracks (now Cathal Brugha Barracks) just off Rathmines Road, they were informed that transport back to England was not available and they were each given a rifle and ammunition and told to protect themselves and the barracks. That night they joined a party of 70 men detailed to escort arms and ammunition to Dublin Castle. They set out on a roundabout route that brought them near the Liffey. As they passed under a street lamp, a volley of rifle shots rained down on them 'from a dozen rifles across the river from the windows of the upper storeys of the Four Courts Hotel'. Davis described the scene:

> Above and around us bullets 'pinged' and broken glass clattered to the footpath. The horses bolted and vanished in the darkness, and the troops did likewise. I ducked for cover with the rest and dodged with several of my comrades round the pillars of a nearby building … I at once knew where to find shelter, and bending as low as I could, I ran forward to the cover of a low stone wall skirting the river. Our men in charge had vanished, our ammunition waggons had done likewise, and apparently no one knew exactly where the barracks lay.

The remaining men, 30 out of the original party of 70, made their way to Kingsbridge Station where they stayed the night, and for the next few days they were assigned to guard duty, though not very conscientiously, judging by Davis's account of Wednesday 26 April:

> I was having a nap in a railway carriage about midday, and failed to hear our guard alarm sound. Waking a few minutes afterwards, the place was a scene of activity. The station was being attacked, and jumping up, I could see plainly that the attacking party had no chance as they were hopelessly outnumbered. However, in the affray, one Tommy officer fell wounded. The end came when a small howitzer opened fire on a group of brick buildings close by, and shot several gaping holes in the walls. At dark the guards were doubled.

The next day he went with a party escorting stores to various parts of the city, including Trinity College, where he 'noticed a digger and several "Enzedders" amongst the armed guard. They were evidently in a similar predicament to ourselves'. Presumably the digger was Private McHugh.

Like Private Chapman, Davis and Grant on their trip to Killarney had met up with two Australian nurses who were staying at Ross's Hotel. Davis recorded how, on the Saturday, the two men visited them:

> Hearing that the Ross Hotel was under observation by the military, my pal and I went over to [visit] two Australian nurses, who journeyed to Killarney with us, [and] were staying there. We found them safe but a little scared as a stray bullet occasionally whistled through their window; and, after a good meal of bread and butter and tea (a contrast to bully beef), we returned to our billett [*sic*].

The nurses may well have been the same VADs that Chapman referred to, as the soldiers and nurses were all in Killarney on that Easter weekend and would have travelled down there on the same train. There were not many Australian VADs in Ireland at the time.

Once the fighting had ended Davis was keen to return to England. On Monday 1 May, he and Grant managed to obtain documentation enabling them to catch the Holyhead ferry that night. They reported for duty at Horseferry Road the next day. Despite efforts by his commanding officer to retain him in London, Davis crossed over to France at the end of July 1916. He continued his service until his war was shortened by good fortune when he was selected in September 1918 for early return to Australia. After receiving the news, he wrote in his diary:

> I feel as if I am walking on air, as out of forty-seven 1914 men I am one of the nine in our Column picked to leave on Monday morning on our homeward journey.

The journey commenced on 27 September 1918, but was interrupted three weeks later at Suez where Davis was hospitalised, a victim of the dreadful pneumonic influenza pandemic, known as the 'Spanish flu', which killed tens of millions around the world. Fortunately, he survived and a month later he was again on his way home, arriving in Melbourne on 21 December 1918.

Bob Grant remained in England where he worked as a driver with the Red Cross and the Australian Motor Transport Section. He became ill with influenza in June 1918 and shortly thereafter suffered an injury to his hand, which saw him returned to Australia in September 1918.

Private Michael John McHugh

Private McHugh, the Australian soldier who assisted in the defence of Trinity College, did not leave any papers and the *1916 Rebellion Handbook* provides no further information about him or his activities at the college. But a combination of his AIF personal file and documents in the Manuscripts Department of Trinity College Library enable the events in which he was involved to be reconstructed.

Born near Cooktown in Queensland in 1893, Michael John McHugh was a labourer when he enlisted in the 9th Battalion on 9 January 1915. On 16 April 1915, he sailed for Egypt with the 5th Reinforcements on board the *Kyarra*, joining the battalion two months later at Gallipoli. This was only a week before the battalion participated in a feint at the Knife's Edge on 28 June 1915, in which it sustained over a hundred casualties.[11] So, he probably saw action fairly early in his service on the peninsula and would have taken part in the bitter fighting during the August offensive.

On 16 September 1915, McHugh was admitted to hospital with influenza and enteric fever and evacuated to Malta on board the hospital ship *Somali*. After a month at the Imtarfa Military Hospital, he was transferred to England on the *Re d'Italia* and admitted to the 1st Southern General Hospital, Edgbaston. At the end of November, he was discharged to duty but did not return to the 9th Battalion until July 1916. In the meantime, during Easter week, he spent an eventful few days in Dublin.

When news of the rising reached Trinity College, the Chief Steward Joseph Marshall directed two porters, whom he armed with Fenian pikes which he had seized while serving in the Dublin Metropolitan Police during the rising of 1867, to lock the front gate and to invite into the college all passing soldiers.[12] Those invited

Private Michael McHugh
(Courtesy of Bill McHugh)

in included McHugh, who is recorded as having served there from 24 April to 5 May.[13] James Glen, a British soldier, was walking down O'Connell Street when he and a colleague were fired upon. In an account of the rising, he wrote:

> We realized that we were probably the target and ran down to O'Connell Bridge, where we were joined by about half a dozen soldiers (Australians and I think one or two South Africans) who were on leave and had been attracted by the firing.
>
> My friend and I ... took the party into College ... The Australians and South Africans volunteered to man the roof overlooking College Green where there were the best opportunities for experienced riflemen.[14]

As noted above, *Blackwood's Magazine* described the shooting of a dispatch rider outside the college, an event that in all probability involved McHugh. James Glen also described that incident:

> One of the marksmen on the College roof shot and killed a motor dispatch rider in SF [Sinn Féin] uniform in the street outside the Provost's house, his body being brought into College through the Front Gate.[15]

The dead insurgent is identified in the *1916 Rebellion Handbook* as Gerald Keogh, aged 20 years.[16] The shooting is also mentioned in a handwritten letter dated 10 May 1916 from Gerard Fitzgibbon, a member of the college Officer Training Corps (OTC), to an acquaintance, William Hugh Blake:

> We had five Anzacs, two, or perhaps three, Canadians ... three South Africans, one in a Kilt ... almost all men on leave or sick furlough in Dublin, who had been fired upon when – unarmed – as they were walking through the streets ... One thing that terrified [?] was early on Tuesday morning, just after Dawn. Three of their dispatch riders came pelting down on bicycles from Stephen's Green, bringing dispatches to the Post Office, and we had twelve or fifteen men posted in windows and on the roof in front of College. They fired on the cyclists. Killed one, wounded another, and the third left his bicycle & rifle & bolted down a side street. No doubt he went back to his headquarters and told them the College was stuffed [?] with armed men. The booty collected was three bicycles, five rifles, 400 rounds of ammunition, & their dispatches, and of course the [corpse]. We planted him out later on to fertilise the Provost's daffodils ... One Anzac got nine, but he was a marksman, and the Anzacs were given all the eligible situations, which it must be allowed they deserved. They were an extraordinary gang. I have never seen their like. The man they shot on the bicycle in the early dawn was riding fast, it was a hard shot at a downward angle from a high window, I believe they only fired four or

five shots and he had two through his head, one through his right lung, and a fourth that hit [?] and winged the second man of the party. If they hadn't concentrated so much they would have bagged all three.[17]

The dispatch rider's body was brought into the college by Acting Porter George Crawford, who the next day wrote in a report:

> At 4.15 A.M. on the 25th I was ordered by Lieut Luce to arouse the Provosts House, so that a Sinn Feiner, who was shot at the foot of Grafton Street, could be brought in that way, three more men and myself succeeded in bringing in the dead body, also two bicycles, two Rifles, 1 Revolver, 1 Bandolier & Kit.[18]

Elsie Mahaffy, the daughter of the Provost of Trinity College, described in her diary kept during Easter week how the dead insurgent was brought into the Provost's house. She wrote that he had been carrying a rifle, a revolver and plenty of ammunition and money, and added:

> For 3 days he lay in College, in an empty room. When necessary he was buried in the Park and later when quiet was restored was disinterred and sent [?] to the morgue, but during the fortnight while he lay in College, though well dressed and from a respectable street, no one ever came to ask for his body.
>
> His friends must have seen him fall but apparently were too cowardly or too callous to come & secure him decent burial.[19]

It is interesting to note that in his letter, Fitzgibbon claimed 'One Anzac got nine' in a way that suggests he meant that the Anzac had killed nine insurgents. But that does not square with the information compiled by historian Brian Barton on casualties suffered by the insurgents, which suggests that Gerald Keogh was the only one killed in the sniping war conducted in the College Green area.[20] Nevertheless, Fitzgibbon was not the only contemporary to claim that the death toll was higher than has been acknowledged. In

Sinn Féin and the Irish Rebellion, a polemical pamphlet published in Melbourne in 1916, the socialist activist DP Russell quoted from a letter said to have been written by a New Zealander, Corporal John Godwin Garland to his father:

> On Saturday morning we killed a woman who was sniping from an hotel window in Dame Street. When the RAMC brought her in we saw she was only a girl about 20, stylishly dressed, and not at all bad-looking. She was armed with an automatic revolver and a Winchester repeater. Altogether we Anzacs were responsible for 27 rebels (twenty-four men and three women).[21]

Russell's pamphlet provides no further information about Garland or the provenance of the letter. However, the *1916 Rebellion Handbook* identified '3/1315 Corporal Garland, New Zealand MC' as one of the colonial defenders of Trinity College. New Zealand military service records confirm that that serial number belonged to Private John Godwin Garland of Auckland, a medical orderly who from December 1915 to October 1916 served on board the NZ Hospital Ship *Marama*. Although Russell's letter writer might have been a real person, the claims made in the letter as published by Russell cannot be verified and are inconsistent with the available evidence on insurgent casualties both as to numbers and gender – not one woman is included among the dead in the list compiled by Brian Barton.[22]

On 5 August 1916, three months after the rising had been put down, a ceremony was held in the Provost's garden at Trinity College to present the commandant of the Officer Training Corps with two large silver presentation cups, each valued at £50 and weighing 170 oz. Silver replicas were presented to all ranks of the Corps who participated in the defence of the college, as well as to certain other individuals including the dominion soldiers who had assisted. By then, however, Private McHugh was in France, having rejoined the 9th Battalion on 29 July 1916, two days after it had been relieved from the desperate fighting around Pozières. The battalion had been severely savaged during the action and McHugh marched in to a badly depleted unit that had lost 17 officers and 299 men during the previous week.[23] Three weeks later, the battalion returned to the front line in the attack on Mouquet Farm, but, unlike Private Chapman, his fellow 9th Battalion veteran of the Dublin fighting, McHugh survived the ordeal unwounded, while the battalion sustained further casualties of 5 officers and 158 men.[24]

Nevertheless, three months later, McHugh once again found himself on board a hospital ship heading to England after being admitted to hospital with appendicitis. He remained in England until 22 November 1917, when he rejoined his unit in France. In July 1917, while at Hurdcott camp in Wiltshire, McHugh received a letter from Lieutenant CL Robinson, Adjutant of the Trinity College OTC, advising him that he was due a silver presentation cup for his part in the defence of Trinity College and requesting an address to which he might send it. Hoping to wheedle a bit of leave in Dublin, McHugh replied:

> I am to get a few days leave to proceed to Dublin and my Colonel is not the kind of man to grant leave without he has a reasonable excuse put before him.
>
> Now just between you and I Sir I wish you would do me a favour by dropping me a line stating that you should like me to be present at your OTC to be presented personally with this cup.
>
> If you could do me such favour Sir I would be very thankful to you.

He must have thought his chances slim because he added an address to which the cup might be sent in the event that it was to be posted. In a letter dated 23 July 1917, Robinson confirmed that he couldn't help and on 1 August 1917 McHugh wrote back acknowledging receipt of the cup and advising that he would call on him personally when he went on leave. Whether he received his Dublin leave and returned to Trinity College is not known.[25]

After returning to France, McHugh was wounded by shrapnel on 21 July 1918 at Méteren near Armentières and once more evacuated to England, where he remained until he rejoined the 9th Battalion at its rest camp at Gorenflos in France, in early November, a few days before the armistice. He returned to Australia in April 1919.

An 'Australian officer … on leave in Ireland'

Another Australian in Dublin during Easter week wrote of his experiences in a letter to Richard Garland, the general manager of the Dunlop Rubber Company. The text of the letter was published in *The Age* newspaper on 1 July 1916. *The Age* did not name the soldier but described him as an 'Australian officer … on leave in Ireland' who had offered his services when the rising broke out. The letter describes a series of events in which members of the Crown forces committed atrocities against Irish civilians, including one of the most notorious episodes of the rising – the murder by Captain John Bowen-Colthurst of three journalists (Thomas Dickson, Patrick J. MacIntyre and the well-known Dublin eccentric Francis Sheehy Skeffington), whom he ordered to be shot by firing squad on the Wednesday morning of Easter week.

Bowen-Colthurst, of an Anglo-Irish family from County Cork, was a captain in the 3ʳᵈ Battalion Royal Irish Rifles, stationed at Portobello Barracks. He had been severely wounded at the Aisne in September 1914, leading to his being invalided home. Unfit for combat, he might have sat out the war in the relative peace of a home posting. However, with the outbreak of the rising, Bowen-Colthurst once again found himself in action. On the evening of Tuesday 25 April 1916, he was given command of a patrol to uncover a group of rebels believed to be holed up in the shop premises of a suspected Sinn Féin sympathiser, Alderman James Kelly, about a kilometre from Portobello Barracks. Earlier that day a young officer, Lieutenant Morris, who was guarding the bridge near the barracks, had detained Sheehy Skeffington as he was walking towards his home in Rathmines followed by a small crowd, who were making a noise and heckling the odd-looking eccentric. That night, on his way out of the barracks, Bowen-Colthurst removed Sheehy Skeffington from the guardroom and forced him to accompany the patrol as a hostage, threatening to shoot him if the party were fired upon. The patrol included the anonymous Australian soldier, who described the evening's events in his letter home.[26]

As the patrol turned into Rathmines Road, it came upon three men who had been at a sodality meeting at the nearby Catholic Church of Our Lady of Refuge.[27] The Australian wrote in his letter:

> Near the barracks we saw three men. The captain wanted to know their business, and one answered back, so the captain just knocked him insensible with the butt of his rifle. The other two ran and one shouted something about 'down with the military' and the captain just shot him dead.

The patrol continued along Rathmines Road to Kelly's shop, where the Australian threw a bomb through the front window, allowing the patrol to charge in. He wrote:

> There was a light showing from a room downstairs. I went down carefully, and told the people there to put up their hands, just allowing them to see a bomb I was holding. This had the right effect, and I went down and found five men and three women. They were marched to the barracks. Two were let go. The three others turned out to be head men of the gang and were shot.

This last sentence is a clear reference to the shooting of the three journalists the next day. The description of them as 'head men of the gang', however, was wrong; no doubt the Australian was taken in by self-serving allegations that Bowen-Colthurst later made about the journalists to cover up his crime.

The Australian was not the only one to believe that fabrication. On Friday 28 April 1916, Mary Louisa Norway, the wife of Arthur Hamilton Norway, the secretary of the General Post Office who was often at Dublin Castle during Easter week, wrote in a letter: 'On Wednesday three of the ringleaders were caught, and it is said they were shot immediately!'[28] Bowen-Colthurst might have got away with it, but for the persistence of a fellow officer in the Royal Irish Rifles, Major Sir Francis Vane, who was not satisfied when

Bowen-Colthurst's immediate superiors refused to charge him. He had simply done his duty under difficult circumstances, was the response, an attitude shared by many in the Anglo-Irish community. In her diary of the rising, Elsie Mahaffy, wrote of Bowen-Colthurst in glowing terms: 'one of the best young men I have ever met' and described Sheehy Skeffington as 'a man whose life and principles were vicious' and the other two shot with him as 'ruffians, editors of sedition & indecent papers'.[29] But Vane took the matter to the top, laying his allegations before the Secretary of State for War, Lord Kitchener, who ordered that Bowen-Colthurst be arrested and charged.

On 10 June 1916, a General Court Martial found Bowen-Colthurst guilty of the murder of Sheehy Skeffington and the two other men. But the court also found he was insane at the time he committed those acts. Therefore, instead of being hanged for the murders, he was sentenced to be detained in Broadmoor criminal lunatic asylum during His Majesty's pleasure. This lasted less than two years, until January 1918, when Bowen-Colthurst was granted conditional release. On 26 April 1921 – five years to the day after the murder of the three journalists – Bowen-Colthurst, with his wife and four children, emigrated to Canada, where he resided until his death on 11 December 1965 at the grand age of 85 years.[30]

Public opinion was not assuaged by the court martial. Sheehy Skeffington's widow, Hannah, mounted a campaign that eventually led to the government's establishing a royal commission under the chairmanship of former Home Secretary Sir John Simon to inquire into the murders. The commission took evidence between 23 and 31 August 1916 and issued its report on 29 September 1916. While stating the obvious, namely, that the 'shooting of unarmed and unresisting civilians without trial constitutes the offence of murder, whether martial law has been proclaimed or not', the report laid no blame on 'the military', whose conduct, it said, 'should be viewed in the light of the abnormal circumstances then prevailing'.[31]

The activities of the anonymous Australian on leave did not end with the raid on Kelly's shop. The letter goes on to describe another tour of duty – one which also had wider implications:

On Thursday night a Canadian and I acted as bombers. In town we didn't see a single civilian – just as well for them, as they would have been shot – and the houses had to be in darkness too. One house had a light in the front window, but one of the officers put half a dozen shots into it, and it soon went out. Our mission was to raid the house of a Russian Countess, who was a keen rebel. The house was empty, and we searched it from top to bottom, finding tons of rebel and incriminating documents.

One of the rebels was indeed a countess – Countess Constance Markievicz – though she was not Russian but an Anglo-Irish woman by the name of Constance Gore-Booth, who was married to a Polish count, Casimir Dunin-Markievicz, whose family owned land in Russian-ruled Ukraine. A prominent figure in the women's Irish nationalist movement, the countess stood for parliament in 1908 and was gaoled in 1911 for her part in demonstrations against King George V's visit to Ireland. While most women participants in the rising acted as nurses or messengers, Countess Markievicz insisted on performing a full combatant role, serving as a member of the Irish Citizen Army and second-in-command to Michael Mallin, commander of the rebel forces at St Stephen's Green. After the surrender she was court-martialled along with other participants in the rising, found guilty and sentenced to death, but with a recommendation of clemency on account of her sex that saw her sentence commuted to life imprisonment.[32]

Thus, on the Thursday night of Easter week, two days before the surrender, an anonymous Australian soldier on leave in Ireland was engaged on a mission to gather and secure evidence that could be used against Countess Markievicz once the rising collapsed, as was clear by then would soon be the case.

The identity of the 'Australian officer' remains a mystery. A list containing the names and units of officers who reported at Portobello Barracks during Easter week does not include any Australian officer.[33] However, the identification of the letter writer as an 'Australian officer ... on leave in Ireland' comes not from the text of the letter itself but *The Age*'s introductory comments. He might not have been an officer at all. In the letter, he wrote, 'They called for bombers and I was turned over to a captain, an enormous man [of] about 6 feet 4 inches'. (A form in Bowen–Colthurst's pension file gives his height in 1935 as 6 feet 3½ inches.)[34] This suggests a degree of subordination that implies he was not an officer. Moreover, an officer, whose role is to lead and direct, is unlikely to have been appointed the raiding party's bomber. These observations apply equally to his account of the raid on the Thursday night. Monk Gibbon, a lieutenant in the British Army Service Corps, was at Portobello Barracks during Easter week. In his war memoirs, *Inglorious Soldier*, he wrote of the Bowen–Colthurst affair and of 'the tall bomber', whom he met the morning after the raid on Kelly's shop, describing him as a non-commissioned officer.[35]

Whoever he was, his letter when published in *The Age* provoked a strong reaction in Australia, particularly from Irish Catholics already incensed by what they saw as Britain's brutal suppression of the rising and the execution of its leaders. Catholic newspapers published comments highly critical of his conduct. A correspondent to the *Tribune*, a Melbourne Catholic newspaper, wrote:

> As a specimen of cold-blooded atrocity I venture to say that the Hun in his worst alleged excesses has not equalled it … The letter of this 'Australian officer on leave', which is a disgrace to Australian manhood … stirs up rebel instincts that I thought had perished.[36]

Attitudes to the Easter Rising

The correspondent's hyperbole illustrates the passion which the letter aroused. And it was not only Catholic newspapers and their readers that were outraged. A few months after the rising, DP Russell republished the letter in his pamphlet *Sinn Féin and the Irish Rebellion*, adding the comment, 'Did Australia's sons in Dublin add lustre to the deeds of the heroes who fought and died in Gallipoli for the "Rights of Small Nations"?'[37]

Russell's question remains. What do we say about the deeds of these Australian soldiers in Dublin during the Easter Rising? Did they have any qualms about fighting Irish insurgents? In attempting to answer these questions, it must be acknowledged that we do not know, and are unlikely ever to know, how many Australian soldiers were in Dublin during Easter week 1916, or who they were, as relevant AIF files were culled in the late 1950s. Nevertheless, it is reasonable to assume that there were more than the handful whose stories are told here, like the unnamed Australian treated at Dublin Castle hospital by a VAD who wrote of her experiences in *Blackwood's Magazine*.[38]

No Australian units were posted there, but Ireland was a popular destination for Australian soldiers on leave, as is discussed in chapter 4. In April 1916, the AIF had just moved from Egypt to France and its administration was still in the process of transferring from Cairo to London. Yet, by then more than 13000 sick or wounded Australians were in the United Kingdom, entitled upon discharge to convalescent leave.[39] We also know that a small number of Australian VADs were in Dublin during the rising, as recounted by Chapman and Davis. They had travelled to Europe, or joined up in England, as volunteers to assist the Red Cross in treating sick and wounded soldiers.

For those Australians who did lend a hand, it would not have been an easy time. They had enlisted and travelled half way round the world to fight Germans, not Irishmen. It was also dangerous work, as attested by Chapman and Davis. But as with so many of the deeds of the diggers during the Great War, one is left wondering what motivated them to do what they did. Veterans of the Dardanelles campaign, who had survived the hellhole of Gallipoli since the landing, would have well and truly lost their thirst for adventure. By September 1915, when Davis, Grant, Chapman and McHugh were on their way to England, morale was low, illness was rife and the glory of war had proved illusory. Men who a few months before had been enthralled by the idea of the great adventure had become envious of the sick and wounded who were being evacuated from the peninsula.[40]

Nevertheless, ingrained in these men was a strong sense of duty that kept them going, long after their martial enthusiasm had waned. In his graphic portrayal of life on the Western Front, *Eye-deep in Hell*, military historian John Ellis wrote:

> In the war as a whole, on all sides, most men simply did what they conceived to be their duty. When they were told to hold, they held; when told to advance, they went forward even to almost certain death. The reasons for this lay in their sense of patriotism, duty, honour and deference to authority; all much more important concepts [then] than they are today.[41]

Private Chapman's diary is lacking in detail and does not tell us what he thought about the rising or his part in its suppression. He was already an experienced soldier, having been on active service at Gallipoli. Yet street fighting against civilian insurgents would have been a completely different kind of war for him. As a soldier he no doubt did his duty, but whether he felt any concerns about fighting the Irish insurgents is not disclosed. Chapman was not a Catholic; he was Presbyterian. Whether his religion contributed to his attitudes to the rising can only be a matter of speculation. Certainly, Private Davis, a Methodist, was not happy about what he was asked to do. He recorded in his diary: 'We were in a very unenviable position, for we personally had no quarrel with the rioters'. But as a pragmatic Australian soldier he did his duty: 'We are making the best of a bad job, but would prefer to be anywhere but in this unenviable city'.[42] Private McHugh was a Catholic of Irish descent, but it seems he too did his duty. Whether he shot the dispatch rider who passed by Trinity College is not known, but by all accounts he would have been on the roof of the college when the event occurred. What he felt about being called to arms by the British military authorities and ordered to fight his 'cousins' has not been recorded and on his return to Australia he does not seem to have spoken much about it, if at all.[43]

But being Irish or a Catholic did not necessarily translate into sympathy for the insurgents or their cause, let alone a propensity to disobey an order to fight against them. When the rising broke out, a majority of the 2400 British Army soldiers in Dublin were Irishmen, mostly from regiments that recruited in the south of Ireland. It was these Irish troops that initially confronted and fought the rebels. It was not until reinforcements from the 59th (North Midland) Division began arriving in the city on the Wednesday that the Crown forces assumed a predominantly English composition.[44] John Dillon, the Irish Nationalist MP who was in Dublin during Easter week and witnessed events there, told the House of Commons:

> I asked Sir John Maxwell himself, 'Have you any cause of complaint of the Dublins [the Royal Dublin Fusiliers] who had to go down and fight their own people in the streets of Dublin? Did a single man turn back and betray the uniform he wears?' He told me, 'Not a man'.[45]

Irishmen in the British Army, including nationalists who before the war had been in the paramilitary Irish Volunteers, had already made a commitment to serve the Empire and to reject the arguments of the advanced nationalists that they were traitors to Ireland and degenerates for having taken the king's shilling. Attempts by the German Army to incite disaffection among the Irish regiments on the Western Front in the wake of the rising were met by derision and defiance. Historian Keith Jeffery has written:

> During May 1916 the 8th (Service) Battalion of the Royal Munster Fusiliers ... found themselves faced by two German placards. One read 'Irishmen! Heavy uproar in Ireland. English guns are firing at your wifes [sic] and children'. The other announced the fall of Kut to Turkish forces. According to the regimental history (not an entirely unbiased source) the men responded by singing 'God Save the King' and captured the placards which were later presented to King George V.[46]

Some Irishmen, like the nationalist intellectuals Tom Kettle and Frank Ledwidge, were troubled by their choice, but nevertheless considered that by enlisting in the British Army they were serving Ireland and the cause of home rule. It was only after the rebel leader

Pádraic Pearse had surrendered and the British began to execute the leaders that the insurgents of Easter week started to assume the mantle of Irish heroes. In the early days of the rising they were largely seen as wreckers who had stabbed Ireland in the back.

It is also the case that the rising was unpopular with those sections of Dublin's inhabitants who were dependent on the separation allowance paid to them while their husbands were serving in the British Army in France, either as regulars or in the New Army. Many of them feared the rising would threaten their economic well-being. Others had lost loved ones during the Gallipoli campaign. To many of them, the rising was an insult to the memory of those who had died fighting for the Empire.[47]

It is not surprising therefore that the immediate response of the Australian Irish to the rising was generally negative, both in Australia and at the front. Even Archbishop Daniel Mannix, who became well known in Australia and overseas as a passionate advocate of Irish independence, initially described the rising as truly deplorable and its leaders as misguided,[48] a sentiment shared by Sergeant James Joseph Makin of the 21st Battalion, a Catholic, who wrote to his mother:

> Is it not deplorable that trouble has broken out in Ireland? It is astounding, in as much as there are thousands of fine men in the Irish regiments here, who are moved by the highest sense of patriotism. Who can deny that these Irish regiments are not among the best of the British fighting units and are fighting to uphold British integrity and traditions? I have mixed with them for a month and I know their spirit. And yet they are having their honour and name filched away by a ruffian horde, blinded by long-past wrongs and kindled by German gold and influence. Let me hope that the trouble will be stamped out this time for good and all, as assuredly it will be, but at the expense of much needed lives at a critical moment. This is another instance illustrating the saneness of the 'Keep your eye on Germany' policy.[49]

The reference to German gold and German policy reflected a widespread belief at the time that the rising was instigated and financed by Germany to distract Britain from the war effort. An intelligence summary issued by the General Headquarters of the Egyptian Expeditionary Force on 28 April 1916 included the following:

> The capture of the notorious SIR ROGER CASEMENT and two German officers (on the very day when the disturbances broke out) whilst being landed off the Irish Coast from a disguised German Auxiliary cruiser has probably robbed the rebellion of all direction ... Inspired articles have already appeared in the Dutch and Italian papers which show clearly that this rebellion has been organized in Germany to co-incide with the approach of the spring when an Allied offensive was to be expected, and also relied [*sic*] to find in Ireland (excused from the Military Service Act) many men of military age who could be used to further the designs of the enemy.[50]

Casement had in fact been arrested on the preceding Friday after he had come ashore from a German submarine with Bob Monteith and Dan Bailey – Irishmen not Germans. Ironically, his intention had been to persuade the Irish rebel leaders to call off the rising because of the inadequacy of German support. Nevertheless, the intelligence report is indicative of the belief that the Germans were behind Irish opposition to the war, a view that had currency well before Easter week. An Australian officer from the 9th Light Horse Regiment had written home in November 1915 that while in Ireland on convalescent leave he had seen 'a full battalion of "Sinn Feiners" at Limerick dressed in German uniforms and armed with Mausers'.[51]

Yet Australian soldiers drew a distinction between Sinn Féiners and the Irish soldiers with whom they had served at the front. On 1 May 1916, Sergeant Makin wrote to his father:

> It is pleasing that the Irish rebellion is not as alarming as
> it was thought and is now dying out. It is most regrettable
> that it should have occurred at this time. It is the fanatical
> Sinn Feiners at the bottom of the trouble, & the Nationalist
> Party under John Redmond is absolutely against them. It
> is astounding when you see the Irish regiments here in
> France, fighting along with the rest of us: – Australians,
> N.Z.ers, & Canadians.[52]

Makin's reference to the Irish regiments and the unity of purpose
of the Empire soldiers touches on one of the key issues that divided
constitutional nationalists from the separatists: the idea that one
could serve the country of your birth and the Empire at one and
the same time, a view shared by most Australians, though not all.
Ironically, in Australia it was not nationalists but Empire loyalists
who opposed the notion of dual loyalty, believing that the Empire
was one and indivisible.[53]

The attitude of many Australian soldiers to the rising is probably
summed up by Private John Collingwood Angus of the 28th
Battalion, who in a letter to his sister on 5 May 1916 wrote:

> Things seem to be pretty lively in Ireland just now, well I
> wish they would send some of our boys there we would make
> things hot enough for them rebels in a pretty short time.[54]

Today, more than 90 years on, we know a lot more about the rising,
its causes and consequences than those in the thick of the action in
1916. But that should not colour our judgment of the deeds of the
diggers in Dublin. In all probability they shared Sergeant Makin's
opinion of the insurgents. And although they might not have liked
doing what they were ordered to do, they would have seen it as
their duty as loyal soldiers of the Empire to answer the call to arms
and 'to resist His Majesty's enemies and cause His Majesty's peace
to be kept and maintained'.[55]

CHAPTER 3

THE IRISH ANZACS

IRISH MEN AND WOMEN IN THE AUSTRALIAN FORCES

The town of Cahir in County Tipperary is situated in a delightful setting on the River Suir at the eastern end of the Galtee Mountains. On a rocky island in the middle of the river stands the town's major tourist attraction: Cahir Castle, reputed to be one of Ireland's largest and best-preserved Norman castles. In its shadow stands a less-well-known landmark, one not mentioned in the tourist books: the town's war memorial, on which are inscribed the names of 'the officers and men of Cahir and surrounding district who gave their lives in the Great War'. An Australian tourist visiting Cahir Castle and used to seeing war memorials in almost every town and suburb in Australia might not pay the memorial much attention. Yet, for reasons discussed in chapter 6, it is quite unusual to find in a town in the south of Ireland such a grand and well-kept memorial to 'England's war' in such a prominent location. On closer inspection, our hypothetical Australian tourist might be surprised to see on the memorial in bold red lettering the word 'Australians', underneath which appear in black lettering the names: D Clohessy, J Lonergan and TP Holloway.[1]

These names belong to just three of the approximately 6600 Irish-born men and women who served in the Australian forces during the First World War, of whom approximately 970 paid the ultimate price.[2] Most of them already called Australia home, having emigrated to the new land of opportunity in the South Seas. Some, however, found themselves in Australia by chance when war broke out and enlisted there rather than returning home to join up, perhaps fearful that the war might end before they did so or in the hope that they might get a free passage home when the AIF sailed.[3] Each has his or her own story to tell, and in this chapter we will look at some of those stories.

Before doing so, it is worth noting that the traffic was not all one way. Scores of Australians, for one reason or another, took part in the war serving in Irish regiments, more than 30 of them being killed or dying of wounds or illness.[4] Among them was Captain Bryan Hughes (an Australian rugby union international and a son of John Hughes, a former Minister for Justice in New South Wales), who was killed in August 1918 while serving with the Royal Dublin Fusiliers. Bryan and his younger brother Gilbert had travelled to England in July 1915 in order to get to the Western Front as soon as possible. Armed with letters of recommendation from Archbishop Michael Kelly, the Catholic Archbishop of Sydney, they both received commissions in the regiment through the intervention of Irish nationalist leader John Redmond. On 27 April 1916, during the Battle of Hulluch in France, Gilbert was gassed and Bryan wounded, with Bryan receiving the Military Cross for his gallantry. Gilbert served out the rest of the war in staff positions in Egypt and Palestine, while Bryan, after recovering from his wounds, returned to France. Twelve months later, during the Third Battle of Ypres (Passchendaele), he was again wounded. Then, on 6 August 1918, while leading a patrol near Hazebrouck in France, he was killed. His battalion's war diary recorded, 'In Capt. Hughes's death the Batt lost a very gallant officer universally popular'.[5]

Who were the Irish Anzacs?

At the outset we need to define who the Irish Anzacs were, a particularly troublesome task given that before the war the Irish, as British subjects, could and did move freely throughout the United Kingdom and the British Empire, particularly after the famine of the mid-19th century. As Richard Doherty and David Truesdale observed in the introduction to their book on Irish Victoria Cross winners:

> In producing a history of Irish VCs the authors faced a problem of definition: what is an Irishman? The purists would argue that only someone born in Ireland may be considered Irish. But this would exclude many sons of Irish parents who were born elsewhere while including the sons of non-Irish parents who happened to be living in Ireland when those sons were born ...
>
> It appeared to the authors that the most acceptable definition – which is really a compromise – is what we have

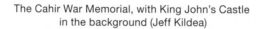

The Cahir War Memorial, with King John's Castle
in the background (Jeff Kildea)

termed the 'Jack Charlton rule': if one or other of a VC's parents were Irish-born, then he is regarded as Irish. Those born in Ireland of non-Irish parents are not excluded from this book, but it is made clear that they were, perhaps, not as Irish as some of those born outside the island.[6]

When dealing with such a relatively small and well-researched group as VC winners, it might be appropriate to apply the 'Jack Charlton rule', named after the English footballer who as manager of the Irish national football team recruited players with tenuous Irish links. However, in the context of this chapter, the place-of-birth criterion is more attractive, for reasons not of purity but of pragmatism. If we were to include those with one or other parent having been born in Ireland, the problems of identifying the potential number of Irish Anzacs would increase manyfold.[7]

Given the estimate of 6600 Irish-born members of the AIF, what does it tell us about the attitude of Irish-born Australians to the war? In 1911, the year of the last census before the First World War, Australia's population was 4 455 005 of whom 139 434 or 3.13 per cent were born in Ireland.[8] Since the figure of 6600 Irish-born AIF members represents only 1.57 per cent of total AIF enlistments of 421 809, it suggests that the Irish-born did not support the war in proportion to their numbers in the general population. This conclusion would seem to be confirmed by the fact that while total enlistments represent 9.47 per cent of the Australian population, the Irish-born enlistments represent only 4.73 per cent of the Irish-born population. However, a closer examination of the 1911 census returns reveals a startling fact about the Irish-born, namely that they were an aging population, with 74 per cent being 45 years and over compared to 19 per cent for the general population. This is due largely to the fact that Irish immigration to Australia peaked in the 1880s and thereafter, particularly following the depression of the early 1890s, declined sharply, with all overseas immigration contributing only 6063 of the total male population growth of 273 889 between the censuses of 1891 and 1911.[9] If one counts only males of military age (that is, between 18 and 44 years), the

The names of the 'Australians' on the Cahir war memorial
(Jeff Kildea)

proportion of eligible Irish-born males to all eligible Australian males is not 3.13 per cent but 1.8 per cent, much closer to 1.57 per cent, the proportion of Irish-born enlistments compared to total AIF enlistments.

The contribution to the war effort of the Australian Irish community, both Irish-born and local, was the subject of much controversy during the war, due in the main to sectarianism, which was chronic in 19th- and early 20th-century Australia.[10] The term 'sectarianism' in the Australian context is pregnant with meaning, which dictionary definitions fail to capture. It derives its distinctive meaning from the fact that religious affiliation was generally identified with the three main national or ethnic groups that constituted European society in Australia: the English, the Irish and the Scots. In early 20th-century Australia, to be Irish was to be Catholic and to be Catholic was to be Irish – a generalisation that is substantially accurate given that overall approximately 83 per cent of Irish who emigrated to Australia were Catholic.[11]

The heaviest Irish immigration occurred in the 1850s and early 1860s, with the 1861 census recording that 15.4 per cent of Australia's population was born in Ireland – significantly higher than the 3.13 per cent in 1911. Up to the 1880s, Irish emigrants to Australia were mainly from the south, particularly the province of Munster. From the late 1880s, however, the emigration map changed rapidly, with the more prosperous regions of Leinster and Protestant Ulster accounting for an increasing proportion until in the early 1900s Ulster took the lead in migration to Australia.[12] The 1911 census records that 70 per cent of Irish-born Australians were Catholics, reflecting the trend towards an increasing proportion of Protestants among Irish immigrants.[13] Even so, the Australian-born descendants of the earlier and larger waves of Irish immigration preserved the predominantly Catholic character of that part of the Australian community with Irish ancestry.

Competition between religions in Australia reflected not only theological differences but also complex ethnic rivalries, particularly those between Irish Catholics, on the one hand, and English

Anglicans and Scots-Irish Presbyterians on the other. With the outbreak of war this ethno-religious rivalry receded as the churches united in support of the Empire's cause. But, following the Easter Rising in April 1916 and the divisive conscription debate later that year, the facade of denominational harmony cracked, as manifested in public discourse by the denunciation of Irish-Australian Catholics for failing to respond to the nation's call to arms. The situation was further inflamed by claims by pro-conscriptionists that the Australian Irish were disloyal and by Prime Minister William Hughes's public slanging match with Archbishop Mannix. Each accused the other of being responsible for the outbreak of sectarianism, and Hughes alleged that Mannix was opposed to all recruiting, not just conscription. In June 1917, however, the Minister for Defence, Senator George Pearce, released embarkation figures which substantially refuted Protestant claims that Catholics were shirking (though the provision of the information did not silence the critics). According to the 1911 census, Catholic males over 20 years of age represented 19.6 per cent of the population; Pearce's figures showed that 18.57 per cent of those who had embarked for overseas service were Catholics.[14] Half a century later, Lloyd Robson's 1973 survey of 2291 enlistment papers provided further refutation of the libel, with his figures indicating that 19.73 per cent of the AIF were Catholics.[15]

The fact that the Australian Irish generally supported the war might come as a surprise to some in the light of the perceived antagonism between Ireland and Britain and the way the troubles there were played out vicariously in Australia with sectarianism rising steadily after 1916. However, the Australian Irish had generally prospered under the British Crown in the broad, new land of Australia and had tended to put behind them the conflicts of the old world: 'They saw their future, and Irish Australia's, successfully merged with the general Australian community, and Ireland happily merged, through Home Rule, with the British Empire'.[16] Tighe Ryan, the editor of the *Catholic Press*, summed up the feeling of the Australian Irish in an editorial early in the war, shortly after the enactment of home rule:

The attitude of Ireland towards the European war is the attitude of the Irish people throughout the world. For it must be remembered that during the past quarter of a century the relations between England and Ireland have been completely revolutionised ... Today Ireland is no longer a garrisoned country. She is as free as Australia and hence we find her sons not only in arms for the defence of her own shores, but fighting in the trenches of France and Belgium against the ruthless militarism and materialistic despotism of the Prussians.[17]

To the Australian Irish, the war also presented an opportunity to rid Australia of its sectarian divide. By sharing in the blood sacrifice, they hoped the wider community would come to accept them for whom they were.

But who were the Irish-born who did enlist? Research by John Connor of a sample of 350 Irishmen who joined the AIF gives a broad view of who the Irish Anzacs were.[18] Connor reports that among his sample almost two-thirds had arrived in Australia after 1909, when an assisted immigration scheme, reinstated following its suspension during the 1890s depression, was at its peak. He notes that in the main they were not youngsters, most having been born in the 1880s. These findings are consistent with the small size of the cohort of military age referred to above. The counties with the largest number of enlistments in the AIF were Antrim, Dublin and Cork, followed by Down, Tipperary, Derry, Clare and Kerry. The majority of enlisters were labourers or farm labourers, for whom a private's pay of six shillings a day might have been an attraction. Interestingly, only about 60 per cent were Catholics when the proportion of Catholics among the Irish-born, according to the 1911 census was 70 per cent. However, this might be explained, at least in part, by a combination of the ageing of the Irish-born population and the fact that the proportion of Protestants was greater among more recent Irish immigrants than in earlier years. A sample of over 600 Irish-born Anzacs from the AIF Database indicates a similar trend, but with a more pronounced Ulster Protestant influence. In that sample Catholics account for just under 50 per cent, while those born in the north-eastern counties of Down, Derry, Tyrone and Armagh (next in order after Antrim, Dublin and Cork) exceed those from the southern counties of Tipperary, Clare and Kerry.[19] In other words, in both surveys Protestants were over-represented among the Irish-born who enlisted in the AIF, a result which is not surprising given the enthusiastic support for the war in Ulster and among Protestants in Australia. Indeed, those born in the United Kingdom, which then included all of Ireland, were overrepresented in the AIF throughout the war. According to historian EM Andrews: 'They were 13.3 or 15.64 per cent of the Australian population, but either 18 or 22.5 per cent of the AIF for the whole war, depending on whose figures are taken. They were more numerous in some formations, however, being 27 per cent of the first contingent'.[20]

Lloyd Robson by his survey demonstrated that the support of the Australian Irish Catholic community for the war continued even after the Easter Rising and its suppression by the British

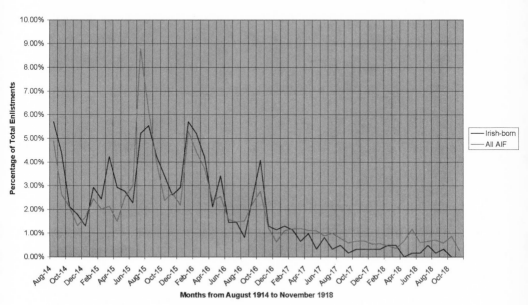

AIF enlistments: Irish-born compared to AIF

government.[21] This continuing support is confirmed in the case of the Irish-born as a whole by comparing the enlistment dates of the AIF Database sample with those of the AIF as a whole. As shown by the graph on page 87, the trend in recruiting throughout the war is remarkably similar, with the exception of the spike in July–August 1915, which is not as pronounced for the Irish-born, though a few months before they had had a boost in recruiting not matched by the general population.[22]

Stories of the Irish Anzacs

The stories of these Irish volunteers are many and varied, but in the space available it is possible to narrate only a few of them. They include those of a Victoria Cross winner, a nurse, two generals, two chaplains, two prisoners of war, a submariner and a few of the men whose names are recorded on Irish war memorials.

The Victoria Cross winner

During the First World War, 64 Australians won the Victoria Cross,[23] many of them bearing Irish surnames: Alexander Henry Buckley, Maurice Vincent Buckley, John Carroll, William Matthew Currey, John James Dwyer, William Donovan Joynt, Thomas James Bede Kenny, Lawrence Dominic McCarthy, Lewis McGee, Frank Hubert McNamara, Martin O'Meara, and John Ryan. Although some of them had recent Irish heritage (for example, Maurice Vincent Buckley's father and both of John Carroll's parents were Irish-born) and other Victoria Cross winners with non-Irish surnames had an Irish connection (Clifford William King Sadlier's father was Irish-born), only one of the 64 was himself Irish-born: Martin O'Meara of Lorrha, County Tipperary.[24]

Born in 1885 to Michael O'Meara and his wife Margaret (née O'Conner), Martin O'Meara emigrated to Australia as a young man, where he worked as a labourer and sleeper-hewer at Bowling Pool, near Collie, Western Australia.[25] In August 1915, at age 29, he enlisted in the AIF and sailed the following December for Egypt, where he joined the 16th Battalion, part of the 4th Division. He arrived too late to serve at Gallipoli but was soon to see action when his battalion sailed to France in June 1916 and took part in the Battle of the Somme from August.

It was during the fighting around Mouquet Farm near Pozières between 9 and 12 August 1916 that O'Meara earned his Victoria Cross. His citation reads:

> For conspicuous bravery. During four days of very heavy fighting he repeatedly went out and brought in wounded officers and men from 'No Man's Land' under intense artillery and machine gun fire.
>
> He also volunteered and carried up ammunition and bombs through a heavy barrage to a portion of the trenches, which was being heavily shelled at the time.
>
> He showed throughout an utter contempt of danger, and undoubtedly saved many lives.

One eyewitness to his deeds, Lieutenant Frank Wadge, estimated that O'Meara had brought in not less than 20 men, mostly from the 15th Battalion and the Suffolk Battalion, and that at times when he was carrying out 'this work of mercy', the high explosive, shrapnel and machine-gun fire was 'intense beyond description', so intense that everyone other than O'Meara believed it impossible to search for survivors. Captain Ross Harwood confirmed the severity of the shelling, describing in his report how on the night of 8–9 August 1916 he watched O'Meara go out into no-man's-land and rescue at least six men, treating them for their wounds before helping carry them to the dressing station. Captain A McLeod reported that in rescuing one man 'O'Meara with great gallantry and utmost fearlessness went through the barrage and subsequently assisted to bring him down to the Regimental Aid Post'. Lieutenant WJ Lynas described O'Meara as 'the most fearless and gallant soldier I have ever seen'. So dangerous were the conditions on the night of 11–12 August, with part of the front trench and the communications trenches having been destroyed by the shelling, that Lynas was not prepared to order any of his men to bring up supplies, even though they were running very short of ammunition and a German infantry assault was expected once the barrage lifted. However, O'Meara, on his own initiative, twice made his way to the battalion dump, staggering back under a very heavy load of much-needed ammunition. During these trips he located three wounded men and carried them back to the dressing station.

On the morning of 11 August, O'Meara was doing scouting duties when, according to Major Black, he climbed over the parapet into a section of no-man's-land, which was being raked by three German machine-guns and bombarded with high-explosive shells, and returned with a wounded man he had found lying in a shell hole. After dressing the man's wounds, O'Meara went back to his scouting duties. The next morning Black ordered his company to evacuate a section of trench that was being heavily shelled. One man failed to get out and was buried. Despite the intense fire, O'Meara rushed to the man's aid and dug him out.

On the basis of these reports, O'Meara's commanding officer, Lieutenant Colonel EA Drake-Brockman recommended him for the Victoria Cross, adding his own personal observation of O'Meara's gallantry. He recounted how, after the battalion had been relieved, he saw O'Meara heading towards the frontline. When he asked him where he was going, O'Meara replied that he had heard that two wounded men of the battalion had not been brought in from no-man's-land. Drake-Brockman added, 'In order to carry out his mission of mercy this man voluntarily returned through the barrage … after having reached a position of comparative safety'.

Charles Bean in the *Official History* wrote that the barrage that fell on the 16th Battalion on 11–12 August was 'furious' and that the battalion 'suffered heavily'. He continued:

> The carriage of water, supplies, and the wounded was sustained largely by the example of one man, Private Martin O'Meara, who four times went through the barrage with supplies, on one occasion taking with him a party, and who thereafter continued to bring out the wounded until all those of his battalion had been cleared.[26]

Eventually O'Meara's luck ran out and on 12 August 1916 he was severely wounded in the abdomen and evacuated to a hospital in England, where he remained until December 1916 before being able to return to his unit at the front. Twice more before war's end O'Meara was wounded in action: in April 1917, when he received a slight wound to the face, and in August 1917, when he suffered a shrapnel wound to the back, once again necessitating evacuation to England. On this occasion he had not long returned to his unit after having taken leave, during which he received his Victoria Cross

Martin O'Meara, VC (AWM H12763)

from King George V at Buckingham Palace on 21 July 1917. He also took the opportunity to visit family and friends in Tipperary, where he was given a hero's welcome. Money was collected for him as a testimonial, but he insisted that this and any other money raised for him be donated to restore Lorrha Abbey, near his home town.[27]

O'Meara was promoted to corporal on 13 March 1918 and to sergeant on 30 August 1918. The next day he once more left the front for England, this time in order to return to Australia. However, this brave and compassionate man, described by Lieutenant Lynas as 'always cheerful and optimistic', was not destined to live the full and productive life which the many wounded men he rescued would have wished for him. Soon after his return to Australia, he was admitted to a mental hospital, the seriousness of his illness evidenced by a letter dated 19 December 1918 from the commandant of the 5th Military District informing Base Records, the Australian Army's records office located in Melbourne, that 'this patient is suffering from Delusional Insanity, with hallucinations of hearing and sight, is extremely homicidal and suicidal, and requires to be kept in restraint. [The doctor] is not hopeful of his recovery in the near future'.

The prognosis proved correct and O'Meara spent the rest of his life in psychiatric institutions, dying on 20 December 1935 at Perth's Claremont Hospital. He was buried with full military honours at Karrakatta Catholic Cemetery, Perth, by fellow Tipperaryman Father John Fahey, whose own outstanding deeds as a chaplain during the war are described later in this chapter (pp. 98-100). Three Victoria Cross winners were the chief mourners, and Senator Sir George Pearce, Minister for External Affairs, who had been Minister for Defence during the war, was one of the pallbearers.

The nurse

According to the AWM, 2139 Australian nurses served with the Australian Army Nursing Service (AANS) and 130 with the British counterpart, the Queen Alexandra Imperial Military Nursing Service (QAIMNS) overseas, while a further 423 nurses served in hospitals in Australia. How many of these were born in Ireland is not disclosed, but the database of the National Archives of Australia (NAA) gives the names of 24 AANS nurses with places of birth in Ireland. Many more bear Irish surnames. Of the 2269 nurses who served overseas, 25 AANS nurses and at least five QAIMNS nurses were killed or died on active service during or in the years immediately after the war due to their war service.[28] One of those who died while caring for sick and wounded soldiers was Staff Nurse Kathleen Power of Piltown, County Kilkenny.

Power was 27 years of age when on 11 August 1915 she applied to enlist in the AANS, having previously trained for four and a half years at Dr Steeven's Hospital, Dublin, and having six and a half years experience in all. She was initially posted to the 10th Australian General Hospital, embarking with 25 fellow nurses at Melbourne on the *Morea*, on 24 August 1915, bound for England. Already on board were 26 nurses who had embarked at Sydney, and a further six would join at Adelaide. However, like the troops almost a year before, the nurses were surprised to find themselves off-loaded in Egypt, where they were assigned to the 1st Australian General Hospital at Heliopolis, Cairo.[29] Power served at a number of Australian military hospitals in Egypt before sailing on 22 July 1916 to India on the *Devanha*, a passenger liner used during the war as a troop and hospital ship.

Conditions on the hospital ships carrying wounded soldiers from the Middle East to India were terrible, particularly during the northern summer, and India was a difficult and dangerous posting because of the physical conditions, the cultural differences and the ever-present threat of cholera. It was the last of these that claimed Kathleen Power. Soon after her arrival at Bombay, she was admitted to the Colaba War Hospital, where she died on 13 August 1916. Just the day before, another Australian nurse, Sister Amy Veda O'Grady, had died of cholera in the same hospital. Both nurses were buried at Sewri Cemetery, Bombay, but later reburied at Kirkee War Cemetery at nearby Poona.

The generals

According to military historian Ross Mallett, the AIF had 68 generals throughout the course of the First World War (one full general, four lieutenant generals, twelve major generals and fifty-one brigadier generals). Of these, only two were born in Ireland, which at first seems a small proportion, but given that the Irish-born comprised but 1.57 per cent of the AIF it is more than par. Of the 68 generals, 49 were born in Australia and only 15 were born in the United Kingdom: eight in England, four in Scotland, two in Ireland and one in Wales. Of the remainder, two were born in India and two in New Zealand.[30] The two Irish-born generals were Lieutenant General James Whiteside McCay, born at Ballynure, County Antrim, on 21 December 1864, and Brigadier General John Meredith, born at Rosenallis, Queen's County (now County Laois), on 11 November 1864.

Another AIF general, Brigadier General John Patrick McGlinn, was the son of Irish parents, having been born in Sydney on 11 April 1869 to John Joseph McGlinn and Bridget Bergin, both of County Tipperary. Not being Irish-born, General McGlinn does not find a place in this chapter. However, because he presided at the court martial of AIF chaplain Father Thomas O'Donnell, arrested in Ireland in 1919 for making traitorous and disloyal statements concerning British policy in Ireland, he does figure in chapter 4 (see p.146).

Lieutenant General James Whiteside McCay

Although born in Ireland, James Whiteside McCay lived almost all his life in Australia. In 1865, before his first birthday, his family emigrated to Victoria, where his father, a Presbyterian minister, took up an appointment at Castlemaine, the town in which he grew up. At 21 years, James, with a friend of similar age, purchased the Castlemaine Grammar School, becoming its principal and gaining a reputation as a good teacher. At the same time he pursued studies in law, which he completed with first class honours in 1897, whereupon he set up his own legal practice as a solicitor. His military career began when he was commissioned in the Victorian Rifles in 1886, and he rose to the rank of lieutenant colonel in 1900.

In 1901 he was elected to the federal parliament and served as Minister of Defence in the government of George Reid between August 1904 and July 1905. With the elimination of his seat in 1906, McCay found himself out of parliament, whereupon he turned his attention to his military interests. On the outbreak of war in August 1914, he was initially put in charge of censorship but was soon appointed to command the AIF's 2nd Brigade. He was fortunate to survive the landing at Anzac Cove as he was shot twice through his cap and once through his shirt without injury, while his brigade lost half its strength in the first two days.

In May, the 2nd Brigade was transferred to Cape Helles to assist the British and French in the Second Battle of Krithia. As related in chapter 1 (pp. 30-31), he climbed onto the parapet of a trench to urge his men forward, risking death from the hail of machine-gun bullets ripping into the ground around him. The brigade suffered terrible casualties, while McCay himself was wounded, his leg broken by a bullet. After returning to duty before his leg had properly healed, he had to be evacuated to Malta, from where he was sent home to Australia in November 1915 to take up the post of Inspector General of the AIF.

Early in the new year he was appointed to command the newly formed 5th Division, which was the first Australian formation to see serious action in France at the Battle of Fromelles on 19–20 July 1916. It was a disastrous introduction to the Western Front for the Australians, with the division losing over 5500 casualties in a poorly planned attack that was intended as a feint to draw German troops from the Somme, where the British offensive was meeting stiff resistance. The Germans, who were well dug in and forewarned by a lengthy artillery bombardment, quickly realised the attack was a diversion, so that it failed in its purpose. Although many in the division blamed McCay for the debacle, his fellow AIF commanders believed the fault lay with the higher authorities. The division took many months to recover and although transferred to the Somme in October 1916, it did not take part in much of the fighting there. In January 1917, McCay was relieved of command and put in charge of the AIF's base depots in England.

Although McCay, all his life, had an uncanny knack of rubbing people up the wrong way, he had his supporters. In Charles Bean's opinion he was unjustly blamed for the failures at Krithia and

Fromelles. Lieutenant General Sir Brudenell White described him as 'one of the greatest soldiers that ever served Australia ... greater even than Monash'.[31] After the war, McCay was appointed to a number of government boards and inquiries, retiring from the army as an honorary lieutenant general in 1926. He died on 1 October 1930.

Brigadier General John Meredith

Unlike McCay, Brigadier General John Meredith spent his formative years in Ireland, receiving his secondary education at Port Arlington, County Laois, before studying medicine in Dublin between 1882 and 1887. After receiving further medical qualifications at Edinburgh and Glasgow, Meredith emigrated to Australia in 1888 and bought a medical practice at Raymond Terrace in New South Wales.

His military career began with the Hunter River Light Horse and he volunteered for service in South Africa as a medical officer in the Citizen's Bushmen's Contingent. After the Boer War, he formed a troop of light horse at Raymond Terrace, rising to major in 1908 and lieutenant colonel commanding the 4th Light Horse Regiment in 1911. In 1908–09 he took his family to Ireland, where he was attached to the 18th Hussars for training.

On the outbreak of war, Meredith was appointed commander of the 1st Light Horse Regiment, which fought dismounted at Gallipoli. After the evacuation, he served in the Middle East, commanding the 1st Light Horse Brigade at the Battle of Romani (3–4 August 1916) with 'much distinction' according to the official war historian,[32] for which he was mentioned in dispatches and awarded the Distinguished Service Order. From February 1917, he commanded the newly formed 4th Light Horse Brigade and was promoted to brigadier general. Just before the Battle of Beersheba (31 October 1917), Meredith relinquished his command to Brigadier General William Grant, and in November 1917 returned to Australia 'for family reasons', his AIF appointment ending in January 1918. He continued to serve in the Australian military until his retirement in 1923. He died on 1 January 1942.[33]

The chaplains

Personal service records at the NAA (series B2455) show that 457 clergymen served as chaplains with the AIF: 193 Anglicans, 87 Catholics, 75 Presbyterians, 60 Methodists and 38 other Protestant denominations. There were two Jewish chaplains and two whose religion is not shown in the NAA records. The place of birth of 379 is shown, of whom 54, or almost 12 per cent, were born in Ireland. Almost one-half of the Catholic chaplains whose place of birth is known were Irish-born (49.32 per cent), while two-thirds of the Irish-born chaplains were Catholics (36 out of 54). The Presbyterians were the next largest group of Irish-born chaplains, with nine (16.67 per cent), all from the north of Ireland. Perhaps the best-known of these was Chaplain General John Laurence Rentoul from Garvagh, County Derry, who was a major controversialist in Australia's sectarian era. Nicknamed 'Fighting Larry', he often engaged his Catholic counterparts, Archbishops Thomas Carr and Daniel Mannix, in spirited debate over the rights and wrongs of Roman Catholicism. At least five Anglicans, two Methodists and a Congregationalist chaplain also came from Ireland.

Although chaplains were not combatants, it did not stop them being killed or wounded or from receiving awards for gallantry and conspicuous service. The names of twelve chaplains appear in the AWM's Roll of Honour, three of them Irish-born: the Reverend David de Venny Hunter of County Down (Methodist) and Father Michael Bergin of County Tipperary (Catholic) were killed in action in September and October 1917, respectively; and the Reverend John Dempsey of Belfast (Congregationalist) died in June 1917 of injuries received when on 15 April 1917 the troopship on which he was travelling, the *Mashobra*, was torpedoed by a German submarine in the Mediterranean. AWM records show that four chaplains received the Distinguished Service Order (including two Irish-born), 25 the Military Cross (including six Irish-born) and 30 were mentioned in dispatches (including six Irish-born), with four (including one Irish-born) being mentioned on two occasions.[34] Chaplains also received honours in the Order of the British Empire for their work, including two Irishmen who were made Officers of the Order: the Presbyterian, the Reverend William Floyd Shannon,[35] and the Catholic, Father Edmond McAuliffe of County Limerick, the latter having rendered distinguished service at Gallipoli and in France.

Father John Fahey, DSO

One of the chaplains awarded the Distinguished Service Order was Father John Fahey, a native of County Tipperary, who had been sent to Western Australia shortly after his ordination in 1907 at age 24. Described by author Myles Dungan as 'an outdoor priest … teak-tough, a fine sportsman and a good shot',[36] Fahey joined the AIF in September 1914 and was assigned to the 11th Battalion. Disregarding an order to remain on board ship, he was the first chaplain ashore at Anzac Cove and for a number of days he and Father McMenamin, a chaplain with the New Zealand forces, were the only clergymen there. Unlike Father Finn, his fellow Tipperary man who was killed at the landing at V Beach (see p. 25), Fahey passed unscathed through the hail of bullets on his way to the beach while men around him fell dead, an eerie experience which Fahey felt compelled to describe in graphic detail in letters home:

> The order was given us to man the boats, and we tumbled in as fast as possible, and pushed off for the shore. It was only 300 yards away but to me it seemed miles, and to have taken hours to reach. There was dreadful slaughter in the boats. I could then see only what was happening in my own. First the 'cox' was shot; then an oarsman fell dead across my feet; then a bullet came through the boat and grazed the puttee on my leg; then another of the men collapsed without a sound, and we knew that he was dead and so on. It was horrible. I never expected to reach the shore alive. There was only one anxiety amongst the men – to reach the shore, and rush the Turks with the bayonet.[37]

Fahey's letters home were published regularly in the Catholic papers in Australia making him 'a household name amongst Australian Catholics'.[38] But his reputation was given international exposure when the Irish journalist Michael MacDonagh wrote an article on Catholic chaplains at the front. In the article MacDonagh quoted from a letter from an officer of the 11th Battalion:

'The "Padre" as he is called by his battalion,' writes the officer in his letter to the Archbishop of Perth, 'fills in his spare time carrying up provisions to the men at the front, and helps the wounded back, and I can tell you he is not afraid to go where the bullets fall pretty thickly'. Since that communication was written Father Fahey has done more in the way of utilising his spare time – he has led the men in a charge against the Turkish entrenchments. On an occasion when all the officers had been killed or disabled, he called on the remainder of the company, 'Follow me, and although I have only a stick you can give the Turk some Western Australian cold steel'. In the engagement Father Fahey was wounded, and the latest account of him is that he is in hospital at Malta.[39]

But was his gung-ho reputation deserved? Although Myles Dungan repeats without comment McDonagh's account of Fahey's leading the charge, Michael McKernan doubts the veracity of such stories.[40] Fahey's service record indicates that, rather than battle wounds, it was a far less romantic ailment, haemorrhoids, that led to his evacuation to Malta. Certainly, he had been tempted on the first day to join in the helter skelter of the Australian troops as they chased Turks up the ridges and through the gullies. He wrote to a priest friend in Australia: 'My first impulse was to grab a rifle and bayonet, and go with them. The cheering and yelling would do your heart good to hear'. But he added, 'after clearing the first ridge, I saw so many wounded and dying that I had to turn my attention to them'.[41] And it was the spiritual and material well-being of the men, rather than fighting Turks, that occupied his time and required his fearless devotion to duty in the difficult and dangerous conditions of the peninsula.

Fahey had high praise for the soldiers he served and they for him. Yet, he was far from the enthusiastic warrior his publicists were keen to portray, even though, on his own admission, he crawled out of his trench one night to souvenir a Turkish Mauser rifle and ammunition belt to keep as a trophy or to use in self-defence.[42] Early in the campaign he recognised that it would be a drawn-out affair: 'It will be a long and costly operation unless something unforeseen occurs, such as the sudden collapse of the Turkish resistance. Gallipoli Peninsula is a fortress, and the operations here are in the nature of a siege'.[43] He was also appalled by what he witnessed:

> War is abominable. I shall never volunteer again in any capacity, for I have seen enough of it. It is not so much personal fear that would deter me, as the awful sights and nerve-shaking ordeals of fire one has to go through. You have no idea what an awful thing shell fire is. I have seen strong men become gibbering idiots as the result of a shell bursting near them and tearing men to pieces. Yet they were untouched. It will shake the strongest nerves.[44]

His horror was heightened the following year by what he witnessed at Pozières. On 29 July 1916, he wrote to Archbishop Patrick Clune, 'Whatever I have said in previous letters about the horrors of war I wish now to withdraw. I must admit that I have not seen the real thing until the last fortnight … It just beggars all description'.[45]

Despite a number of close calls at Gallipoli, where he was buried in his dugout by a shell-burst, his pack was struck by shrapnel, his overcoat was penetrated by bullets, and objects were shot out of his hand, Fahey continued unscathed to minister to the men until he took ill and was evacuated to England in November. For his service during the campaign, he was awarded the Distinguished Service Order for 'gallantry under fire' and was also mentioned in dispatches. Following his convalescence, he rejoined the 11th Battalion in France in March 1916 and served with it until November 1917. By then he had become the longest-serving front-line chaplain of any denomination. He returned to Australia in March 1918 and resumed pastoral duties in various Perth parishes for the next forty years, until his death in 1959.[46]

Father Michael Bergin, MC
(AWM P04475.001)

Father Michael Bergin, MC

Another Tipperary man, Father Michael Bergin, also served with distinction as a chaplain in the AIF, although he never set foot in Australia. Born at Roscrea in 1879, Bergin was ordained in 1910 and sent by the Jesuit Order to Damascus. When war broke out he was interned by the Turks, but later released and expelled from Syria. He made his way to Cairo in January 1915 and fell in with the Australians, who were arriving there in increasing numbers. Although not then a chaplain, he ministered to the men, saying mass and hearing confessions. When it came time for the troops to sail to Gallipoli, he was told he could not accompany them because he was a civilian. Undeterred, he joined the 5th Light Horse Regiment as a trooper.

After landing at Anzac Cove he was appointed a chaplain and served in that capacity until he fell ill with typhoid in September 1915 and was evacuated to England. By the time he was well enough to return to Gallipoli the Anzacs had been evacuated, so he continued on to Alexandria, where he remained until June 1916, when he travelled to France with the 13th Brigade. He served as chaplain to the men of the brigade until the night of 11 October 1917, when he was severely wounded at Zonnebeke in the Ypres salient when a German shell exploded near the advanced aid post where he was working. The next day, aged 38 years, he died and was buried in the churchyard at Reningelst near Poperinghe in Belgium.

Three weeks before his death, his brigade commander had recommended him for the Military Cross. The recommendation included the following:

> In the line or out Padre Bergin is always to be found among his men helping them when in trouble and inspiring them with his noble example and never-failing cheerfulness. These are the characteristics which have endeared him to all and which make him such a valuable asset to the Brigade.[47]

The award was not made until after his death.[48]

The prisoners of war

Just over 4000 Australians were taken prisoner during the First World War, including about 200 captured by the Turks at Gallipoli and in Mesopotamia, Syria and Palestine, and 3850 captured by the Germans on the Western Front. A total of 395 Australians died in captivity, at least two of whom were Irish-born.

Air Mechanic David Curran

In 1902, David Curran, a young carpenter and joiner from Downpatrick, County Down, left Ireland to make a better life for himself in the colonies. At first he went to Cape Town, but after five years he moved to Australia, where at age 29 he settled in Melbourne. He enlisted on 25 June 1915 in the Australian Flying

Corps (AFC) and was posted to the Australian Half Flight in Mesopotamia (now Iraq) on 18 September 1915.

With Turkey entering the war on Germany's side on 31 October 1914, Britain's oil fields in Persia (now Iran) came under threat. Within a week of Turkey's declaration of war, the 6th Indian Division landed at the head of the Persian Gulf in Turkish-administered Mesopotamia and advanced north along the River Tigris to where it meets the Euphrates at Kurna, the reputed site of the Garden of Eden. Not content with having secured the oil wells, the Mesopotamian Expeditionary Force continued its advance northward towards Baghdad– and ultimately to disaster.

At the request of the Viceroy of India, the Australian government dispatched four officers and 41 airmen of the AFC – the so-called Half Flight. This small force arrived at its base at Basra, just south of Kurna, on 26 May 1915, and began securing the flanks before the advance on Baghdad. In the words of the RAAF historian Alan Stephens, 'Like the Anzac campaign, the Half Flight's war was to be heroic, bloody, and ultimately tragic'.[49]

The advance began on 12 September 1915 and was initially successful when later that month the 6th Division under Major General Sir Charles Townshend captured Kut-el-Amara (now Al Kut) in a brilliant tactical victory. However, on 24 November the advance halted and turned into a retreat when Townshend's force, stretched to the limit of its logistical support, suffered a decisive defeat at Ctesiphon, requiring the exhausted and demoralised survivors to fall back on Kut, harried all the way by Turks and Arabs. The depleted force of 3000 British and 10000 Indian troops reached Kut on 3 December 1915. Although 30 Squadron, which included the Half Flight, was ordered to leave the town, several British pilots and observers and most of the non-commissioned officers and mechanics were left behind, including nine Australians, among them David Curran.

As their Anzac compatriots were preparing to evacuate the Gallipoli peninsula, men of the Australian Half Flight were settling in for what would be a 147-day siege in the most appalling conditions.

Attempts to relieve the besieged British and Indian force were beaten off by the Turks who, reinforced by troops buoyed by their victory at Gallipoli, inflicted heavy casualties on the relief column of the British Tigris Corps. Townshend's men seemed doomed. Last-minute negotiations by the soon-to-become-legendary Captain TE Lawrence, who offered the Turkish commander Khalil Pasha one million, then two million pounds sterling for the release of the British force, proved unsuccessful.

Townshend surrendered to the Turks on Saturday 29 April 1916 (the day Pádraic Pearse surrendered his small band of Irish rebels to Brigadier General Lowe in Dublin). It was one of the worst defeats ever suffered by the British Army.[50] The following Saturday, the remnants of the defeated army, some 9000 in all, 44 of them from 30 Squadron, including David Curran and his Half Flight comrades, began a forced march to Anatolia (Asia Minor), 1100 kilometres away. In the words of historian Martin Gilbert, it was 'a veritable death march'.[51] On their journey north, they passed through Baghdad, Tikrit, and Mosul. Those who did not die along the way through beatings, exposure, fatigue and starvation were put to work in railway construction on the Taurus Mountains, where more died of typhus, malaria or dysentery, exacerbated by malnutrition and exposure. Only 2000 survived their captivity.

Among the survivors of the Kut debacle were six of 30 Squadron's 44 mechanics, two of them Australians: Acting Flight Sergeant James McKenzie Sloss and Air Mechanic Keith Liston Hudson.[52] Sloss recounted after the war:

> Whilst being driven to our place of internment I suffered, almost beyond human endurance (being beaten by rifle & whip). To fall out was (in most cases) to die. The food we were given consisted of *Atta*, wheat (mostly whole) with no wood to cook it, & in the journey of about 600 miles we had meat on the track 5 times & very little at that.
>
> The Arabs in some part were hostile … but by far the posters of the column [the Turkish troops escorting the prisoners] were the chief offenders.[53]

Air Mechanic Curran managed to march as far as Nisibin (now Nusaybin) near what is today the Turkish-Syrian border, where he died in about July or August 1916. Air Mechanic Hudson told the Australian Red Cross, '[Curran] suffered badly from fever on the desert march and from exhaustion and exposure followed by malarial fever, for which he had practically no treatment. Formerly he was a strong, powerful man but became a walking skeleton'.[54] Captain Thomas White, who had been captured by the Turks in late 1915 and reunited in captivity with some of his fellow Australians, reported, 'It is doubtful if the graves of A.M. [Air Mechanic] Curran and Cpl. Soley would be known as Nisibin was one of the worst halting-places, and the hospital perhaps the worst on the line of march traversed by the Kut-el-Amara men'.[55]

Sloss described conditions at Nisibin as follows:

> Turkish hospital at Nisibin was nothing less than a death trap. 6 men of my unit entered with me. Only 2 came out. When to [*sic*] weak to visit rear [they] were placed in a separate room & left to die, laying in their filth for days. [emphasis in handwritten original]. At this place I saw Turkish orderlies choke one of our men with water because he was not dead. They were wanting to bury him.
>
> The Armenian doctor came sometimes once a day. There was little or no medicines. Sanitation, I cannot describe it. The rooms were overrun with lice. Throughout Turkey sanitary arrangements are very crude and filthy. All clothing worn by me during my stay in Turkey was supplied by American or Dutch consuls or representatives.

Curran had not made contact with his family since leaving home in 1902, and his parents knew neither whether he had married nor his address in Australia. But once they received notification of his capture in January 1917 they commenced an extensive correspondence concerning his imprisonment with Australian defence authorities and the offices of the Australian Red Cross Society in London. Unbeknown to them and to Australian authorities, Curran was by then dead. Throughout the first half of 1917, Curran's parents continued to receive messages of hope from the authorities and the Red Cross:

> I have to inform you that your son ... is reported to have been taken Prisoner of War at Kut, and is believed to be at present interned in Turkey. [30 January 1917]

> We have your son's name on our lists and believe him to be at Afion-Kara-Hissiar, a Camp in Asia Minor. [12 March 1917]

> You will be glad to hear that our parcels are at last being received by our Turkish Prisoners of War. Your son acknowledged one of our parcels lately, his [postcard] being dated 4th April. It is so nice to feel that we have at last got into communication with them. [26 May 1917][56]

This last communication was the cruellest of all. It was simply untrue. The error, when discovered, was blamed on a 'young assistant'. The postcard reputedly from David Curran was in fact a postcard the Red Cross had sent to him but which the Turkish Red Crescent Society had returned undelivered. The Red Cross office first learned Curran's real fate in July 1917 when it received a letter from Captain White in Afion Kara Hissar prison camp, who wrote, 'I was sorry to hear of the deaths of Munro, Lord, Rayment, Williams, Adams, Soley and Curran'.[57] No further details were provided. Rather than informing Mr and Mrs Curran directly, the Red Cross office wrote to a family friend, Mrs Maggie Malone:

> We have heard news, unofficially, of the death of David Curran. We were waiting for official information before writing to his parents. Perhaps it would be best if you were to tell them that we have received this information, and that we fear there is not much hope of it turning out to be untrue. We heard it from a letter of one of the other Prisoners, so he could hardly make a mistake.[58]

After Mrs Malone showed the Currans the letter, Mrs Esther Curran wrote to the Red Cross:

> We hope the sad news is not true and are anxiously waiting
> for further news from you. If it is true we want you to
> get all information you can from the Prisoner of War who
> communicated the news to you concerning his death.[59]

But the Red Cross could not provide anything more substantial. It
did advise that its informant was Captain White, which prompted
Mrs Curran to write to him in September 1917. White replied to
Mrs Curran from captivity in November 1917, advising in a postcard
that David 'was reported to have died in hospital at Nisibin near
Mosul in Aug 1916, the cause of death not being stated'.[60] However,
judging from the tenor of her 1918 letters, it is not clear whether she
received it. To add to Esther Curran's woes, her husband Samuel took
ill at the end of 1917 and died early in the new year. Mrs Curran's
correspondence with the Red Cross continued, apparently without
satisfaction, until March 1919, when the Prisoner of War Office in
London closed. As late as March 1920, she was still writing to the
Australian Department of Defence seeking further information,
but to no avail. It is not known whether Mrs Curran ever received
sufficient information to put her troubled mind at rest.

David Curran was initially buried in the Nisibin cemetery. After
the war the Imperial War Graves Commission relocated the remains
of servicemen buried in that cemetery to Baghdad (North Gate) War
Cemetery 'in order to secure the reverent maintenance of the graves
in perpetuity'. However, Curran's grave could not be found. His name
is inscribed on a memorial erected at the Baghdad (North Gate) War
Cemetery to the memory of the 265 British Empire servicemen who
died as prisoners of war and whose graves were lost.[61]

Private Michael Lomesney (aka McBarren)

It is not only defenders but also attackers who can end up as prisoners
of war. If an attack is not well coordinated, some of the attackers
may advance further than others and find themselves cut off. This
was the fate of Private Michael Lomesney, who, as a member of
the 13th Battalion, took part in the First Battle of Bullecourt on
11 April 1917.

Born in County Cork in 1882, he had emigrated with his family to Australia at age seven years and was educated at St Patrick's Primary School, Bega. He was a miner at Coledale, south of Sydney, when he enlisted in the 13th Battalion in April 1916 under the name McBarren. Why he changed his name and why he used 'McBarren' is not known.[62] Five months later, he was on board the *Euripides* with the battalion's 20th Reinforcements sailing to England, where he underwent further training before joining the battalion in France on 2 January 1917. He was just in time to take part in the battalion's assault on Stormy Trench, north-east of Guedecourt in early February 1917, for which Australia's most highly decorated soldier Captain Harry Murray received the Victoria Cross. Two months later he was in the thick of things at Bullecourt, his first major battle. It was also his last, as he was to spend the rest of the war in captivity.

On the orders of General Hubert Gough, the Irish-born commander of the Fifth Army, the 4th Australian Division attacked the strongly fortified Hindenburg Line without the usual artillery barrage, on the basis that tanks would cut a path through the wire for the infantry to follow. In Charles Bean's assessment it was 'an experiment of extreme rashness', which had been opposed by the Australian commanders.[63] It proved a costly failure, embittering the Australians against both their British commanders and the new wonder weapon, the tank. Most of the tanks broke down before reaching the start line so that the soldiers had to advance without an artillery barrage and with only 4 of the promised 11 tanks, which moved so slowly in the heavy going across soft farmland covered in snow that soon the troops outran them. Remarkably, the 4th Division achieved what most informed observers would have thought impossible – the breaching of the supposedly impregnable Hindenburg Line without artillery support, but by doing so they wedged themselves in the German strongpoint and soon came under murderous machine-gun and artillery fire from the German defenders. They received no artillery support as the Australian artillery commander, unsure of the location of the Australian troops, refused to provide the much-needed covering fire. The choice for the soldiers caught in the German lines was to stay where they were, at the risk of being killed or captured, or to attempt to withdraw to the Australian lines under winnowing fire. Of those who opted to return to their lines, few made it back – even fewer unscathed. Lomesney's brigade had gone into battle that day 3000 strong; in the engagement it suffered 2339 casualties. Of the 4th Division's total casualties of over 3300, about 1170 were captured, in Bean's words 'much the largest number of Australians taken by the enemy in a single battle,' accounting for just over 30 per cent of all Australian prisoners captured on the Western Front.[64]

Among the prisoners was Private Lomesney. According to Bean, the Australian prisoners at Bullecourt were well treated by the Germans who captured them. Their greatest risk in the initial days of their captivity was of being killed or wounded by Allied shelling as they made their way to the German rear, and some were. However, upon reaching Lille their humane treatment came to an end as they were paraded through the streets of the French city, then split into parties of about 100 each and imprisoned in Fort Macdonald. Charles Bean describes their conditions:

> Each party was thrust into a room of the fort to which it is no exaggeration to apply the word 'dungeon'. These chambers, large enough for perhaps 25 men, were floored with stone or concrete with little light or air. For all purposes of sanitation, there was placed in the corner a single tub, which quickly overflowed. The men were allowed neither straw nor blankets, but must sleep on the bare damp floor, and were fed with one slice of bread daily and coffee 'substitute'.[65]

It was later explained to the prisoners that their treatment was an act of retaliation against the British employment of German prisoners in work details within range of the German guns. As a consequence, parties of Australians were sent to work in the artillery zone on and near the battlefield. In Bean's words, 'They were purposely underfed and overworked, under fire'. Some died of hardship, others of shellfire before the British and German authorities reached agreement in July 1917 for the removal of prisoners to an agreed distance from the front. In the meantime, however, the Germans deliberately misled the Red Cross as to the prisoners' true location, claiming they were in prison camps in Germany, a deception which added to the men's deprivation because they could not receive the Red Cross parcels which were being sent to them at these camps.[66] In Lomesney's case, the Red Cross received a report from the Germans dated 23 June 1917 stating he was in the prison camp at Limburg.[67] Bean asserts that, apart from this period, the German treatment of the prisoners was moderate, though some commandants and subordinates gained a reputation for brutality.

In the second week of November 1918, as news of the armistice spread among the prisoners, there was much rejoicing at the prospect they would soon be going home. At this time Lomesney was an inmate of the Schneidemuhl camp in Prussia (now Pila in Poland) and had been assigned to a *Kommando* (work party) that was working near Posen (now Poznan). He had previously been at Friedrichsfeld near Mannheim in Germany. On 4 November, he wrote to the Red Cross acknowledging receipt of a food parcel it had sent him. It was to be his last contact with the organisation. Like so many other soldiers who had survived the fighting and the privations of imprisonment, Lomesney was struck down a few days later by the Spanish flu. He died on 20 November 1918, nine days after war's end. A fellow prisoner, Sergeant Reginald Camden, wrote to the Red Cross reporting his death and those of two other Australian prisoners. In the letter he wrote:

> Now that we all expect to be home so soon I don't think I need trouble with any complaints; in fact there is nothing to complain of only this terrible Spanish grip which is slowly and surely carrying off our boys. It will be an awful sad time for the friends and loved ones of prisoners for them to receive word that the men they are expecting home have died.[68]

Initially buried at Lobsens Catholic Cemetery near the prison camp, Lomesney's body was exhumed in 1926 and reinterred at Poznan Old Garrison Cemetery, as part of a program by the Imperial War Graves Commission to gather together in the one cemetery the graves of Commonwealth servicemen who had died in Poland as prisoners of war.

Tragic though the news of Lomesney's death must have been for his mother, Ellen Lomesney, at least she knew his fate and the location of his last resting place, the Australian authorities having advised her of the reburial. Such was not the case with her other son Maurice, whom she also lost to the war, and his ultimate fate remains unknown. He too, it seems, had enlisted under an assumed name and thereafter was not heard from. As late as June 1923, Mrs Lomesney was still writing to the officer in charge of Base Records inquiring whether they had managed to trace his whereabouts.

The submariner

Another Irish-born Australian prisoner of war, but one who lived to tell the tale, is the leading character in one of the First World War's greatest stories of daring. It concerns the Australian submarine *AE2*, which on the day the Anzacs were landing at Gallipoli set out on a voyage to penetrate the Dardanelles in order to disrupt Turkish shipping bringing supplies to the peninsula. At a time when submarine warfare was in its infancy, requiring great skill and courage merely to survive let alone fight, the *AE2* managed to breach the Turkish defences and to sink a Turkish vessel before it, too, was sunk in the Sea of Marmara. One of the forgotten episodes of the Gallipoli campaign, this amazing voyage recently captured the imagination of the Australian public when in 1998 Selçuk Kolay, Director of the Rahmi M Koç Museum in Istanbul, located the wreck of the *AE2* on the sea floor.[69]

The captain of the *AE2* was Lieutenant Commander Henry Hugh Gordon Stoker, known as Dacre Stoker (in honour of his godfather) and a cousin of Bram Stoker, the author of *Dracula*. Born in Dublin in 1885 into a prominent medical family, Stoker determined at age 12 on a naval career rather than follow family tradition. Serving as a midshipman and surviving the brutality of the system as it then operated, he was promoted to sub-lieutenant in 1904, whereupon he volunteered for the new submarine service, attracted by the higher rate of pay. At age 23, he was promoted lieutenant and given his first command of a submarine, which he promptly crashed, though without long-term damage to his career. In 1913, while based at Gibraltar, he volunteered to join the submarine service of the new Australian navy, which involved his taking command of the *AE2* and sailing it, in the company of another submarine *AE1*, to Australia, setting out on 2 March 1914 from Portsmouth and arriving in Sydney on Sunday 24 May, much to the bemusement of thousands of Sydneysiders out and about celebrating Empire Day.

Stoker found Sydney much to his liking, but the frivolities of a self-confessed philanderer were brought to a sudden halt within a few weeks with the news that war had been declared. The two submarines were ordered to patrol the waters of the Pacific to hunt for German cruisers and shipping. The dangers of submarine operations were well illustrated when, on 14 September 1914, the *AE1* disappeared without trace off Rabaul. To this day it has never been found.

After returning to Australia, and with the Pacific clear of German ships, Stoker was determined to get involved in the war in Europe. So he went to the top, lobbying the Minister for Defence, Senator George Pearce, on the benefits of dispatching the *AE2* to Europe. This unconventional move by an unconventional man proved to be successful, and the *AE2* left Sydney in late December 1914 for Melbourne, where it linked up with the transports carrying the second contingent of the AIF to the European war. Like the soldiers and the nurses, the crew of the *AE2* found, once they arrived at Suez, that their orders had been changed, and that they were now required to remain in the Mediterranean in readiness for the push into the Dardanelles. Because of damage sustained in an accident, the *AE2* missed the first stage of the campaign, when in March 1915 the British and French navies unsuccessfully attempted to force a passage through the Dardanelles, losing in the process three battleships sunk and three others seriously damaged. It was thereafter decided to give the army the task of capturing the Gallipoli peninsula to make the Dardanelles safe for the ships.

And so, in the early hours of 25 April 1915, as the Australians were coming ashore at what is now called Anzac Cove, the *AE2* began its perilous, final voyage. Sailing underwater through the Turkish minefields, where its crew was unnerved by the sound of mine wires scraping against its hull, it managed to torpedo a Turkish destroyer before running aground under the muzzles of land-based guns. Fortunately for Stoker and his crew, these guns could not aim low enough to fire upon the *AE2*. After refloating his vessel, Stoker evaded Turkish gunboats that were in hot pursuit and managed to pass through the Dardanelles to reach the Sea of Marmara. For four days, the *AE2* remained at large, making a nuisance of itself among the Turkish shipping before being hit while under heavy fire. Although the *AE2* had caused little direct damage, its presence had forced the Turks to abandon reinforcing Gallipoli by sea, an outcome that might have proved decisive had the Allied land forces performed better in the finely balanced jousting that occurred in the first days of the Gallipoli campaign.

Faced with the inevitable, Stoker decided to scuttle his submarine and surrender. He and his crew spent the rest of the war in Turkish captivity, during which time Stoker twice escaped, on both occasions being recaptured. After the war, he was awarded the Distinguished Service Order – a recognition that was perhaps too little and too late: two British submarine commanders who had followed the *AE2* through the Dardanelles and returned to tell the tale each received immediate recognition in the form of the Victoria Cross.

In 1920, Stoker retired from the navy and took up an acting career in England, appearing in plays, films and television dramas. During the Second World War he rejoined the navy serving in an administrative capacity. He died in 1966.

Remembering the Irish Anzacs

The above are just some of the Irish men and women who served in the Australian forces during the First World War. There were thousands more, many of whom are remembered on war memorials erected in their former home towns in Ireland. Some of the Irish public memorials listing the names of Australian servicemen are identified in appendix 1.[70]

The difficulties of locating Irish war memorials that record the names of Australian servicemen vary between north and south. For reasons outlined in the introduction to this book and covered in more detail in chapter 6 (pp. 218–25), few public memorials were erected in that part of the country which today is the Republic of Ireland, so the main difficulty there is to find a memorial at all. In Northern Ireland, where war memorials are as ubiquitous as they are in Australia, the principal problem is finding memorials that include a roll of honour that identifies the country of service. Even so, such war memorials, whether in the north or the south, tend to record only those who died in the war and not those who survived, unlike most memorials in Australia. An exception is the war memorial at Ballycastle, County Antrim, which includes the names of seven Australians, only one of whom, Private David Rennie of the 2nd Battalion, died in the war.

Of the war memorials listed in appendix 1, the one with the highest number of Australian names is the Carlow War Memorial, with 11 out of a total of 472. It was unveiled at a ceremony in September 2002, evidencing a recent trend in the south towards greater recognition of those who died in the First World War. In Northern Ireland, where remembrance has always been strong, new memorials are springing up as well. In Ballymoney, County Antrim, six black marble tablets bearing the names of those from the district who died in the two world wars and in Korea were erected on the facade of the Royal British Legion Hall in February 2000. Those killed in the First World War account for over 300 of the almost 400 names on the memorial, 9 of them members of the Australian forces. Each of their stories has been researched and recounted in *Ballymoney Heroes 1914–1918*, by Robert Thompson, who was responsible for initiating and seeing the memorial project through.[71] Thompson has written similar books on other towns in Northern Ireland, including Bushmills, County Antrim (1995, 2003); Portrush, County Antrim (2001); and Coleraine, County Derry (2004), some of which mention Australians.

An early form of commemorative publication was *Ireland's Memorial Records*, which lists the names of 49 000 Irishmen said to have died while serving in various Allied forces during the First World War. Compiled by the Committee of the Irish National War Memorial under the direction of Field Marshal John French, 1ˢᵗ Earl of Ypres, it was published in 1923. Only one hundred copies of the original publication were ever produced. Its 3177 pages in eight volumes are beautifully illustrated by decorative artist Harry Clarke, who used a combination of Celtic and Art Deco motifs, silhouette battle scenes, medals and insignia, and religious and mythological scenes.[72] Its accuracy is not its strong point and it contains only 204 entries on Irish-born soldiers who died while serving in the Australian forces, when the true figure is closer to 970, as noted above (p. 80).

In some places where a war memorial does not include a roll of honour, local authorities have commissioned research leading to the publication of a book listing the soldiers from the town or district who died during the world wars. An example of such an enterprise is Colin Moffett's *Newry's War Dead*, which includes the names of three Australians.[73] In 2002 Paul Maguire, published *Follow Them up from Carlow*, in connection with the inauguration of the Carlow County Memorial.

As well as these sources, newspaper records have also proved useful in tracing the Irish Anzacs. During the war, families would submit memorial notices for publication in their local or national newspapers. For example, the *Irish Times* of 26 June 1917 included the following notice:

> **Edwards** – Killed in action Arthur Cecil Edwards Australian Imperial Force, third son of Mr and Mrs James Edwards, Quinsboro House, Bray. 'Greater love hath no man than this.'[74]

Among the 188 names on the war memorial at Bray, County Wicklow appears 'Edwards, A.C.', without any further identifying information. The *Irish Times* notice provided the only lead.

Serendipity also played a part in the research for this book. On the Drogheda War Memorial, which identifies each soldier's regiment or country, the following appears: 'Pte H. Donegan AIF'. A search of the Commonwealth War Graves Commission (CWGC) index turned up two entries for H Donegan: Private Harry Donegan and Private Herbert James Donegan, both Australians, with the latter having been born in Western Australia. The service record for Private Harry Donegan shows that he was born in Bray, County Wicklow. Sure enough, on the Bray War Memorial, a few places above 'Edwards A.C.', appears 'Donegan, Henry'. Presumably Donegan moved from Bray to Drogheda, earning himself recognition on both towns' memorials.

The most recent medium, the internet, provides another useful source and another form of commemoration – the virtual war memorial. An example is the website *Ballymena in World War One*, which records the names of hundreds of Irishmen from Ballymena, County Antrim. It not only lists the usual identifying details but includes a collection of pictures and reports from the files of a contemporary newspaper, the *Ballymena Observer*. It includes the names of 11 soldiers who died while serving in the Australian forces.[75] In the south, the Fame of Tipperary Group has a virtual war memorial commemorating those from County Tipperary who served in the war, including the three Australians on the Cahir war memorial (see p. 80).[76]

Behind each of the unadorned names on the memorials in their various forms, there is a story to be uncovered. Here are just a few of them.

Private Samuel James MacFarlane (Portrush War Memorial, County Antrim)

The sole Australian listed on the Portrush War Memorial is Private Samuel James MacFarlane of the 13th Battalion AIF, who died of wounds received at Gallipoli on 20 August 1915, aged 21 years. Robert Thompson's book on Portrush's war dead has an entry for MacFarlane that includes a poignant photograph of his parents taken in 1915, his father wearing a black armband and his mother a black dress. His family had opposed Irish home rule, with his parents subscribing to Ulster's Solemn League and Covenant, a remonstrance signed on 28 September 1912 by almost 450 000 opponents of home rule, pledging their uncompromising opposition to the Home Rule Bill then before Parliament. Samuel himself had served in the Ulster Volunteer Force, an anti-home rule paramilitary force, before emigrating to Australia just prior to the war. He served in the New Guinea campaign before going to Gallipoli. After being wounded there, he was evacuated to a hospital ship, where he died and was buried at sea.[77]

Second Lieutenant Everard Digges La Touche (Newcastle War Memorial, County Down)

The rather unusual-looking war memorial at Newcastle, County Down, includes the name of another avowed opponent of home rule who emigrated to Australia before the war: Everard Digges La Touche. The memorial is in the form of a lion reclining on a plinth on which are inscribed the names of the fallen, including Everard and his brother Averill. Everard was killed at Gallipoli, while serving as a second lieutenant with the 2nd Battalion AIF, and Averill at Loos in France the following month, fighting with the Royal Irish Rifles.

Born at Burrendale, Newcastle, County Down, in 1883, and ordained as an Anglican clergyman at Durham in the north of England in 1908, Everard earned a reputation as a gifted theological scholar, receiving a doctorate from Trinity College for his book *Christian Certitude: Its Intellectual Basis* and being appointed to the prestigious post of Donnellan Lecturer in Theology at the college in 1911–12. He emigrated to Australia in 1912 for health reasons and held a number of ecclesiastical offices there prior to the war. In 1914, he proposed a motion at the Anglican diocesan synod in Sydney that the diocese affirm 'its protest against the attempt to force Home Rule upon the unwilling Protestants of Ireland' and collected signatures for a letter that appeared in the *Sydney Morning Herald* opposing home rule.

On the outbreak of hostilities he voiced a fervent belief in the righteousness of the war against godless Prussianism and applied to be appointed as a chaplain. When his application was refused, he enlisted as a private soldier. By then he was 31 and had a wife and two young children, who were still living in Ireland. Three months later he was discharged as medically unfit.[78] But this did not deter La Touche, and, following an operation to correct his medical condition, he re-enlisted and was selected for officer training. He was too late to participate in the landing at Gallipoli, instead arriving on the peninsula on the evening of 5 August 1915, the day before the start of the August offensive. He pleaded to join the attack at Lone Pine and was given permission to do so. However, his part in serving the Empire in what he believed was its righteous cause was cut short when he was mortally wounded in the opening minutes of the assault and died soon after. The family suffered a double blow: his wife's brother, Sergeant William Ernest King of County Galway, was killed in the same battle, also serving with the 2nd Battalion. They are both buried in the Lone Pine Cemetery at Gallipoli.[79]

Private Patrick Morgan (Portadown War Memorial, County Armagh)

The attitude to home rule of Private Patrick Morgan of the 3rd Battalion, whose name is recorded on the Portadown War Memorial, is not explicitly known but can be deduced from his sister's comments on the circular she completed for the Official War Historian. In answer to the question, 'Any other biographical details likely to be of interest to the Historian of the A.I.F. or of his Regiment', she wrote, 'His great grandfather died fighting for Ireland in 1798 and his grandfather received wounds of which he died in 1867'. (The years 1798 and 1867, along with 1916, are hallowed in Irish nationalist historiography as occasions when the Irish asserted their independence from Britain. 1798 was the year of the rising of the United Irishmen and 1867 the Fenian Rising.) A ship's fireman who had emigrated to Australia in his late twenties, Patrick seems to have shared their fighting spirit, for he was recommended for a Distinguished Conduct Medal for his actions at Lone Pine on 6 August 1915. The recommendation read:

The war memorial at Newcastle, County Down
(Jeff Kildea)

Volunteered for a storming party under Capt. Scott, 4th
Bn. for the capture of an important length of enemy
trench which was taken in the face of heavy bomb fire.
This action was of great value to the defence in opening
up communication with neighbouring units and in keeping
down hostile bomb fire.[80]

Unfortunately, he did not survive the battle, being killed in action
the next day, less than three months after he had enlisted.

The Irish and the Anzac tradition

The Irish Anzacs, like their fellow Australians, were ordinary men and women thrust into extraordinary circumstances. Some acted seemingly in total disregard for their own survival, such as Private O'Meara; some performed their duties with a high degree of skill and determination, such as Captain Stoker; while others showed remarkable compassion for their fellow-man, such as Chaplain Bergin. For the most part, however, they just survived – existing from day to day in the most appalling conditions imaginable, resigned to their fate. For every one who received a medal for bravery, there were many more whose deeds of valour went unrecognised, but there were also many others who cowered in fear at the bottom of a trench, their resilience crushed by ceaseless shelling, the ravages of rats, lice and assorted vermin, and the mud, the blood and the gore of the battlefield. Through it all, though, there emerged a camaraderie that sustained them to the end, giving rise to the digger legend, which has contributed so much to Australia's national mythography. Just as in Australia the Irish were the leaven in the Australian mix, as Patrick O'Farrell has so eloquently described in *The Irish in Australia*, so, too, in the First World War did the Irish play their part in building that most enduring edifice of Australian national identity, the Anzac tradition.

CHAPTER 4

SIX-BOB-A-DAY TOURISTS

AUSTRALIAN SOLDIERS ON LEAVE IN IRELAND

'Six-bob-a-day tourists' is an epithet frequently applied to Australia's soldiers of the First World War. Quintessentially Australian, it is an expression manifesting the self-deprecating irony that characterised much of the digger slang: boastful yet understating the gravity of the soldiers' task and the dangers they faced.[1] Even so, it was not an inaccurate description: privates in the AIF were paid six shillings a day (one of which was deferred to be paid on discharge), the highest pay given to a private in any army during the war.[2] As for 'tourists', Richard White has contended, albeit somewhat speculatively, that in some respects Australian soldiers were in fact tourists.[3] During the First World War, more than 300 000 Australian soldiers travelled overseas, an exodus the size of which would not be seen for another two generations, when cheap flights would bring international travel within reach of the masses. Just as today Ireland is a popular destination for Australians holidaying in Europe, so it was then, when 'Blighty leave' gave the troops an opportunity to travel throughout the United Kingdom, which at that time included Ireland.

For many Australian soldiers, leave in Ireland meant visiting the place where they, their parents or grandparents were born, or a place where friends and close relatives lived; for others it was about as far away from the war as you could travel on a 10- or 14-day leave pass. For a few – those determined to excuse themselves from further military service – Ireland was a perfect haven for absentees and deserters.

Australian soldiers as tourists

In support of his 'Australian soldier as tourist' thesis, Richard White argues that 'a desire to see the world ... was probably a much more significant motive for enlistment than is often recognized'.[4] The recruiting authorities clearly thought so. In 1917, the New South Wales Recruiting Committee issued a leaflet entitled 'Free Tour to Great Britain and Europe: the Chance of a Lifetime', which offered a 'personally conducted tour whereby you can see the world and save money at the same time'.[5] Another leaflet promised the recruit he would 'broaden his mind and enrich his memory with the knowledge of other peoples and with the sight of other lands', while a recruiting poster announced, 'Free Trip to Europe: Invitations Issued To-day'.[6]

White also details the many ways in which an Australian soldier's war experience mimicked that of the tourist. All undertook a long and leisurely sea voyage in one of the great ocean liners of the day, leased from one of the major shipping companies, while being farewelled with the same rituals of streamer-throwing, gift-giving and band-playing, stopping at the same ports of call, and being entertained by the same equator-crossing ceremonies and deck games as the more conventional tourist. Moreover, when Australian soldiers went on leave they did so as tourists, unlike their German, French, British and Irish counterparts for whom leave meant returning home to see the family. They saw the same sights as tourists, used the same guides and guidebooks and sent postcards home.[7] Many soldiers were prepared to overstay their leave, and face punishment for doing so, in order to see properly the country they were visiting. Cameras, an essential part of the tourist's kit, were ever-present, even when banned, and there was widespread collecting of souvenirs, whether taken from dead Germans or of the more conventional variety. According to White, many of the soldiers' memoirs were typical of pre-war Australian travel literature, with titles such as *Diggers Abroad* and *Digger Tourists*. One soldier, whose travels to Ireland are discussed in this chapter, Lance Corporal Leonard Clyde Bryant, called his war journal, 'Diary on My Travels'.[8] Nevertheless, despite this, White is careful to point out that although the Australian soldier 'had more than a touch of the tourist in him ... that is not to suggest that his war was simply a kind of holiday'.[9] Rather, he was 'given two profound, overlapping experiences. The first was the horrific experience of modern warfare ... The second experience was that of travel to Europe, a peculiarly military variety of "tourism", but tourism nonetheless'.[10]

While an ever-expanding volume of literature has extensively described the first of these two experiences, little has been written on the second. Apart from theoretical contributions by White[11] and James Wieland,[12] James Curran (a student of White) has written about Australian soldiers on leave in Paris,[13] Peter Cochrane has researched soldier-photographers of the First World War,[14] and Robin Gerster and Peter Pierce have edited an anthology of Australian military travel, in which they make the point that 'The reality of what lay at the end of the journey often made a mockery of this ardour for travel'.[15] John Ellis included a chapter on rest and leave in his study of the soldiers' life on the Western Front, but it covers all combatant nations, with only passing reference to Australian soldiers, and concentrates mainly on the rest areas behind the lines.[16] While Suzanne Brugger discusses Australian soldiers on leave in Egypt and Bill Gammage in his classic study of the AIF devotes a few pages to leave in England, the most detailed narrative account of Australian soldiers on leave is by Michael McKernan.[17] Drawing on their letters and diaries as well as accounts in the English press to track their activities in England and the local response to them, McKernan argues that when the novelty of the quaint colonials with their distinctive uniform and raw manners wore off, Londoners began to resent the high jinks of larrikin diggers. Furthermore, anticipating White's thesis, he asserts there was 'an important sense ... in which the Australians were "tourists" and their experiences in themselves are informative and entertaining'.[18] This chapter adds to this small body of literature by examining the experiences of Australian soldiers on leave in Ireland, a subject not previously covered.

Going on leave

Australian soldiers going on leave to Ireland would either travel there from one of the military establishments in England or would pass through England on their way from the front, in both cases often spending a few days in London. The usual means of getting from London to Ireland was to take the night train from Euston Station to Holyhead, from where the ferry crossed the Irish Sea to Kingstown (now Dún Laoghaire), and then to travel by train the 10 kilometres into Dublin, arriving before 9 am. At Kingstown, volunteers from the Women's League would provide the men with hot coffee and cake as they disembarked. Another option was to depart Euston about 8.30 am and arrive in Dublin about 6 pm. This had the advantage of allowing the soldier to see the English and Welsh countryside from the train, though it also used up one of his valuable days.

Leave from the front was allocated on a roster basis and its availability was contingent on whether the soldier could be spared when his turn came up. Corporal Noel Michael Keating of 13th Brigade Headquarters, who had been in France for 12 months without leave, wrote in his diary for 13 August 1918, 'To-night I was granted leave to UK by the Staff Captain, which was cancelled almost immediately afterwards by Brigade Major who says he wants all his NCOs till after this offensive'. On 28 August, he recorded, 'My leave has again been deferred a couple of days. I have now to get all the officers' records of the Brigade complete before I can go'. The next day he was told he could take his leave and on 1 September 1918 he set out for Boulogne to take the channel ferry to Folkestone.[19]

For front-line men, the journey from their unit to the embarkation port could be frustratingly slow, particularly if the roads to the railhead were choked with military traffic or were in poor condition. At stations serviced by special leave trains, there could be a further delay as soldiers were not permitted to take local trains. Lance Corporal Leonard Clyde Bryant of the 2nd Field Ambulance described in his diary a 'very slow and dreary trip' of 16 hours in a cattle truck from Corbie to Boulogne, which he said should have taken 4 hours 30 minutes. He then had to wait two hours for the train to Calais because it was running late.[20]

Departing soldiers were also obliged to attend the divisional depot to have their leave pass checked, to receive instructions on sexual hygiene and standards of behaviour, and to clean themselves and their clothing. The regulations were quite strict on such matters: the diggers were not to go on leave with the mud of the trenches staining their uniforms, though a desire to impress women was a far greater incentive in that respect than any military regulation. As for sexual hygiene, venereal disease was a serious problem in the AIF throughout the war despite monetary penalties, warnings and exhortations, with Australian soldiers recording among the highest infection rates of all the Allied armies.[21]

Colonel AG Butler in the *Official History of the Australian Army Medical Services* devoted a chapter to the issue, in which he noted that in 1916 venereal diseases among Australian troops in Britain accounted for almost 15 per cent of hospital admissions, declining to just under 13 per cent in 1917 and rising to 13.7 per cent in 1918. This compared with rates of around 3 per cent for British troops.[22] Butler gave as one of the main reasons for the disparity the fact that 'VD in the Army was pre-eminently a disease of leave-time, and to dominion troops "leave" did not mean "home leave" ... The incidence of VD in the AIF troops in France did not greatly exceed that among the British, whereas in Great Britain it was approximately four times as great'.[23] Ireland was not immune from the problem. Butler's *Official History* includes a table showing that Ireland was the source of 19 cases of venereal disease reported during the four weeks ending 30 December 1916, out of a total of 567 for the United Kingdom. As a result, early treatment was made available at military hospitals in Ireland as well as in Great Britain.[24]

Horseferry Road, Westminster, London,
where AIF Headquarters was located
(AWM D00796)

If the army had difficulty in stamping out venereal disease, so, too, did the soldiers have difficulty in eliminating another common affliction – lice. While a thorough cleansing might shed the lice from their bodies, it was difficult to eradicate the eggs lying dormant in the seams of their clothes, which would hatch before long to renew the soldier's discomfort during his leave. Second Lieutenant Charles Richard Carleton, MC, of the Royal Australian Engineers wrote to his mother, 'On reaching England I practically only had what I walked about in and was as chatty as ——'. (In digger dialect, a chat was a louse and to be chatty was to be verminous.)[25]

Cleaned and preened, it was then a matter of getting on board a cross-channel ferry, not an easy task when military demand for transport was high, though in such cases the men might be credited with extra leave to make up for the delay. The channel crossing was often slow and unpleasant due to bad weather and the need for the ferries to sail a zig-zag course as a precaution against submarines. Arriving in England, the soldier would take a train to London and report to AIF Headquarters at 130 Horseferry Road, Westminster. Here the soldier could store his kit, receive advice on accommodation and travel and draw money on his pay book, including a furlough allowance of 1s 9d per day.[26] Nearby were the War Chest Club, the YMCA kiosk and the Anzac Buffet, where the soldier could drop in for a snack and a yarn. They were staffed by Australian women volunteers and provided meals and teas, reading matter from home, a piano, gramophone and billiards. The men could obtain relatively cheap accommodation at the YMCA, the Union Jack Club, Peel House or at numerous soldiers' homes, but many preferred to stay in hotels and boarding houses.

It was not only the men from the front who passed through London. From mid-1916, tens of thousands of Australian soldiers were housed on the Salisbury Plain in training camps for reinforcements newly arrived from Australia, or in command depots, which managed the transition back to their units of sick and wounded soldiers after their discharge from hospital. The hospitals and convalescent homes themselves accommodated thousands of Australian soldiers.[27]

Those granted leave from these establishments and intending to visit Ireland would usually travel to London to catch the boat-train to Kingstown. One who did so was Gunner Joseph Patrick Byrne of the 7th Field Artillery Brigade, who in July 1916 was granted four days disembarkation leave from Lark Hill training camp, which he took in Ireland where he had close relatives. With one day's travelling in each direction, including time spent reporting at AIF Headquarters, he could manage only two days in Dublin, one spent meeting relatives ('Uncle Mike dead spit of dear old dad') and the other sight-seeing.[28] To avoid London, an alternative route from the Salisbury Plain was to travel by train to Bristol, then through the Severn Tunnel to Cardiff and from there to Fishguard to catch the ferry to Rosslare, County Waterford.

The presence in London of thousands of soldiers on leave provided new marketing opportunities for those in the travel industry.[29] *The Overseas Soldier's Guide to London* sold for 6d, while London Underground advertised *Half Day Tours Around London for Men on Leave*. Under the auspices of the Australian Military Office, Thomas Cook & Son offered organised tours to different parts of the United Kingdom. One of its brochures, 'Tours for Convalescent Australian Soldiers in England, Scotland and Ireland', advertised a seven-day round trip to Ireland including a night each in Cork and Killarney, two nights in Dublin and a night in Belfast, all for ten pounds, including travel, accommodation, tours, meals, transfers, tips, and the services of a guide throughout the tour.[30]

Michael McKernan has written that London was the place to which most Australian troops were drawn back.[31] No doubt this was true, but in time and for reasons which McKernan himself advanced, London became less welcoming and less friendly. Private Roland Henry Simpson of the 9th Battalion wrote to his mother in January 1918, 'London I know nearly as well as Brisbane but there is nothing in it & everybody robs you. It is rotten'.[32] Lieutenant James McKenna wrote of his impressions of London, 'the Big Smoke is a fine place for fine people, but a young officer with only his pay behind him had better not pass all his leave there'.[33] Air raids and the blackout were other irritants. A raid occurred the first night Private Verdi Schwinghammer of the 42nd Battalion arrived there in March 1918, with several people being killed.[34] Private Frederick Thomas Heming of the 54th Battalion received a similar welcome on his arrival, confiding to his sister Violet, 'It puts the wind up you to hear the guns and the bombs falling'.[35] Colonel Joseph Livesley Beeston of the 4th Field Ambulance, after walking back to his London hotel one night, wrote in his diary, 'it is nearly as dangerous as the beach at Anzac [Cove]. The crossing of darkened streets and rushing about of cars makes it difficult'.[36]

Ireland, on the other hand, remained a popular leave destination for Australian soldiers. On 1 September 1918, Simpson, now a lance corporal, wrote to his mother after his second visit to Ireland, 'Well I had a real tip top furlough this time in Ireland I am quite satisfied that it is the best place to go & have a good time'.[37] Lieutenant Carleton, who had been given five weeks leave starting on 12 December 1917, chose to take it in Ireland. He explained to his mother that he returned to London for a medical board examination on 28 December before going back to Ireland on 30 December as he preferred to return to Dublin than stay in London where he knew no one.[38]

For those with friends and relations there, Ireland was an obvious place to visit. Colonel Beeston, a native of Newcastle in New South Wales, had studied medicine in Ireland and had met and married his wife there. On his return to Dublin 33 years later in November 1915, he went to his former digs at 127 Leinster Road, tracking down old acquaintances and visiting St Peter's Church, where he had been married.[39] Sergeant Daniel Joseph Scanlon of the 49th Battalion, who was born in Ipswich, Queensland, took the opportunity in December 1916 to visit family in Ireland. In a letter to his niece, he reported on his trip:

> Last Sunday week I arrived back from 6 days leave spent in Ireland. The time was not enough so I could only spend one day with my uncle. Annie Scanlon wrote to me while I was in France giving me their address. They have a nice comfortable house and farm & are doing well. You may be

sure I had a warm welcome. When I get my full leave I intend to see my mother's people & visit Ennis again.

Annie wrote to Scanlon's brother John:

> Well John you will be surprised to here [sic] that we had brother Dan here in Ireland he came to visit us unexpected which came to a great surprised [sic] to us to see him the time you send me his address I wrote to him & never got answer untill [sic] he came to the house & when he came in we did not know him & he said I am Dan Scanlan [sic]. So we had hearty welcome for him & received him with the greatest of kindness ... he came about 11 o'clock & went about 10 o'clock ... all the neighbours & friends came to see him.[40]

Lieutenant McKenna from Melbourne also received a warm welcome from his relatives when he visited them in Arigna, County Roscommon, in December 1917:

> Aunt welcomed me most warmly. Inside, uncle shook hands again and offered me a hundred thousand welcomes to the cabin of my forefathers. I was rather affected by it all, too, although I don't think I showed it. Then our cousins came in – Mary, Terry, John, James and Annie. It was some welcome, I tell you Nick. I never saw a welcome like it and I expect to see another anything like it only when I get back to a place called Coburg, about 12,000 miles from here.[41]

But the hospitality could be overwhelming, as McKenna complained to his brother:

> We get home to find the place crowded with relatives and friends, come to see me. Aunt wanted me to eat, but I implored mercy, for I have been eating all day. Every house I went into required an eating bout. My hosts and hostesses were not content unless I was gorging myself. Tom's sister was quite surprised and a little offended because I could not bear 9 potatoes off my plate and swallow a jug full of very rich milk. I tried hard to please and found that I could hardly

get up the boreen [laneway] leading to uncle's. Then aunt wanted me to eat more and I had to crave mercy. Having escaped that, I had to get out and be introduced all round. Almost every family for miles around was represented.

In February 1917, Carleton wrote to his mother about the prospect of his getting leave in England, adding, 'If I am there for any time will of course go to Erin. Can't remember the place where you came from. Should love to know so please drop me a line'.[42] However, it was not until December 1917 that he made it to Ireland, after having been wounded and receiving five weeks leave. He told his mother, 'Am hoping to be able to look up some of the old places about which you & father have often spoken, and will let you know the result of my investigations'.[43] Like future generations of Australians who would travel to Ireland with the same purpose in mind, Carleton began to search for his roots.

He first tried to locate the house where his father had lived in Dublin, but without success, though he managed to find Aunt Lizzie and to visit Aunt Carrie at St Stephens Green. He then set out for Portarlington in Queens County (now County Laois) to look for where his mother had lived. He later wrote to her that while strolling around Deerpark he met a woman from whom he inquired the way to the station:

> After telling me she said 'You are very like one of the Dignams, were you looking for anyone?' We then got talking and she informed me that she was a sort of cousin of mine being a Miss Cobb – now Mrs Shan.

Mrs Shan then took him to see 'your Uncle Jonathan Dignam who now lives in your old home'. She also took him to visit his mother's old teacher, where they had afternoon tea. They kept him so long that he missed the train to Dublin and had to 'square' the guard of a goods train to take him back so he could catch the morning ferry.[44]

Private Alfred John Johnston of the 9th Light Horse Regiment also went searching for his roots. Having arrived in Dublin on the morning of 11 November 1915, he and a mate, Private Charlie

Cotton, took the 3 pm train to Oldcastle, County Meath, from where they travelled 16 kilometres to Lisduff, County Cavan, in a jaunting cart.[45] It was cold there and snow was on the ground. Johnston's aunt and his cousin Maud greeted them, the uncle having died just a few weeks before. The next day they cycled to the Johnstons of Soonah (Aughwelia), who said they thought he was just like his father. On 17 November, Johnston cycled to Cavan township, about 16 kilometres away, and took the train to Clones to visit his Uncle Charlie. Next day he visited a cousin at Kilnaleck.

Readers who have themselves undertaken such roots-seeking visitations to Ireland, will readily relate to these experiences. For an Australian with Irish heritage, leave in Ireland could be a busy diversion from the war, but the country also attracted those with no prior Irish connections. It was remote from the war, both geographically and metaphorically, and reminders of the conflict, such as food shortages and rationing were largely unknown. Private Schwinghammer, who visited Dublin in March 1918, wrote in his memoirs: 'It is a fine city. Food was good and plentiful as the Irish people were not rationed. The whole city was brilliantly lit up (as it was too far away for air raids) – quite a contrast to the English and Scotch cities'.[46] Carleton wrote to his father, 'Food is infinitely more plentiful here than in England. Food restrictions are almost unknown, every place is brilliantly lit up & the people hardly know there is a war on'.[47] Reporting on his trip to Portarlington, he told his mother of the 'afternoon tea of home made bread & scones & real butter – a luxury which I had not tasted for over a year. It is always margarine now in England'.[48]

Ireland also had outstanding scenic beauty, on which the soldiers commented in their letters and diaries. According to Private Heming, 'Ireland is some place so pretty with the fields and hedges and their whitewashed cabins. There is no doubt that Ireland is the Emerald Isle'.[49] Furthermore, its people were warm-hearted and hospitable, even to strangers. Lance Corporal Simpson wrote, 'They all have very old ideas and superstitions. But no one could wish for a more homely lot of people & it is a pleasure to talk to a sensible & decent girl that is very hard to find in England. They will all invite you home & treat you like one of their own'.[50] Private Schwinghammer noted, 'The Irish people were very kind to us'.[51]

Scenic beauty and friendly people are characteristics of Ireland that continue to attract tourists. In fact, many soldiers' accounts of their leave there could have been written by modern-day tourists: their letters and diaries refer to visits to Dublin Castle, St Stephen's Green, Trinity College to view the Book of Kells, and Phoenix Park including Dublin Zoo; inspections of the Guinness brewery; and train trips to Cork with excursions to Blarney Castle to kiss the Blarney Stone. But the most popular destination of all was Killarney in County Kerry. As related in chapter 2 (pp. 55, 58), Privates Chapman and Davis visited there in April 1916 before returning to Dublin during the early stages of the Easter Rising. Chapman in his diary was succinct:

> 22/4/16: Left for Killarney at 7.15 am arrived at 12.30 pm. Had two Australian Sisters with us, enjoyed the trip alright, beautiful scenery. Had a drive round the lakes in the afternoon. Rather cold – a very bad day for photography.

> 23/4/16: Had a great day – did a whole days trip. Got horses and did some riding. Got a good view of lakes and country surrounding – covered 50 miles by land and water.

But Davis was more expansive and he related his first impressions:

> We found Killarney a very quiet and old fashioned place. Half the population rode around the town on donkey carts and the shawls worn by the women and covering the head and shoulders was in great prominence. I was struck by the real Irish expressions. Every Irishman, without exception, has a clear representation of the little map of Ireland on his face. We soon got busy to see the sights of the much talked of beauty spots around here.[52]

Davis and his mate Bob Grant stayed at Graham's Glebe Hotel, which published a brochure advertising three separate one-day excursions, being pretty much the standard tours offered by Killarney's tour operators even today. 'No. 1 Excursion' comprised a drive to the Gap of Dunloe, a pony ride or walk to the Upper Lakes for lunch, a boat ride down the lakes past Eagle's Nest Mountain, Shooting the Rapids and Innisfallen Island to Ross Castle, and a drive back to the hotel; 'No. 2 Excursion' included a drive to Muckross Abbey and along the shores of the lakes past Colleen Bawn Rock to Colleen Bawn Cottage and on to Torc Waterfall before returning to the hotel; and 'No. 3 Excursion' comprised a drive through Lord Kenmare's Deer Park, a walk through the Glen, and a drive to Aghadoe Heights and along the shores to Ross Castle and Ross Island before returning to the hotel. The Glebe Hotel brochure also offered walks in and about Killarney as well as excursions further afield and activities such as fishing and golf.

On their first day in Killarney, Davis and Grant took No. 2 Excursion and the next day No. 1 Excursion. During the latter tour they came across some local entrepreneurs ('queerly garbed mountain folk') who were keen to relieve the cashed-up Australians of some of their money. 'The first invited us to test out their home-brewed whisky (kill or cure), 6d. a taste. Another mountaineer, blowing an echoing sound on his bugle, held out his hand for 6d. He was sure the echo was worth 6d. anyway.'[53] That evening, Davis and Grant left Killarney to return to Dublin to witness a far more spectacular series of events during Easter week.

In August 1918, Lance Corporal Simpson took all three excursions on three separate days, and on his fourth day in Killarney returned to the Gap of Dunloe.[54] The following month Corporal Keating stayed at the Alexandra Hotel and met up with three Australians and two Americans, with whom he took a trip around the lakes, visiting Muckross Abbey. The next day they went by jaunting cars to Kate Kearney's Cottage, where they hired ponies and rode through the Gap of Dunloe and then went by boat to Ross Castle. 'One of the best scenic trips I've ever had,' Keating wrote in his diary.[55] In his four days at Killarney he, too, managed to cover all three excursion routes, while on his way back to Dublin he stopped off at Cork, visiting Blarney Castle, where he kissed the Blarney Stone. So, too, did Lance Corporal Bryant, who in September 1917 spent two days in Killarney and went on No. 1 and No. 2 excursions.[56] Sergeant Arthur Morrison Dick, MM, of the 2nd Machine Gun Battalion also had two days in Killarney in March 1918, visiting the lakes and the surrounding sights.[57]

Of the many Australian soldiers who visited Killarney during the war, Corporal James Nelson of the 10th Field Artillery Brigade was probably unique in that he chose to take his Australian bride Joy there on their honeymoon. Joy (whose maiden name was also Nelson, though the couple were not related) and her sister Hope had been holidaying in England when war broke out. Unable to arrange transport back to Australia, the two young women from Walcha, New South Wales, were biding their time in England when they met Jim and his brother Albert, two of the six Nelson siblings from Coonabarabran, New South Wales, who had enlisted in the AIF. Albert was a lance corporal in the 33rd Battalion. On 25 February 1918, Jim and Joy were married at Walthamstow, north London, a month after Albert and Hope were married there. Unfortunately, Jim and Joy were not destined to live a long and happy life together. Having been wounded and gassed on four occasions, Jim fell ill after returning in early 1919 to Australia and was admitted to Sydney's Callan Park Hospital, where he died in 1921.[58]

In May 1919, after the armistice, Lance Sergeant Frederick August Stichnoth of the 41st Battalion visited Ireland, spending three days in Killarney. In a letter to his parents, he wrote, 'Killarney is glorious. We've been on the move ever since we came here in Jaunting cars etc from early morn till late at night'.[59] The letter was written on three black-and-white postcards depicting scenic views around the lakes. He added, 'I just noticed these PCs are printed in Germany but they don't seem to care here'. After returning to Codford Camp in England, Stichnoth sent more letters to his parents describing his leave in Ireland, some of them on colour postcards of Killarney and other places he had visited there.[60] Private Schwinghammer was in Killarney in June 1919, having returned to Ireland for a second time: 'I palled up with an American soldier and we had a very enjoyable three days here. Saw all of the beautiful sights and went

Off to the lakes: Corporal James Nelson next to his bride Joy on a jaunting cart in Killarney
(Courtesy of John Gallagher)

all over the famous lakes in boats (shooting the rapids &c). It was midsummer and everything was beautiful and green'.[61]

Apart from Dublin and Killarney, Belfast was another popular destination for Australian soldiers on leave, though it was somewhat different to what they experienced in the south. Simpson told his mother, 'The people are altogether different up there but all the places I went I liked, they are a long way better than London or England ... We went to see the people where we were invited in Belfast. They were very nice'.[62] The city itself did not have as many attractions for young Australians, except for those interested in its industrial sights, such as the Harland and Wolff shipyards, where the *Titanic* had been launched just a few years before. Lance Sergeant Stichnoth, who had headed north after leaving Killarney, stayed five days in Belfast, visiting several spinning and weaving works, a brewery and a distillery, as well as the shipyards, where he saw a ship launched.[63] Private Robert Andrew Tulloch of the 15th Battalion, who spent four days in Ireland out of his eight days leave, wrote home, 'I ... went through a big printing works in Belfast, also seen the big docks there which is something to see'.[64] Schwinghammer was another to visit the Harland & Wolff shipyards, having travelled to Belfast from Killarney.[65]

However, Belfast did not provide the same range of activities as Dublin or Killarney. Bryant spent his two days there roaming the city 'as there are no sights to see' and having a 'good flutter around' to break the monotony.[66] Nevertheless, on each of his two nights in the city he went to a show, unlike Stichnoth, who told his parents that because there were not many theatres he would take rides in jaunting cars in the evening instead.[67] Even so, Belfast was a base from which the diggers could sample the scenic beauty of the north. During his stay there Stichnoth travelled to Portrush and the Giant's Causeway on the north Antrim coast, which he described as 'a wonderful piece of nature's work'.[68] Tulloch went as far afield as Donaghmore in County Tyrone.[69]

Because they were well paid, Australian soldiers could afford to lodge at some of the best hotels. Lance Corporal Bryant stayed at the Metropole Hotel in Cork, which he described as 'the finest and biggest of its kind in the Emerald Isle'.[70] Sergeant Francis Thomas Coleman, on leave from his staff job at the 3rd Australian Divisional Headquarters, and his mate Driver Boxer Ware of the 3rd Division Motor Transport Company stayed three nights at the salubrious Shelbourne Hotel during their stay in Dublin. Their fateful decision to return to London, boarding RMS *Leinster* for the crossing, is described in chapter 5 (p. 153).

For officers, there was another option. Lady Frances Ryder conducted the Dominion Services Hospitality Scheme, whereby servicemen from all parts of the Empire were put in touch with families willing to give them a taste of home life during weekends and leave periods.[71] One such family was the Somers of Marlay

Grange, Rathfarnham, south of Dublin. Lieutenant Carleton spent his convalescent leave there in December 1917. Upon arrival at Kingstown pier, he was met by a prepaid taxi and taken to Marlay Grange

> to be shown into a snug little room by a brass buttoned blue coated flunky. He brings you hot water & hot towels & brushes your clothes whilst this chicken washes & changes into slacks, then pilots you down into the drawing room to make the acquaintance of Mrs Summers [*sic*] – a fashion plate lady in evening dress.[72]

There were two other Australians staying there when he arrived and another came the next day. The house, comprising 30 rooms, was set in 200 acres of ground at the foot of the Dublin Mountains, containing woods, a private golf links, tennis courts and a croquet lawn. Carleton told his mother, 'This is the most glorious place right in amongst the hills, equally distant from Dublin & Kingstown and the people are really charming ... I would be quite satisfied to remain here for the duration!'[73]

'A perfect haven for absentees and deserters'

Despite his wish to remain in Ireland, Lieutenant Carleton did return to the front, unlike many Australian soldiers who decided to extend their leave or not return at all. In fact, Ireland became quite a haven for absentees and deserters. Absence without leave and desertion were serious problems in the AIF, a fact acknowledged even by Charles Bean, the unswerving admirer of the Australian soldier.[74] Unique among the armies on the Western Front, the Australian army was precluded by legislation from imposing the death penalty for desertion, being deprived of a form of punishment which Bean described as 'the recognised preventative of desertion'.[75]

While some deserters remained behind the lines in France, sometimes mixing with other troops or joining gangs of like-minded men who lived off the proceeds of crime, others either made their way to the United Kingdom or failed to return from Blighty leave. Private George Davis, who worked as a driver at AIF headquarters and had an ear for scuttlebutt, wrote in his memoirs,

> According to Headquarters' reports, the number of diggers who have not returned from their furlough is very high – quite a few thousand. Most deserters are reported dressed in mufti and favour Ireland, where they evidently get more sympathy.[76]

Davis's reference to Ireland is supported by official documents, including a report by Lieutenant Colonel John Williams, the Assistant Provost Martial, who visited Ireland in April 1918 and reported:

> [Ireland] is a perfect haven for absentees and deserters ... There are 'Sinn Feiners' and other people, who not only harbour absentees and deserters, but provide them with civilian clothes, food, and accommodation, free of charge, in order to hide their identity, and very frequently find them some reasonably lucrative employment.[77]

Another racket Williams noted was that Irish doctors were willing to give a medical certificate for a small fee, certifying that a soldier was unfit to travel or return to his unit, when there was nothing wrong with him. He also reported that the British authorities believed that absentee soldiers were supplying arms to civilians. His remarks referred only to the south of Ireland, for he added, 'In Belfast I found things altogether different. The general population are sympathetic, and the police difficulties are little worse than they are in this country'. In June 1918, Williams returned to Ireland with a small detachment of military police where he made 'several arrests'.[78]

In his report, Williams stated that in some parts of Ireland the Royal Irish Constabulary was unwilling to assist the military police, of if they did, it was in a half-hearted manner. This fact might explain how Private James Carroll of the 58th Battalion was able to live in Ireland for 18 months after deserting in October 1916. Born in County Sligo, he was working in Australia when war broke out and enlisted there. When he went home to Sligo on leave, he found his family in dire straits and decided to stay. He later told the Australian authorities that he had reported his situation to the Royal Irish Constabulary, but that no action was taken against him until a warrant for his arrest was issued in April 1918 and he was taken to England. Due to illness, Carroll was allowed to return to Ireland, where he died in 1919, as related in chapter 5 (pp. 200–201).

One Australian soldier who was not so fortunate in his dealings with the local police was Private Clarence Wilbur Baker of the 5th Pioneer Battalion, who was arrested in Belfast on 20 November 1917 wearing mufti. At Baker's court martial, Sergeant James Wilkin of the Royal Irish Constabulary gave evidence that he was on duty at the railway station when he saw 'a remarkable looking stranger come off the train' (Baker was almost 190 centimetres tall). Wilkin approached the man and asked his name. 'I am an American and my name is Harris W. Regan,' he replied. When the stranger was unable to produce any identification, Sergeant Wilkin took him to the police station, where after further questioning the man identified himself as Private Baker.

Before the war, Baker had been a pacifist and an international socialist, having worked for the cause in both Australia and America. When the war broke out, he modified his pacifism and enlisted, but after two years he claimed to have reverted to his earlier beliefs. He applied for a discharge but was refused. Accordingly, when he was granted leave he went to Ireland, where he intended getting work as an optician, his civilian occupation. While in Dublin, he made contact with members of Sinn Féin and became interested in their cause. When his room was searched after his arrest, police discovered a quantity of literature on Ireland's struggle for independence. He was found guilty of 'conduct to the prejudice of good order and military discipline' and sentenced to 112 days detention at the AIF Detention Barracks at Lewes in England. After serving 61 days of the sentence, he was released to his unit in France, where, after a week, he was sent back to England for return to Australia and discharge from the AIF as an undesirable.[79] In Australia, Baker resumed his prewar pursuits, being one of the founders of the Communist Party in 1920, and spending further time in gaol for his political activities.[80]

Australian soldiers and rebel Ireland

The revolutionary situation in Ireland sometimes intruded into the otherwise peaceful ambience that made the country such a respite from the war. In May 1918, leave to Ireland by members of the AIF was temporarily suspended[81], presumably due to concerns over increased anti-government activities by advanced nationalists, while on occasions a situation could develop that was unpleasant for a man wearing the king's uniform. In February 1917, when contemplating a trip to Ireland, Lieutenant Carleton wrote to his mother, 'They say a uniform is very unpopular over there just now but that will probably die off'.[82] In December 1917, during his stay at Rathfarnham, he wrote: 'Kakhi [sic] is pretty well as popular as —— well what? – say, "work"! Frequently, murmured insults are to be heard as one passes, and I had a small stone shyed at me by a kid near Kingstown'.[83] Even so, there was a certain fascination with the emerging revolutionary movement. Carleton added, 'I should love to go a trip [sic] into the really "hot" districts but it's hardly worth the risk on one's own without mufti'. Private Ken Murray of the 38th Battalion was also circumspect. In a letter to his father in March 1918 he wrote:

> There was not so much bother on St Pats day as I was led to believe there would be. Beyond a fight between the Sinn Fieners [sic] and the police in the small and early hours of Sunday morning, nothing happened. Nevertheless there were some streets in the city in which it was unsafe for a man in khaki to venture. Needless to say we did not venture.[84]

A safer option was a visit to Sackville Street (now O'Connell Street) to see the ruins of the buildings destroyed during the Easter Rising. In fact it became *de rigueur* for Australian soldiers on leave to do so. Private Chapman, having helped to suppress the rising, was given time off from his duties three days after the rebels surrendered. He noted in his diary, 'Got a pass in afternoon from 2 till 9 am following day. Went and saw ruins of buildings in Sackville Street'. Two days later he went back for another look before departing Dublin that afternoon.[85] Private Davis also had a last look before leaving Dublin on 1 May 1916, noting, 'Sackville Street is in ruins, and the shops are looted. The Hotel Metropole, where we previously stayed, is in ruins, the GPO is razed to the ground'.[86]

On 1 September 1917, Lance Corporal Bryant arrived in Dublin and saw various sights including 'where the Rebellion took place in 1916'. On his last night in Dublin he 'visited a famous Sinn Fein play the "King of Dublin" and it was humorous and well played and acted'.[87] In December 1917, Lieutenant McKenna passed through Dublin on his way to County Roscommon but stayed there on the way back:

> I like Dublin and spent another afternoon and night there
> on the way back, staying at the Shelbourne Hotel, a place
> prominent in accounts of Easter Week. It commands St.
> Stephens Green which was occupied by the Sinn Fein in
> force. I 'did' Dublin thoroughly. I saw all the places which
> had figured in the revolt, particularly the GPO which was
> the Headquarters of the rebels and which is now merely
> a skeleton. It took fire and was completely burned inside,
> whilst the outside walls still stand intact.[88]

Private Simpson, who was in Dublin in January 1918, wrote to his mother of a visit to Phoenix Park:

> There was five of us standing talking one was a big red faced
> Irishman. A mob of Sinn Feiners went by and he said come
> on now me boys sing God Save the King. It's only a rumour
> they did not go crook on him. They never play God save the
> King after a programme at the theatres & the people have
> no time for soldiers in Dublin. Sackville Street was blown
> about pretty well at the time of the riot the walls of the Post
> Office are the only parts standing and most of the other
> buildings are in ruins.[89]

Private Tulloch wrote after his visit in June 1918, 'I seen the buildings in Dublin are blown to bits, the time the Rebellion was on'. His letter is on a series of postcards of scenes of Dublin, including one of Sackville Street before the rising, on which he marked the buildings that had been destroyed.[90] Corporal Keating arrived in Dublin on the morning of 5 September 1918. After checking in at the Soldier's Club he went for a walk 'and [saw] many interesting places and scenes of the Revolution'.[91]

Apart from the risks associated with wearing the king's uniform in a country becoming increasingly hostile to the British Empire, there were other, more serious, ways in which an Australian soldier on leave might find himself caught up in the troubles of revolutionary Ireland. At about 10 pm on 29 June 1919, police observed two Australian soldiers, one of them Sergeant John Clark, MM, walking alongside a man holding a Sinn Féin flag (now the national flag of Ireland) at the head of a crowd of between 1000 and 1500 people crossing the O'Connell Bridge. Clark was wearing a Sinn Féin ribbon and some in the crowd were calling out 'Up Sinn Féin'. The police broke up the procession and arrested Clark. Stones were thrown by the crowd and a revolver shot was heard and a policeman wounded. For his part in the procession, Clark was charged with conduct to the prejudice of good order and military discipline. At his court martial in August 1919, he said that he had been drinking in a bar when news was announced of the signing of the Paris Peace Treaty and that he had joined the procession thinking it was in celebration of the peace. He said he did not know how he came to be wearing green, white and orange ribbons but said they may have been pinned on him by the crowd. He claimed he was not aware of their significance as he had no knowledge of, or opinions on, Irish politics. The charges were dismissed.[92] Clark might have had more adventures in Ireland, if his obituary is to be believed:

> He himself would not talk on the subject of war a great deal, although on occasions when he did he revealed many of the amusing sides of army life. On one occasion while he and a companion were on leave in Ireland he was mistaken for another person and appeared certain to be executed, and it was not until the final hours before the time for his shooting that his identity was established and he was released.[93]

Another member of the AIF who was court-martialled for apparent sympathy with Sinn Féin was Chaplain Thomas Joseph O'Donnell. A native of Buninyong, Victoria, Father O'Donnell, while a priest in the Archdiocese of Hobart, had been an outspoken supporter of conscription during the war, enlisting as a private soldier because Archbishop Mannix at first would not approve his application to be a chaplain. When his appointment came through, he set sail for the front in February 1918, equipped with letters of recommendation from Prime Minister Hughes to Field Marshal Haig and General Birdwood, and joined the 11th Battalion in France.[94] Father O'Donnell was as ardent a supporter of self-government for Ireland as he was of conscription. After the war, he took leave in Ireland and met Arthur Griffith, the founder of Sinn Féin, at the Gresham Hotel in Dublin, presenting him with a pistol that had once belonged to John Mitchel, a leader of the Young Ireland movement responsible for the abortive 1848 rising. Father O'Donnell then toured Ireland and, like many other Australian soldiers, went to Killarney, where he stayed at the International Hotel.

On 10 October 1919, O'Donnell, wearing his military uniform, was having an animated conversation in the hotel dining room with an Ulster businessman, a Mr Marsh, whom O'Donnell had just met that evening, when, it was later alleged, he uttered 'violently disparaging remarks about HM the King, the Royal Family, Mr Lloyd George, and the whole British Government'. The conversation was overheard by Second Lieutenant JS Chambers of the King's Liverpool Regiment, who asked O'Donnell to desist, whereupon it is alleged he told Chambers to mind his own damn business. O'Donnell and Marsh then left the room. Not content to leave the matter rest, Chambers reported the incident to the local military authorities, who forwarded the information through Cork district headquarters to Irish Command in Dublin, who in turn reported it to the War Office. Meanwhile, Father O'Donnell had left Killarney for Cork, returning to Dublin on 14 October. That afternoon, two military police interviewed him at his hotel and he was ordered into close arrest. Although AIF Headquarters was alerted, nothing was done for a few days, by which time O'Donnell had made application to the High Court for a writ of habeas corpus to secure his release from custody, a civil proceeding that attracted the interest of the press. Prime Minister Hughes, having heard of O'Donnell's predicament, sent him a telegram of support, advising that he had cabled the Secretary of State for the Colonies suggesting that a regrettable mistake had been made. On 25 October 1919, however, the High Court ruled that, despite some irregularities in the arrest, O'Donnell's detention was lawful and he was committed to the custody of Lieutenant G Francis of AIF Headquarters, who escorted him to London.

In a lovely piece of irony, Father O'Donnell was held overnight in the Tower of London, for centuries a place of incarceration of many Catholic martyrs and where Sir Roger Casement was imprisoned after his arrest in 1916. This was purely by chance because, it being a Sunday when they arrived in London, AIF Headquarters was closed; in such a situation, the usual place for accommodating officer prisoners in London was the depot of the Royal Fusiliers (City of London Regiment), which happened to be in the Tower. The next morning, Father O'Donnell was taken to AIF Headquarters and released into open arrest.

The case had reached a stage where it was no longer possible to brush it under the carpet and AIF Headquarters felt obliged to prosecute O'Donnell on the charge that had been brought against him on the word of a junior officer, namely 'Conduct to the prejudice of good order and military discipline in that he ... made use of traitorous and disloyal language concerning His Majesty the King and the British Government', which was later amended to 'using disloyal words regarding the Sovereign'. On 26 November 1919, the court martial opened in front of Brigadier General JP McGlinn (the Sydney-born son of Irish parents from County Tipperary; see p. 94), four colonels, one major and two captains, all AIF, with a Grenadier Guards captain as judge advocate to advise the court on military law and court-martial procedure. O'Donnell was represented by two King's Counsels and a junior barrister, while the prosecution also had a King's Counsel. After a hearing lasting two days, the tribunal reached a verdict of not guilty. O'Donnell received from the War Office £1060.12s.11d for his costs plus £700 as compensation. On 2 December 1919, Father O'Donnell resigned his commission and was demobilised in London, making his own way back to Australia via the United States. On his return to Australia, he continued his priestly ministry in the Archdiocese of Hobart until his death in 1949.

All good things must come to an end

Thousands of Australian soldiers took their leave in Ireland during the war, but only a few have left written accounts of their time there, giving us but a small insight into what they did, saw and felt. But for all of them the time came when they had to leave that scenic, friendly sanctuary and return to the hellish world they inhabited at the front. Nevertheless, some never made the journey back, either because Ireland became their last resting place after they were struck down by disease, enemy action or misadventure, as recounted in chapter 5, or because they were among that band of deserters who, with the help of Sinn Féin, disappeared into Irish civilian life.

For the vast majority who did return to the front, not all did so with regret, despite the good time they had had in Ireland, for they were returning to their mates, their adopted family with whom they shared a unique bond. HR Williams wrote,

> To every Australian soldier, his company, his battalion, was his home. Here lived our truest and most trusted companions, brothers who would share their last franc or crust with each other, bound together till victory or death. Home and civilian associates were only misty memories.[95]

Lieutenant Carleton expressed a similar feeling somewhat differently:

> This country [Ireland] with its familiar names has set me thinking more & more of you all. In fact, France is perhaps best after all, as one is least homesick there.[96]

CHAPTER 5

WATTLE AMONG THE SHAMROCKS

AUSTRALIAN WAR GRAVES IN IRELAND

I first conceived the idea of writing about Australian war graves in Ireland after visiting Grangegorman Military Cemetery in Dublin, not far from Phoenix Park, the vast and popular parkland that lies on the city's western edge. Hidden behind a high stone fence, the graveyard is easily missed. The taxi driver who dropped me there said that in all the years he had driven along Blackhorse Avenue he never realised there was a cemetery behind that wall. In fact, while looking for the entrance, he pulled over to ask directions of a woman walking along the street.

Pushing open the heavy, iron gate on a cold but sunny January morning, I entered a peaceful park whose lush, verdant lawn was punctuated by headstones and tall evergreen trees that filtered the winter sun. A bitumen path bisected the park. I walked up and down its length trying to spot the graves of the seven AIF soldiers I knew to be buried there. Four of them had drowned when RMS *Leinster*, the mail boat operating between Kingstown (now Dún

Laoghaire) and Holyhead in Wales, was torpedoed and sank just one month before the end of the war, while the other three had died of illness, two of them succumbing to the 'Spanish flu' pandemic that swept the world at war's end.

Not far into the graveyard, on the right of the path, row after row of headstones stood, marking the graves of the military passengers of the *Leinster*. As I wandered up and down the rows, looking for the distinctive rising-sun badge that designates an Australian war grave, the enormity of this little-known maritime tragedy became more real. In the worst loss of life of any incident in the Irish Sea, more than 500 of the *Leinster*'s 770 passengers died that day. On board were thirteen soldiers of the AIF plus two Australians serving with the New Zealand army (one a nurse), all of them returning from leave in Ireland. For them, the war in France would have already seemed so far away; in fact, it *was* virtually over. Australian battalions were being withdrawn from the line and, thanks to the armistice on 11 November, were never to return to the front again. Tragically, the war from which these antipodean tourists had all but escaped brutally sought them out, in the form of the German submarine *UB-123*, whose torpedoes crashed through the steel hull of the *Leinster*, sending it to the bottom in just fifteen minutes. Seven of the Australian soldiers died, but only four bodies were recovered. It was the last resting place of these four soldiers that I was now trying to find.[1]

After retracing my steps without locating any Australian graves I was close to giving up; had my trip been wasted? Eventually, I sought assistance from one of the cemetery staff, who pulled out a large map of the graveyard and laid it out on a bench in the toolshed. Using the reference numbers I had obtained from the Commonwealth War Graves Commission (CWGC), he quickly located the grave sites and led me straight to the spot. Although the Australian graves are in a separate section from the main group of *Leinster* victims, they are not far off the bitumen path, up and down which I had walked without spotting them. They are in two rows: four graves in front, numbered RC 1 to RC 4, for the Catholics, and, a few metres back, separated by a decent interval to maintain denominational propriety, another row of three graves, numbered CE 1 to CE 3, for the Protestants. Together they form 'some corner of a foreign field that is for ever Australia', to misquote Rupert Brooke. Nearby lies the Australian Kiwi soldier.

As I read the names and inscriptions on the headstones, I began to wonder: of the thousands of Australians who travel to Ireland each year, touring Dublin and Phoenix Park, how many ever visit these graves; how many even know about them; how many would be bothered to spend the time to find them? In recent years, Gallipoli and the Somme have become places of pilgrimage for increasing numbers of Australians wishing to pay homage to the fallen. But what of those who fought at Gallipoli or on the Western Front and whose remains lie buried not on those battlefields but in graveyards elsewhere, such as in Ireland? At a time when interest in Australian servicemen who fought and died in the First World War continues to grow, it seems to me that this national enterprise of remembrance should not lose sight of those who made the ultimate sacrifice but whose remains lie far from the well trodden paths of Gallipoli, Flanders and the Somme. Wherever you are in Ireland, be it Dublin or Belfast, Cork or Donegal, you are not far from an Australian war grave. The number of these graves is not large, but they are dotted throughout the island of Ireland as if laid out as markers for a Cook's tour of the Emerald Isle (see the map on pp. 154–55).[2]

This chapter tells the stories of the Australian service personnel of the First World War and of some of the Australians serving in Allied forces who are buried in Ireland or who died in the seas off Ireland and whose bodies were never recovered.

Killed in action in the seas off Ireland

The seas off Ireland have always presented dangers for mariners. During the war, those dangers were magnified as a result of the Germans deploying submarines and laying mines, which accounted for the loss of many Aliied ships, both naval and civilian. Australian soldiers and seamen were among the victims of this form of warfare.

The Australian graves in Grangegorman Military Cemetery.
Two are obscured by flax bush. (Jeff Kildea)

The sinking of RMS *Leinster*

On 10 October 1918, 22 Australian servicemen died in all theatres of the war. Of that number, seven were killed in a single incident, the sinking of RMS *Leinster* in the Irish Sea. The man sent to Dublin by AIF Headquarters to investigate the loss of these Australian service personnel was Warrant Officer Sydney Ernest Yeomans. His task was made difficult by the absence of a complete list of names of those who had embarked that morning. In the normal course of events soldiers travelling by ship were required to complete an embarkation card and to hand it in as they boarded, thus enabling a list of military passengers to be prepared (in any case not an ideal system, Yeomans noted in his report, as there was no process to verify each soldier's identity). But just before the *Leinster* sailed, the third mail train from Dublin arrived late and there was a last-minute surge of soldiers trying to get on board, many of them anxious to return to England before their leave ran out. As a result, 18 soldiers were able to board without embarkation cards, among them at least five of the Australian survivors, according to their own testimony. Furthermore, the embarkation officer, Captain Harold Locke of the Royal Irish Regiment, who sailed with the ship, drowned in the sinking and no passenger list was found on his body.

The slip-up with the embarkation cards was more than just an administrative problem on the day. Weeks later, Warrant Officer Yeomans and AIF Headquarters were still investigating six cases of alleged sightings of Australians who were unaccounted for. As noted in chapter 4, Ireland was a popular destination for deserters. Fearing that absentees in Ireland might take advantage of the fact that the authorities were unsure as to the identity of the missing, AIF Headquarters in London sought to ensure that the mix-up remained secret. This might explain the doggedness with which Yeomans sought to verify witness accounts of the presence on board of men who were thought to be missing.[3] Even so, not all claimed sightings were cleared up.

Private Boxer Allen Ware (lost at sea)

Private Boxer Allen Ware, a native of Adelaide, was a 19-year-old wool classer when he enlisted in January 1916. Although initially posted to the Light Horse, Ware soon transferred to the Army Service Corps, where he trained as a driver. In November 1916, he embarked for overseas with the 3rd Division Supply Column, where he became best mates with Sergeant Francis Thomas Coleman, a civil servant from Sydney. In France, Ware joined the 3rd Division Motor Transport Company, while Coleman was posted to the staff of the 3rd Australian Divisional Headquarters. In September 1918, Coleman was given Blighty leave; he delayed it for a week so that he could travel to Britain with Ware.

The two men caught the channel ferry from Boulogne on the morning of 4 October 1918 and spent the first three days of their leave in London with Corporal Edward McCarty, a medical orderly with the Australian Flying Corps, whom they had met on the ferry. They stayed at the Queens Hotel in Leicester Square until 6 October, when McCarty left for Liverpool and Coleman and Ware made the overnight crossing to Dublin, where, making the most of the generous pay Australian soldiers received, they stayed three nights at the salubrious Shelbourne Hotel. The two friends had intended going on to Cork, but on the morning of 10 October, in what proved to be a fateful decision, they decided to catch the mail boat in order to spend the rest of their leave with McCarty and other friends in London.

Carrying more than 770 passengers and crew, including 489 military personnel, the *Leinster* set out from Kingstown just before 9 am on an overcast and hazy Thursday morning.[4] The sea was rough, following recent storms, but the *Leinster* still made good headway in the heavy swell. About 50 minutes out of port, Coleman and Ware were standing on the ship's port side when, gazing out over the grey, choppy sea, Coleman observed an object in the water heading towards the ship. It soon dawned on him that it was a torpedo. Unable to do anything about it, he followed its course through the water and watched it strike the port side bow, bringing the vessel to a halt and causing it to settle slowly by the head.[5]

In fact, the *UB-123* had fired two torpedoes in quick succession, the first one missing the *Leinster*; it was the second Coleman saw. In order to avoid the second torpedo, the mail boat's skipper, Captain Birch, had ordered the ship to be swung hard to starboard, but to no avail. The torpedo ripped into the hull on the ship's port side

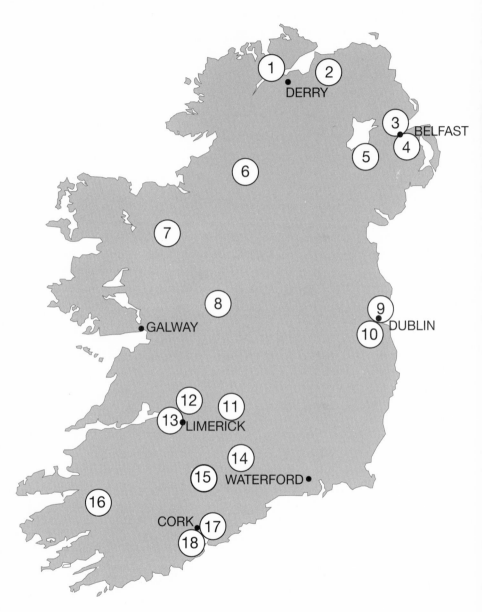

Australian war graves of the First World
War in Ireland

1. Upper Fahan (St Mura's) Church of Ireland Churchyard, County Donegal
   Able Seaman Frederick Allen Sheedy RAN

2. Macosquin (St Mary) Church of Ireland Churchyard, County Derry
   Lance Sergeant William Hugh Moore

3. Belfast City Cemetery, County Antrim
   Lieutenant Reginald Leopold MacLean

4. Belfast (Balmoral) Cemetery, County Antrim
   Private James Cowan

5. Lurgan New Cemetery, County Armagh
   Private James Balfour Leathem

6. Boho Church of Ireland Churchyard, County Fermanagh
   Sergeant Thomas Robert Reid

7. Kilturra Old Graveyard, County Sligo
   Private James Carroll

8. Cam Cemetery, County Roscommon
   Private John Michael Doyle

9. Grangegorman Military Cemetery, County Dublin
   Private George Bardon
   Private Joseph Thomas Barnes
   Private Charles Michael Byrne
   Private Edwin Johnson Carter
   Private Joseph Gratton
   Private Arthur Andrew Murphy
   Private Michael Ernest Smith

10. Mount Jerome Cemetery, County Dublin
    Lieutenant George Gilmour Allardyce
    Private Philip Douglas Davis

11. Glenkeen Old Graveyard, County Tipperary
    Private John Quinane

12. Bridgetown Catholic Churchyard, County Clare
    Private John Joseph Hickey

13. Limerick (King's Island) Military Cemetery, County Limerick
    Corporal John Taylor Anderson

14. Powerstown (St John) Catholic Churchyard, County Tipperary
    Private John Parnell Darmody

15. Mitchelstown Catholic Churchyard, County Cork
    Private John Joseph Cahill

16. Killarney New Cemetery, County Kerry
    Private Robert Emmett Kinchington

17. Midleton (The Rosary) Catholic Churchyard, County Cork
    Gunner Ambrose Augustine Haley

18. Blackrock (St Michael) Church of Ireland Churchyard, County Cork
    Private Thomas Paget Sudlow

and passed through, blowing a hole in the starboard side as well. The *Leinster* continued its 180-degree turn until it was facing back towards Kingstown.[6] The *Leinster*'s crew quickly and methodically began to lower the lifeboats and to throw rafts into the water. At this stage there was no panic and for ten minutes the passengers quietly watched the crew go through their drill, waiting anxiously but patiently for the order to board the lifeboats. As a precaution, Coleman and Ware put on their lifebelts, but Coleman was not unduly troubled, believing the ship would hold until the rescue boats arrived. Suddenly, however, the eerie silence was broken by the sound of another explosion as a third torpedo hit amidships, practically severing the vessel and smashing two of the lifeboats. Then another explosion rent the air – this time it was the boiler exploding. Pandemonium immediately broke out and terrified passengers began jumping into the sea. Coleman and Ware leapt for their lives and began swimming away from the sinking ship to avoid being sucked under as the *Leinster* began to plunge. Within 15 minutes, it had gone under.

As Coleman bobbed about in the heavy swell, he heard Ware call his name. 'I turned towards him,' he later wrote to a friend of Ware, Corporal Russell, 'He seemed to be going well, and [was] not unduly distressed'. Coleman called out to him to make for a raft, which he himself eventually did. With the help of a New Zealander, Coleman scrambled aboard. 'On looking back I could not see Boxer and I thought at the time he might have went to one of the Boats'. Coleman and the New Zealander had great difficulty holding on to the raft as the sea was running very high, and frequently Coleman fell off, fortunately being able to scramble back each time. Many of those who drowned that day were washed off the life rafts in the heavy swell. After two hours in the water, Coleman was eventually rescued by a British destroyer, HMS *Lively*. On returning to Dublin, he visited the local military hospitals in a vain attempt to trace his friend. At the mortuary he looked among the unidentified dead but none resembled Ware. 'I cannot think what has become of him,' he wrote to Corporal Russell. 'I cannot think in what way he was not picked up'.

Private Joseph Gratton (Grangegorman Military Cemetery, Dublin)

During his ordeal, Coleman saw another Australian, Private Joseph Gratton of the 4th Machine Gun Battalion, clinging desperately to a lifeboat, which was too crowded to take him aboard. Private Gratton, a 28-year-old plumber from Toowoomba, Queensland, had enlisted in the 4th Pioneer Battalion in May 1916. In October 1916, he had sailed for England on the *Boonah*, arriving early in the new year.

After further training, Gratton transferred to the 42nd Battalion and then to the 4th Australian Machine Gun Company (later designated the 4th Machine Gun Battalion) before proceeding to France in October 1917. After five months in the field he took leave in Paris, and in September 1918 was again granted leave, this time in the United Kingdom. However, soon after arriving in London he fell ill and was admitted to hospital. After three days, he resumed his leave and travelled to Dublin, where a cousin, May Hamberry, was living. Gratton was on his way back to rejoin his unit when he boarded the *Leinster*.

To Coleman's observation, Gratton seemed to be in an exhausted condition as he clung to the lifeboat, and he later learned from a Scottish officer that Gratton had subsequently drowned. The Scottish officer, Captain Hugh Love Parker of the 3rd Battalion Cameron Highlanders and Adjutant of the *Leinster*, told the Australian Red Cross of Gratton's final moments:

> I spoke words of encouragement to him but it was obvious his strength was failing fast. Every time I spoke to him he smiled but never answered. The seas kept breaking over us & this combined with the cold and exposure, undoubtedly caused his death. Ultimately he let go his hold & sank smiling to the last. In all my experience (which includes several fronts) I have never seen a braver death.[7]

Private Michael Ernest Smith (Grangegorman Military Cemetery, Dublin)

Private Michael Ernest Smith was also on the *Leinster* that morning, returning from leave with his 19th Battalion mate Private John Arthur Meigan. Smith, originally from Cobar, was working as a

A contemporary drawing of RMS *Leinster* sinking
(Courtesy of Philip Lecane)

labourer in Sydney when he enlisted in February 1916 at age 22, a year after Meigan. It was not until September 1916 that he joined the 19th Battalion in France, but in November he was wounded by shrapnel in the fighting around Flers in the final stage of the Battle of the Somme and admitted to the 6th Australian General Hospital at Rouen, rejoining his unit on Christmas Day 1916.

Smith might have met up with Meigan in England nine months later when he took UK leave, but both men were back with the 19th

Battalion in September 1917 in time to take part in the Third Battle of Ypres (Passchendaele). In the spring of 1918, the 19th Battalion helped halt the German advance that broke through the line and threatened the Allies with imminent defeat. The battalion also took part in the Allied counteroffensive in the late summer at Amiens and in the legendary attack on Mont St Quentin at the end of August. A month later, Meigan and Smith exchanged the mud and the trenches for the streets of London, Dublin and Belfast, having gone on leave together on 26 September. At the end of their fortnight's furlough, as they stood on the deck of the *Leinster* watching Ireland recede into the mist, they would not have known that their mates from the 19th were taking a well-earned rest after the battalion had fought its last battle of the war around Montbrehain the week before. Cruelly, however, the war, now over for their comrades in France, was about to come to them.

When the torpedoes struck, Meigan and Smith shook hands, for the last time as it turned out, and jumped into the sea. After about 15 minutes of bobbing helplessly in the swell, Meigan managed to swim to a life raft where 14 others were clinging, but Smith was not with him. Meigan told Warrant Officer Yeomans that on reaching the raft he called out, 'Are there any Australians here?', to which one man replied, 'Yes. I am an Australian. I belong to the Australian Flying Corps'. Meigan and the man clasped hands for a while, but the raft overturned when struck by a large wave and Meigan saw the man no more.[8] The identity of this soldier remains a mystery as the list of Australian dead, missing and survived does not include anyone from the AFC. Meigan claimed also to have seen another Australian on the ship, a soldier by the name of Brissett, with whom he had stayed at Robertson's Temperance Hotel in Belfast a few days before.[9] But it is more likely he saw him at the wharf, as Brissett was fortunate enough to miss the boat.[10]

Meigan was in the water for two hours before being picked up by HMS *Mallard*. He landed at Kingstown with two other Australian survivors, Corporal John Brendan Murray and Driver Frederick Leonard Hopkins, both of the 1st Division Motor Transport Company. Meigan was downcast, telling them he believed his cobber

Smith had drowned. Unfortunately, he was right, for the next time Meigan saw Private Smith was at the mortuary in Dublin where Warrant Officer Yeomans had asked him to identify the body.

When Yeomans had first arrived in Dublin on the day following the sinking, he had gone straight to King George V Military Hospital, where the bodies of military personnel recovered from the tragedy had been taken. Among the corpses lying in the mortuary he discovered three bodies already identified as Australians, while the identity of three corpses remained to be determined – one of them turned out to be Private Smith. The three identified Australians were the machine-gunner Private Gratton and two infantrymen, Privates Barnes and Carter.

Private Joseph Thomas Barnes (Grangegorman Military Cemetery, Dublin)

Joseph Thomas Barnes, BA, of the 48th Battalion was a 37-year-old school teacher from Payneham in South Australia when he enlisted in July 1917. He was married to Muriel Thirza Barnes, whose 19-year-old brother Private Norman Cox of the 52nd Battalion had been killed at Mouquet Farm near Pozières the previous September. Barnes landed in England just after Christmas 1917 and following three months further training proceeded to France, where he was assigned to the 48th Battalion, a unit comprising men mainly from regional South Australia and Western Australia. On 3 May 1918, a month after arriving at the front, he was on his way back to England after having been wounded at Monument Wood near Villers-Bretonneux where his battalion had been engaged in a fierce struggle with the position's German defenders. Judging by Charles Bean's description of the battle, Barnes was lucky to have survived:

> This position ... when bristling with machine-guns had been taken and lost by the Western Australians of the 48th Battalion at so heavy a cost [that in July 1918] their bodies still lay thickly before the trenches ...[11]

Having recovered from his wounds, Barnes was returning from convalescent leave when he boarded the *Leinster*. A friend, Lance

Corporal Michael Denis Roach of the 12th Field Ambulance, had seen him on the ship, but it is not known what happened to him after the torpedoes struck; that is, until Warrant Officer Yeomans found his body in the Dublin mortuary.

Roach himself was lucky to survive. After the third torpedo hit the ship, he jumped overboard like many others and swam on his back for about ten minutes before finding a raft. He did not last long there, being pulled under by another soldier, so he swam to a lifeboat, which he found was full of water. Clinging to the boat was another Australian, Private James Henry Moore of the 1st Australian Machine Gun Battalion. When the lifeboat eventually capsized, its erstwhile occupants struggled to hold on to the upturned boat in the heavy swell, and Roach watched helplessly as a man and a young woman, washed off the boat for the fourth time and too exhausted to climb back on, drowned in front of him as they struggled to keep each other afloat. 'I do not know the young lady's name,' he later told Warrant Officer Yeomans, 'but she was very plucky'. Roach and Moore managed to hang on until picked up by HMS *Helga*, the vessel that two and a half years earlier had shelled rebel strongholds in Dublin during the Easter Rising.

Private Edwin Johnson Carter (Grangegorman Military Cemetery, Dublin)

Private Edwin Johnson Carter of the 29th Battalion, a 5th Division unit, was born in 1884 at Brunswick in Melbourne and when he enlisted in January 1916 was a farmer in the Warrnambool area of Victoria. He trained in Australia and Egypt prior to sailing to England, where he arrived in June 1916 for further training before proceeding to France in September. He was admitted twice to hospital with illness before being wounded in action on 9 August 1918 at the start of the great advance that spelt the end of Germany's hopes of defeating the Allies. He, too, was returning from convalescent leave when he boarded the *Leinster*. Lance Corporal Roach reported seeing an Australian of the 5th Division on board the ship, but, as with Private Barnes, Carter's movements after the submarine attacked are unknown.

Lieutenant Francis Patrick Laracy, MC (lost at sea)

Lieutenant Francis Patrick Laracy's presence on the *Leinster* was noted by a number of witnesses, perhaps because he stood out – he was a tall man and his left arm was in a sling. Born at Toowoomba, Queensland, in 1891, Laracy was studying to be a chemist at Sydney University when he enlisted in the 1st Field Ambulance in August 1914, rising to the rank of sergeant. Two years later he transferred to the 1st Battalion and was commissioned as a second lieutenant. Wounded three times, once at Gallipoli and twice in France, he was recommended for the Military Cross for conspicuous gallantry and leadership, which he had shown on 12 July 1918 during his battalion's attack on the enemy around Merris in northern France, where he was wounded.[12]

For Laracy the war was over: his wound, the result of a German bullet which struck him in the left forearm, where he had previously been wounded in October 1916, had earned him a trip home. He had already received his orders to return to Australia, but had decided to visit relatives in Kilkenny before taking the ship home. His body was never recovered. Five days after the sinking of the *Leinster*, his Military Cross citation appeared in the *London Gazette*.

Lance Corporal Frederick William Knuckey (lost at sea)

Another Australian soldier who disappeared without a trace that day was Lance Corporal Frederick William Knuckey of the 38th Battalion, a 38-year-old bank manager from Bendigo, Victoria. He had enlisted in February 1916 and was gassed in November 1917 during the Third Battle of Ypres (Passchendaele), the 38th Battalion's most costly operation of the war, resulting in 62 per cent casualties. This kept him out of the line for three months. He had hardly returned to his unit in Belgium when the battalion was rushed south to help stem the German offensive of March 1918. In May, he went to England on leave, but this was interrupted when he was admitted to hospital with myalgia (muscle pain). Its underlying cause must have been serious as he was in hospital almost two months before being discharged to the No. 1 Australian Command

Depot at Sutton Veny in Wiltshire. While waiting to be posted back to his unit that he went on leave to Ireland. Although his body was not recovered, his name was among the early lists of those missing from the *Leinster* and presumed drowned. In March 1918, a Court of Enquiry held at AIF Headquarters, London, returned a finding: "Drowned at Sea: ex. RMS Leinster as a result of enemy action on 10.10.18".[13]

Nurse Winifred Starling (lost at sea)

Another Australian casualty whose body was not recovered was Nurse Winifred Starling. Born at Petersham in Sydney in 1878, she studied nursing at Sydney's Royal Prince Alfred Hospital and at the Chelsea Children's Hospital in London. In August 1915, she volunteered her services to the war effort, being appointed to Sutton Veny (Warminster) Hospital and No. 2 New Zealand General Hospital, Walton-on-Thames, where she was serving when she took leave in Ireland.[14] Nurse Starling had just been given a new posting on a hospital ship heading to New Zealand, and, like Lieutenant Laracy, had made the fateful decision to visit friends in Ireland before returning to the antipodes.[15]

Lance Corporal Peter Freitas (Grangegorman Military Cemetery, Dublin)

The other Australian serving with the New Zealand forces was Lance Corporal Peter Freitas of the New Zealand Army Service Corps, a native of Guildford in Sydney.

The names of those who died in the sinking of the *Leinster* and whose bodies were never recovered are inscribed on the Hollybrook Memorial, set in a beautiful park opposite the General Hospital, high on a hill above Southampton harbour. On the waterfront at Dún Laoghaire the anchor of the *Leinster* is on display as a memorial to all those who perished that day, just one month before the armistice that saw the guns fall silent.

Other naval actions

Apart from the seven members of the AIF and the two Australians serving in the New Zealand forces who died in the sinking of the

Leinster, another six Australians drowned in the seas off Ireland as a result of enemy action. Two were serving in the Royal Australian Navy, two in the Royal Navy and two in the Mercantile Marine. Of the six, two are buried in County Donegal, while the bodies of the other four were never recovered. For those four, no headstones mark their watery graves, though their names are inscribed on memorials at Hollybrook and Plymouth in England.

Able Seaman Frederick Allen Sheedy (Upper Fahan [St Mura's] Church of Ireland Churchyard, County Donegal)

On 25 January 1917, the *Laurentic*, a White Star liner which had been converted during the war to a troop transport and then an armed merchant cruiser with a crew of 474 under the command of Captain Reginald Arthur Norton, RN, was sailing from Liverpool to Nova Scotia, carrying five million pounds worth of gold bars destined for the United States to help pay for Britain's war purchases. That morning, she called at the British naval base HMS *Hecla*, Buncrana, County Donegal, on the east shore of Lough Swilly, and shortly after 5 pm continued the journey on a bitterly cold evening.

Just under an hour after leaving port, as the *Laurentic* was rounding Fanad Head, County Donegal, travelling at full speed and without lights, there was a violent explosion abreast of the foremast on the port side. This was followed about 20 seconds later by a similar explosion, also on the port side, abreast of the engine room. Captain Norton put the telegraph to 'Full speed astern' and gave the order to turn out the lifeboats. He tried to radio for help, but the second explosion had knocked out the dynamo, leaving the ship without power and in darkness. He ordered rockets to be fired to signal the ship's distress. These were seen by lighthousemen and boats were dispatched.

Although Norton was unsure of the cause of the explosions, telling the coroner a week later that it could have been either torpedoes or mines, the Admiralty put out a statement that it had been established that a mine, not a submarine, was responsible for the vessel's loss.[16] There does not seem to be any controversy about this, and most accounts attribute the cause to mines laid by the German submarine *UB-80* a few days before. That being so, the *Laurentic* was extremely unlucky to have been in the wrong place at the wrong time.

It is not known how many died in the explosions, but, tragically, many more died in the ensuing hours through exposure to the extreme cold, even among those who had secured places in the lifeboats. Trawlers began arriving two hours after the distress rockets were fired, but it was dark and many of the lifeboats had fired off all their flares before help arrived, making them difficult to locate. Captain Norton was picked up at about 1 am, seven hours after the explosion, and all the men in his boat were still alive. But it would be almost 24 hours before the last of the survivors was rescued. One boat, picked up the following afternoon, contained 17 frozen bodies; another contained 5 survivors out of 20, the remainder being frozen. Many did not make it into lifeboats. One newspaper report claimed that close to 100 bodies were washed ashore.[17]

In all, 121 survived, while 354 sailors, seamen and marines perished, among them a young Australian rating, Able Seaman Frederick Allen Sheedy RAN, who had taken passage on the *Laurentic* to rejoin his own ship HMAS *Sydney* after attending gunnery school in England. Sheedy, originally from Adamstown near Newcastle, New South Wales, had moved with his family to Fremantle, Western Australia, before the war. He was the son of James and Annie Jane Sheedy, who also lost another son to the war. Less than four months before the sinking of the *Laurentic*, Frederick's older brother James, of the 12th Field Ambulance, had died of wounds on the Somme, aged 23. Frederick was only 19 years old when he died, but he was already a veteran, having joined the navy in January 1913, and having been a member of the crew of HMAS *Sydney* when it took part in the capture of German New Guinea in September 1914 and engaged the German raider *Emden* in the Indian Ocean on 9 November 1914.[18]

On 31 January 1917, a long procession set out for St Mura's Church of Ireland, Upper Fahan, County Donegal, comprising 68 coffins of victims of the tragedy, each wrapped in the Union flag and borne on Army service wagons, with many of the survivors marching behind. Interestingly, denominational differences, so important in those days, were played down. Men of different religions were buried together, while Catholic, Anglican and Presbyterian clergymen officiated in turn at the graveside. Today, the mass grave site is marked by a memorial in the form of a Celtic High Cross on a red granite plinth, on which are inscribed the names of the dead. The memorial incorrectly lists Sheedy's surname as 'Sheehy' and describes him as a gunner in the Royal Marine Artillery. According to Peter Threlfall, an English researcher writing on the *Laurentic*, the memorial is replete with errors. [19]

Sailmaker Francis Leonard Royle (Upper Fahan [St Mura's] Church of Ireland Churchyard, County Donegal)

In his research, Threlfall came across another Australian who died in the tragedy. He was Sailmaker Francis Leonard Royle of the Mercantile Marine Reserve. Born in 1891, in West Melbourne, the son of Francis and Elizabeth Ann Royle (née Brown), he joined the White Star Line before the war, serving on RMS *Olympic* (sister ship of the *Titanic*). Royle was living in Wallasey, Liverpool, England, when war broke out and on 24 August 1914, he joined the crew of the *Laurentic*, serving on it throughout its time as a troop transport and an armed merchant cruiser and ultimately losing his life on the ship's final and fatal voyage. He had a brother, Herbert George Royle, who was wounded eight months later while serving with the AIF's 29th Battalion in France. Sailmaker Royle is also listed incorrectly on the *Laurentic* memorial as a gunner in the Royal Marine Artillery.

Almost immediately after the *Laurentic* went down, the British government set about recovering the 35 tonnes of gold which had been stored on board. But the task proved difficult and it took seven years to recover 3189 of the 3211 ingots, each weighing more than 10 kilograms, by which time it was deemed no longer cost-effective to continue the salvage operation, leaving 22 ingots to be found, an enticement for salvagers and divers to the present day.[20]

Commander Thomas Wyburn Biddlecombe (lost at sea)

Less than two months after the *Laurentic* sank, Australia's fledgling navy lost another member serving in a Royal Navy ship off the Irish coast: Commander Thomas Wyburn Biddlecombe. Biddlecombe had emigrated to Australia in 1906 from his native England in order to join the Commonwealth Naval Forces, forerunner of the Royal Australian Navy (RAN). Born in 1880 at Shapwick, Bridgwater, Somerset, Biddlecombe had served in the merchant navy and the Royal Naval Reserve, rising to the rank of lieutenant, before his move to Australia.[21] On 10 July 1911, when the RAN came into being, it had two new ships, the River class torpedo boat destroyers *Parramatta* and *Yarra*, the latter under the command of Lieutenant TW Biddlecombe.

By the time war broke out, Biddlecombe had been promoted to lieutenant commander and was captain of a light cruiser, HMAS *Pioneer*, which in December 1914 was ordered to the East African coast where the German cruiser SMS *Königsberg* had taken shelter in the Rufiji River, about 130 kilometres south of Dar-es-Salaam. Biddlecombe was made senior officer of the northern section of the blockade and, after a stand-off of three months, British naval vessels eventually shelled the *Königsberg*, reducing it to a wreck and forcing its crew to flee. In May 1916, Biddlecombe transferred from the *Pioneer* to the RAN's London Depot so that he might gain experience as an executive officer on a bigger ship.

Unfortunately, the Australian authorities failed to ensure there would be a position for him before they sent him to England, and he found himself cooling his heels as an 'understudy' to the commander of *HMS Benbow*, having no responsibilities and gaining none of the experience as executive officer that he needed for promotion.[22] Nevertheless, Captain Clinton Baker wrote to the Admiral commanding the First Battle Squadron, reporting on Biddlecombe's good service on the *Benbow*, saying he was fit to be second-in-command of a battleship or large cruiser and recommending him for confirmed rank of commander.[23] But, as luck would have it, an opportunity came up that both suited Biddlecombe and resolved the difficulty of finding him an appropriate posting. He was said to be 'specially pleased to have been selected for this duty', command of HMS *Warner*, a ship whose name did not appear in the Navy List as the service was 'of a strictly confidential nature'.[24] So secret were its activities that a month later, after Biddlecombe was reported missing and possibly a prisoner of war, the Australian Naval Representative in London, Captain Francis Haworth-Booth, reported to the Navy Office in Melbourne:

> I much regret to report that the very secret nature of the service on which the Officer indicated was employed, renders it impossible for me to furnish details of the circumstances; Admiralty will not issue any further information other than contained in my telegram, and it will not be practicable to make official enquiries as to the welfare or otherwise of the officer in question. He took very great risk, well knowing what he was doing, and therefore he and every single man who has undertaken similar service are most unquestionably specially gallant and brave and I fear there is nothing to be done except wait and hope that the Officer in question has been made a prisoner, and will in due course communicate directly or indirectly with his friends.[25]

The secrecy arose from the fact that HMS *Warner*, a 1300-ton converted cargo ship, was the Q-ship *Q27*, one of the Royal Navy's decoy or special service ships, referred to by the Germans as 'trapships', employed to counter Germany's campaign of unrestricted submarine warfare against merchant shipping.

Early in the war, the British realised that German U-boats preferred to surface in order to attack small merchant ships, using their deck gun so as to preserve their torpedoes for bigger prey. So the Admiralty requisitioned a number of smaller, older ships and fitted them with concealed armaments, with a view to enticing German U-boats to approach them on the surface. When the submarine was in range, the Q-ship would raise the White Ensign and begin firing. The ruse worked well for a while until German submarine commanders learned to be more cautious.[26] Biddlecombe had done well to get this posting. According to Lieutenant Commander Harold Auten VC:

> Competition to get into the service was tremendous. The barracks were filled with officers and men who had volunteered, and everyone considered himself extremely fortunate if he were appointed to one of these ships.[27]

On 13 March 1917, the *Warner* was off the west coast of Ireland sailing east – a tempting target for the German submarine *UB-38*. However, the U-boat commander was not easily fooled and he decided to remain submerged, firing a torpedo that smashed into the boiler, causing an explosion that sent the *Warner* to the bottom in less than five minutes. Six of the crew were rescued by the German submarine, while others were later picked up by a British submarine. For months, the fate of the *Warner*'s skipper remained unknown. Shortly after the sinking, one of the crew members rescued by the British raised a false hope that he had survived. In a letter to Biddlecombe's wife five days after the sinking, FJ Yuile, who was then in England, wrote that Biddlecombe had last been seen on a raft with the navigation officer. He assured her that his captain had been picked up by the German submarine. But five months later the truth emerged when another survivor, Richard Lake, wrote to Mrs Biddlecombe from a prisoner-of-war camp in Germany that Commander Biddlecombe was not among those rescued by the Germans and that he had still been on board when Lake, one of the last to leave, had jumped into the sea. Lake said he had no doubt that his skipper had gone down with the ship. In October, another prisoner, Lieutenant Dean Gardner, RNR, confirmed Lake's conclusion. He wrote to Mrs Biddlecombe, saying he could give her little hope of Biddlecombe's survival as he saw him at his post on the bridge as the ship tipped and sank. He confirmed that Biddlecombe was not picked up by the U-boat.[28]

By the time Gardner's letter arrived, Mrs Biddlecombe already knew the truth. On 29 August 1917, the Melbourne *Argus* quoted a German newspaper report of the sinking of the *Warner* that confirmed the loss of its skipper.[29] The Admiralty soon concurred and Mrs Biddlecombe was informed. A short while later, on 22 September 1917, *The Times* included the following in its report of those killed in action: 'BIDDLECOMBE – Reported "missing" since 13th March last, now officially reported "killed in action"'. Curiously, the secrecy surrounding Biddlecombe's activities continued, with his place of death being given in some official documents as Zeebrugge in Belgium, a 'fact' still recorded on his service record card.[30]

Signalman Frederick Thomas Whitchurch (lost at sea)

Another Australian sailor killed in action while serving with a Q-ship off the Irish coast was Signalman Frederick Thomas Whitchurch, RN, from Townsville, Queensland. On 11 February 1918, Whitchurch was a member of the crew of HMS *Cullist* (also known as HMS *Westphalia*, previously the 1470-ton cargo ship *Jurassic*) when it was torpedoed by *UB-97* in the Irish Sea north-east of Dublin.

Sub-Lieutenant Roy Norman Clare Hodge (lost at sea)

Apart from Q-ships, the Royal Navy employed armed merchant cruisers in its fight against German submarines. These were passenger liners converted to warships, many of which were deployed with the 10th Cruiser Squadron in the North Sea and the North Atlantic to maintain the blockade against Germany and to escort convoys, thus freeing up regular navy cruisers for other duties. Among them was HMS *Viknor*, an aging, 5386-ton passenger ship originally known as the *Atrato* and then the *Viking*.

On 13 January 1915, the *Viknor*, under the command of Commander Ernest Ballantyne, RN, and with a crew of 22 officers and 273 ratings, including Sub-Lieutenant Roy Norman Clare Hodge, RNR, from Grange, South Australia, was off Tory Island on the north-west coast of Donegal, when it sent its last message at about 4 pm. The ship had been proceeding towards Liverpool with a complement of German prisoners, including Baron Hans Adam von Wedel of the German Secret Service, but it never arrived at its destination. Its fate became apparent when large quantities of wreckage and some bodies washed ashore along the north coast of Ireland. Because there were no survivors, mystery still surrounds the ship's disappearance. The Admiralty reported it had struck a mine, as the Germans had recently sown mines in the area, but others claimed the *Viknor* was unstable in rough weather and that it had probably capsized and sunk in the heavy seas.[31]

Steward Frederick Thomas Adams (lost at sea)

The sinking of an armed merchant cruiser off the north Antrim coast on 1 March 1918 claimed the life of another Australian, 28-year-old Steward Frederick Thomas Adams of the Mercantile Marine Reserve. From Croydon in Sydney, Adams was a steward on board the 17 515-ton HMS *Calgarian* when it was torpedoed off Rathlin Island by *UB-19*, the same German submarine that had carried Sir Roger Casement to Banna Strand, County Kerry, two years before.

Died of injuries sustained in battle

Seven Australian soldiers buried in Ireland died of battle-related injuries or their consequences: two in Ireland and five in England.

Victims of shell shock

In chapter 4, we saw how Ireland played host to thousands of Australian soldiers on leave. However, the experience was not always joyful and for some their leave in Ireland proved tragic. Of these, Corporal John Taylor Anderson and Private John Joseph Hickey died in unusual circumstances, attributable directly or indirectly to shell shock, a psychological injury known today as post-traumatic stress disorder (PTSD), which was then little understood.

According to historian George L. Mosse, shell shock was one of the most widespread battlefield injuries during the First World War.[32] The term came to cover a range of debilities, many of which had nothing to do with shells or shock, and terms such as 'war neurosis' and 'neurasthenia' or even 'NYDN' ('Not Yet Diagnosed Nervous') were frequently used interchangeably. Military medical opinion was divided as to the cause of shell shock: some doctors believed it to be a manifestation of cowardice, malingering or moral weakness; others recognised it as a treatable psychological disorder induced by experience of war. The latter view gained increasing support as the war progressed, but even so it would be more than 50 years before the condition came to be understood and more effective treatment was devised.[33]

Corporal John Taylor Anderson (Limerick [King's Island] Military Cemetery, County Limerick)

Melbourne-born John Anderson was a marine engineer when he enlisted as a sapper in the 2nd Field Company Engineers on 18 August 1914. He was then 27 years old and unmarried. He was tall (almost 6 feet) and dark, and had tattoos on his chest and right arm. Anderson nominated his father, Captain John Taylor Anderson, of the Victorian Stevedoring Company, as his next of kin. The following month he transferred to the 3rd Field Company.

On 22 September 1914, Anderson embarked on the troop transport *Geelong*. Following service in Egypt with his unit, which was engaged in bridging the Suez Canal, he was sent to Gallipoli, having recovered from a bout of influenza contracted a few weeks before the landing. At Anzac Cove, he was promoted to corporal in July, but in mid-September, following the most intense fighting of the campaign, he once again found himself in hospital. Initially, the diagnosis was an abscess of a bone cavity, which cleared up without treatment. Nevertheless, he was evacuated from Anzac to a hospital ship and thence to Malta, where it was noted he was jumpy and irritable, and suffering from insomnia, cramps and low appetite. The doctors diagnosed 'debility' and 'neuralgia', vague terms that suggest they were casting around for a proper diagnosis. Yet his symptoms were severe enough to warrant his being transferred to England, where on 4 November 1915 he was diagnosed as having 'shell shock'.

Corporal Anderson was discharged from hospital on 20 November 1915 and sent on leave. We can only speculate as to the fragility of his mind, particularly given the circumstances of his death. For on the morning of 18 December the maid at Geary's Hotel, Limerick, where he was staying, found him dead in his bed, fully dressed. According to evidence given at the coroner's inquest, Anderson had arrived in Limerick the night before and had met on the train Robert Ryan, the proprietor of Geary's Hotel. Anderson was asleep when Ryan entered the compartment. On waking, he told Ryan he had no money or friends in Limerick. The kindly publican invited him to stay at the hotel. He was last seen alive at about 10.30 pm after he had had a drink with Ryan. He told Ryan he had come to Limerick on a mission of charity and that he was anxious to see the parents of a girl he had met in London, with a view to their doing something for her. He also told Ryan he had been shot through the left lung in the fighting, and in the legs and a hand, which was bandaged (though his medical records do not support that claim). Doctor JF Shanahan, who made 'a superficial examination of the body', attributed death to natural causes and the jury returned a verdict in accordance with the medical evidence. Corporal Anderson was laid to rest in the Limerick (King's Island) Military Cemetery. A sister living in England had cabled the coroner that it was impossible for her to come to Ireland, and asked to have a wreath of violets placed on his grave.[34]

Private John Joseph Hickey (Bridgetown Catholic Churchyard, County Clare)

Private Hickey was a seaman when in February 1916 he enlisted in the AIF at Melbourne, aged 21 years. Despite, or because of, his previous employment, he had difficulty accepting the discipline of army life. After sailing to Egypt in April 1916 aboard the *Euripides*, he soon found himself in trouble with the authorities. On 16 May 1916 he was found guilty of being absent without leave (AWL) and received seven days Field Punishment No. 2, which meant that during the term of his punishment he could be 'kept in irons' (that is, in fetters or handcuffs) or given hard labour. Posted to the 60th Battalion, he embarked for France in June 1916 and was wounded in action the next month at the Battle of Fromelles. Evacuated to

England, he was assigned to No. 3 Command Depot, where once again he came under notice, being found guilty of insubordination and threatening to strike a non-commissioned officer, for which he was awarded 28 days detention. In December 1916, Hickey rejoined his unit in France, but in September 1917 he was buried during a bombardment in the lead up to the Battle of Polygon Wood and suffered shell shock. While being treated at Etaples in October, he again absented himself, for which he was confined to camp for seven days. The next month he was convicted of drunkenness and sentenced to 14 days Field Punishment No. 1, similar to Field Punishment No. 2, but also allowing him to be tethered to a fixed object for up to two hours a day. After rejoining his unit in December, he was fortunate enough to be sent on leave the following month, during which he made his way to Ireland to visit his father's family in County Clare.

On 26 January 1918, Private Hickey was found seriously injured, lying on the railway track between Sallins and Straffan in County Kildare. He was still alive, but only just. Rushed to the military hospital at the nearby Curragh Camp, he was admitted with a compound fracture of the right leg as well as a compound fracture of the skull. His injuries were so horrific that at the railway station a doctor had removed his right arm, which was hanging by a nerve, while at the hospital doctors amputated his right leg. After initially rallying, Hickey eventually succumbed to shock and haemorrhage and died the following evening at six o'clock. A coronial inquest held two days later found that he had died of injuries suffered after being accidentally struck by a train. The coroner noted that he had no evidence as to how Hickey came by his death and he attached no blame to anyone. No mention appears in the report of his having suffered shell shock. Private Hickey's body was claimed by his uncle, Thomas Hickey of Ballybrack, County Clare, and taken by train to Limerick, where it was buried in the churchyard of the Catholic church in the nearby village of Bridgetown. The funeral was attended by his uncle and aunt, four cousins and twenty-five friends.[35]

Died of wounds

We can only speculate whether Corporal Anderson and Private Hickey died because of their war-related injuries. No such doubt exists in the case of five Australian servicemen who died of wounds in England and whose bodies were transported to Ireland for burial by their families. In all but one of those cases the headstones over the graves were not erected by the CWGC but are family monuments. In the case of the exception, Private James Cowan, the CWGC headstone is located next to the family monument on which his name also appears.

Private James Cowan (Balmoral Cemetery, Belfast)

Private Cowan was born in Melbourne in 1887, the son of John Cowan of Glasgow and Sarah Apsley Cowan (née Craig) of Belfast. Thereafter the family moved to Fremantle, Western Australia, where James attended Fremantle Grammar School. He enlisted in November 1916 and a month later was on his way to England on board the *Berrima* with the 8th Reinforcements of the 48th Battalion. It was not until July 1917, after training with the 12th Training Battalion on the Salisbury Plain, that he joined the battalion in France. The 48th Battalion was a unit of the 4th Division, which had just come out of the Battle of Messines, where it had been part of II Anzac Corps, fighting alongside the 16th (Irish) Division and the 36th (Ulster) Division. The 4th Division men were expecting a rest; instead they were allocated to I Anzac Corps and ordered to prepare for the Third Battle of Ypres (Passchendaele). Australian casualties in the campaign exceeded 38 000, among them Private Cowan, who received gunshot wounds to the back and right knee as his battalion prepared to support the Anzac Corps assault on Passchendaele. He was evacuated to the 24th General Hospital at Etaples, but his knee became infected and when gas gangrene set in, his right leg was amputated. Five weeks later, he was transferred to England, where he was admitted to the Birmingham General Hospital on 22 November 1917, his stump still in a very bad condition, complicated by persistent gangrene. Two days later, before his mother's family

The grave of Private James Cowan
(Jeff Kildea)

was informed of his presence in England, he haemorrhaged and, despite an operation which he survived, he sank very quickly and died shortly before midnight.[36]

The next day his uncle arrived at the hospital and arranged for his body to be taken to Ireland, where he was laid to rest in the family plot at Balmoral Cemetery, Belfast, alongside his grandparents and an uncle, Captain William Craig, who died on 9 June 1917 off Le Havre when his ship, HMS *Harbury*, was torpedoed. A cousin, Lieutenant James Basil Cowan, also from Melbourne, was killed in October 1918 while flying over Belgium in a Bristol aircraft of the 48th Squadron of the Royal Air Force (RAF). He was one of the 200 members of the AIF, including aviation pioneer Charles Kingsford-Smith, who transferred to the Royal Flying Corps (later the RAF) in 1917.[37]

Private John Joseph Cahill (Mitchelstown Catholic Churchyard, County Cork)

Another Australian buried in a family plot is Private John Joseph Cahill of the 23rd Battalion who was a 26-year-old butcher from Ballarat when he enlisted in September 1914. He embarked on the *Wiltshire* in March 1916 and after training in England proceeded to France in September, joining his unit on 1 November. One week later he received a wound to the head, necessitating his return to England and admission to Reading War Hospital. He was transferred the following month to the 2nd Australian Auxiliary Hospital at Southall near London, and, pending his return to France, was given furlough, which he overstayed by four days, for which he received four days field punishment and the docking of eight days pay.

On 20 January 1917, he rejoined his unit in France, but two months later he was wounded again during the fighting near Arras, this time in the right thigh, fracturing his femur. At first he was treated at the 11th Stationary Hospital at Rouen in France, but in mid-April he was transferred to England. On admission to the Royal Victoria Hospital, Netley, near Southampton, his general condition was reported as good, with the wound still discharging but clearing rapidly. His medical report also indicated that he was unfit for further active service, with the consequence that he would be returned to Australia for discharge. He continued to do well until the middle of May, when complications developed and septicaemia set in, with the result that he died of his wounds on 17 June 1917. His uncle, who was present at his death, arranged for the body to be taken to Ireland, where it was laid to rest in the Catholic churchyard at Mitchelstown, County Cork. The headstone, which is adjacent to the church, lists the names of eight members of the

Cahill family and the months and years of their deaths so that the inscription for Private Cahill reads simply, 'John J Cahill, June 1917' with no indication that he was a member of the AIF or that he died on active service.

Private John Parnell Darmody (Powerstown [St John] Catholic Churchyard, County Tipperary)

It is not clear whether the omission of the service information from Cahill's headstone was deliberate, though it is possible given the anti-war feeling in Ireland, as discussed in chapter 6. However, there was no such inhibition in the case of Private John Parnell Darmody, even though his middle name suggests an Irish nationalist family connection. His headstone bears the inscription: 'Erected by John Darmody of Queensland in memory of his son John Darmody who died from wounds received in France 24th Aug 1916 aged 25 years'. There then follow the names of another six members of the first-named John Darmody's family: his parents, his aunt, two brothers and another son.

Private Darmody was born at Normanton in the Gulf Country of North Queensland and was a 24-year-old railway porter when he enlisted in the 26th Battalion in May 1915. He sailed with the battalion's 2nd Reinforcements on the *Shropshire* on 20 August 1915, but was too late to participate in the fighting at Gallipoli and did not join his unit until January 1916, when it had returned to Egypt. The battalion was transferred to France in March 1916 and from the end of July was engaged in the fighting at Pozières. It was here on 5 August that Darmody received shrapnel wounds to the left leg and shoulder, resulting in his being evacuated to the 13th Stationary Hospital at Boulogne and on 10 August to the 1st Southern Hospital, Birmingham, England, where he died of his wounds a fortnight later. An uncle arranged for the body to be taken to Powerstown, near Clonmel, County Tipperary, where it was buried in the Catholic churchyard in the Darmody family plot next to the church.

Lieutenant George Gilmour Allardyce (Mount Jerome Cemetery, Dublin)

Lieutenant George Gilmour Allardyce of the 4th Battalion was also interred in a family plot in Ireland after he died from wounds received in France. Born in Dublin, the eldest son of George and Janet Allardyce, he was an undergraduate of Trinity College Dublin, where he was a member of the OTC. He was living in Melbourne when he enlisted in the AIF on 11 November 1914. His attestation paper gives his age as 21 years and 4 months, but the inscription on the family headstone states he was in his 23rd year when he died in May 1918, some three and a half years after enlisting. Thus, in reality he was only 19 when he enlisted and would have required parental consent, which was not readily available as his father was living in Dublin at the time. His attestation paper also states he was a student, but there is no explanation as to what a 19-year-old medical student from Dublin was doing in Australia. Letters he wrote to his father suggest he may have been visiting friends, though they also indicate he was looking for work as a clerk – perhaps to finance his holiday.[38]

He would have preferred to have served in the British Army, and he wrote to his father that he was sorry that war had broken out while he was away from home as he would otherwise have received a commission. He saw enlistment in the AIF as a means to that end, and expected to be sent to England. When the AIF was diverted to Egypt and then France, he applied twice for a commission in the British army. His applications having been turned down, he eventually resigned himself to serving in the AIF for the duration of the war.

On 22 December 1914, Allardyce embarked on the *Berrima* with his unit, the 4th Field Ambulance, which, after training in Egypt, landed at Gallipoli on 27 April 1915. His letters suggest that his work as a stretcher-bearer was hard, but that his living conditions were quite good and he was well fed. However, by mid-August the shine had rubbed off somewhat, as he wrote to his father, 'We are all looking forward to being relieved now, I know I for one am absolutely fed up with war now'.

He was involved in the August offensive, in which Irish troops served alongside the Anzacs (see chapter 1, p. 32), and he wrote home that he had met 'a few Dublin fellows who are here in the Irish Rifles'. During the offensive, he was admitted to hospital on 23 August 1915 with influenza, but according to a letter to his father he may also have received a small bullet wound to the leg. Evacuated to Mudros on the island of Lemnos and thence to the 2nd Australian General Hospital at Helouan in Egypt, he eventually recovered after a number of relapses. In April 1916, still in Egypt, he transferred to the 14th Field Ambulance, newly formed as a result of the reorganisation of the AIF. After another bout in hospital in late May and early June 1916, he sailed from Alexandria to Marseilles, where he arrived on 30 June 1916.

He served with the 14th Field Ambulance in France, then took leave in the United Kingdom in December 1916. This may have been unsettling, for, after returning to the front, he wrote to his father in February 1917, 'I wish this war would come to an end one way or another. I think if the troops of both sides who are doing the fighting downed tools, it would be the best way of closing the war up'. His despondency would not have been helped by the fact that in May 1917 he was hospitalised for a week, after being gassed.

On 30 May, he transferred to the 4th Infantry Battalion and was selected for officer training, which he underwent at No. 2 Officer Cadet School, Cambridge, from September 1917, eventually receiving his commission on 2 February 1918, when he was appointed a second lieutenant. At the end of March, he returned to the 4th Battalion in France, but on 15 April, outside of Hazebrouck, he was hit by a fragment from a high-explosive shell, which passed through the back of his head. Evacuated to England on 17 April and admitted to the 3rd Southern General Hospital at Oxford, he wrote to his father two days later describing at length and in vivid detail the circumstances of his being wounded. The letter is upbeat, giving no hint as to the severity of the wound, which ultimately proved fatal. But he may not have been downplaying the extent of his injury, as a medical report of 4 May 1918 describes the wound as 'slight not permanent' and estimates the period of incapacity as seven weeks, though it notes he was complaining of headaches and was feeling weak. In the letter, Allardyce promised his father he would write again and describe his situation at the hospital. However, it is the last letter in the file. Whether he wrote again is not known, but the medical documents in his service record indicate that the headaches intensified and after an operation to drain an abscess he died of meningitis on 18 May 1918, three days after being promoted to lieutenant.

His body was taken to Ireland and buried at Mount Jerome Cemetery, Dublin, on 22 May 1918. In attendance were his father George, his brother Ransome and his uncle Robert S Swirles. His body lies alongside those of his mother, who had died in 1911, and his brother William (Billie), who as a surgeon probationer aboard HMS *Negro* had died in a collision in the North Sea in December 1916, aged 20.

Private Thomas Paget Sudlow (Blackrock [St Michael] Church of Ireland Churchyard, County Cork)

Four young men of the Sudlow family, originally from England but living in Western Australia when the war broke out, enlisted in the AIF: all were wounded and two did not return. One of them, Private Thomas Paget Sudlow, a farmer from Western Australia's Katanning district, is buried in the graveyard at St Michael's Church of Ireland, Blackrock, a suburb of Cork City.

Soon after the war began, Thomas, aged 30, enlisted, with his brother Francis Paget Sudlow, in the 11[th] Battalion, and the two young men served together at Gallipoli. Thomas had had previous military service: a short stint with the Royal Naval Reserve just before he emigrated to Australia and, as his attestation form enigmatically records, '6 mo[nth]s – Transport Section – Germany Army'. Another brother, Geoffrey Charles Sudlow, enlisted at about the same time, but in the 16[th] Battalion, and he too served at Gallipoli, where he was wounded in the right shoulder in June and repatriated to Australia. Francis, however, was not so fortunate. Promoted to sergeant on 15 May 1915, he was killed four days later during the massive Turkish attack intended to drive the

Anzacs off the peninsula. For six hours, the Turks hurled wave after wave of their men at the defenders, suffering some 10 000 casualties, 3000 of them killed. By contrast, the Anzacs lost 484 men, 160 killed, among them Sergeant Sudlow, who was buried in Victoria Gully cemetery by Father John Fahey, chaplain to the 11th Battalion, whose exploits are discussed in chapter 3 (pp. 98–100).

Thomas survived the Gallipoli campaign and sailed to France in March 1916 with the battalion. Its first major action was at Pozières in the Somme valley in July. However, Thomas's part in the battle was short-lived, as he suffered a gunshot wound to the chest on 22 July 1916, the day before the 1st Division's attack on Pozières. He was evacuated to Rouen and then to England, where he died on 12 August 1916, at the Royal Victoria Hospital, Netley. His sister, Miss K Sudlow, arranged for his body to be transported to Cork City, where she was living at the time.

Having recovered from his wound, Geoffrey sailed from Australia to England once more, with the 2nd Reinforcements of the 51st Battalion, in April 1916. But after suffering a fracture of his previously wounded shoulder at a training camp on the Salisbury Plain in August 1916, he was once again returned to Australia and discharged from the AIF. Not content to sit out the rest of the war, he re-enlisted in January 1917, but to no avail; two months later he was discharged as permanently medically unfit.

Another brother, Arthur Sudlow, enlisted in March 1917 and served with the 11th Battalion in France, where he was wounded on 11 May 1918, necessitating the amputation of his right leg below the knee. He eventually returned to Australia in May 1919.

Died of illness

The remaining Australian soldiers buried in Ireland died in either England or Ireland of a variety of illnesses, including the Spanish flu.

The curse of the 'Spanish Lady'

A form of pneumonic influenza, the Spanish flu[39] spread throughout the world in 1918–19, killing millions of people. Estimates of the total deaths at the time were in the order of 20 million, but over the years further research has seen that figure climb to 50 million, with a caveat that 'even this vast figure may be substantially lower than the real toll, perhaps as much as 100 percent understated'.[40] Compared to the estimated 14 million deaths, both military and civilian, attributable to the four years of the war, it is a staggering statistic, particularly as the pandemic's death toll occurred in less than one year.[41] An effective maritime quarantine spared Australia from the worst effects of the disease, delaying its onset until early 1919, when its virulence had lessened, with the result that Australia recorded the lowest death rate of any country with a large European population.[42] Even so, more than 12 000 Australians died in the space of six months once the quarantine barrier broke down.[43]

On the Western Front and in Britain and Ireland, Australian soldiers were exposed to the full brunt of the disease, which is thought to have spread in three waves: the first in the northern spring and summer of 1918; the second, and most virulent, in the autumn of 1918; and the third in the winter and spring of 1919. While Australia's mortality rate was 2.3 per 1000, in the United Kingdom it was more than double that: 5.8 in England and Wales and 4.04 in Ireland.[44] With understatement typical of a veteran of the Western Front, Private Verdi George Schwinghammer of the 42nd Battalion, whose visit to Ireland in early 1918 is related in chapter 4, wrote of an outbreak of the disease among the troops in December 1918:

> The influenza epidemic now broke out amongst us and it was sad to see so many of our men dying with the 'flu – ones who had gone through the war without a scratch. Strict precautions were taken. Our clothes were put through fumigators, etc. For a few weeks it was very severe and many of the men were sent to hospital – several of them dying. The man next to me in my billet … a fine, big, strapping chap, died from it. After four weeks the severity of it seemed to have spent itself and we soon forgot about it.[45]

Corporal Noel Michael Keating of 13th Brigade Headquarters, who visited Ireland in September 1918, wrote laconically in his diary of the first outbreak of Spanish flu in July 1918:

> Monday, July 1: Spanish influenza amongst us. One case in the orderly room.
>
> Tuesday, July 2: Some of the lads still suffering from the Spanish 'flu.
>
> Thursday, July 4: The Spanish epidemic seems to be spreading. Cpl White is down, Cpl Hammond is down, Dave is sick. Sgt Harvey is still down and I feel very seedy. A great rush of work and only Corporal Martin and I to carry on.
>
> Friday, July 5: Dad's birthday. I have a slight attack of the Spanish 'flu and put in a rotten night. Being feverish I went outside for a while and a shell burst 30 yards away from me. So between the influ[enza] and the Hun bombardment and plenty of work things not too pleasant.

Both Schwinghammer and Keating were fortunate enough to survive not only the war but also the pestilence that came with the peace. Many did not, including, on my estimate, six of the 25 Australian servicemen of the First World War buried in Ireland. Although none of the service records of these six men specifically identifies the cause of death as Spanish flu, instead using terminology such as 'Died of Disease: Pneumonia', the clustering of their deaths from pneumonia around the time of the pandemic strongly suggests Spanish flu as the underlying cause. As explained by John Barry in *The Great Influenza*:

> Influenza is a viral disease. When it kills, it usually does so in one of two ways: either quickly and directly with a violent viral pneumonia so damaging that it has been compared to burning the lungs; or more slowly and indirectly by stripping the body of defenses, allowing bacteria to invade the lungs and cause a more common and slower-killing bacterial pneumonia.[46]

Private John Quinane (Glenkeen Old Graveyard, County Tipperary)

One who succumbed during the first wave was Private John Quinane, a native of Victoria, who had enlisted in Sydney on 19 February 1916, aged 27. On 22 August 1916 he embarked on the *Wiltshire* and arrived at Plymouth on 13 October 1916, marching in to No. 3 Command Depot at Wool in Dorset on the same day. He proceeded to France on 8 January 1917 and joined the 45th Battalion ten days later. But the atrocious conditions in which the men were forced to fight proved too much for the stocky labourer from Colac, who was admitted to hospital suffering from trench feet, resulting in his being evacuated to England, where he was admitted to Birmingham Hospital and then the 3rd Auxiliary Hospital, Dartford. Trench foot is an infection of the feet caused by cold, wet and insanitary conditions, such as men standing in waterlogged trenches for extended periods without changing their socks or boots. Quinane was given 14 days furlough on 5 April 1917 and thereafter spent two and a half months at No. 1 Command Depot, Perham Down, before returning to France on 5 July 1917 and rejoining his unit three weeks later. Although he missed the Battle of Messines in June, he was in time to participate in the nightmare of the Third Battle of Ypres (Passchendaele).

During the winter of 1917–18, the 45th Battalion, as part of the 12th Brigade of the 4th Division, rotated in and out of the line. After the German army broke through the Allied lines in March 1918, the 45th Battalion became embroiled in a last–ditch fight to contain the German advance in the vicinity of Dernancourt near Albert in the Somme region. These were desperate times, with the outcome of the war literally hanging in the balance. On 28 March, the battalion lost 48 men, including 11 killed in defending the vital rail link between Albert and Amiens. Charles Bean recorded: 'The men of the 12th Brigade, who had now been moving, marching, digging, and fighting for three days and three nights almost without sleep, were in a daze of exhaustion'.[47]

On 29 March 1918, as his company was getting ready to return once more to the front line, Quinane received a gunshot wound to the foot when his own rifle discharged. His company commander Captain Jack Holman, on inspecting the men prior to moving out, had seen Quinane trying to load his rifle and had ordered him to unload before walking on. After Holman had gone about 10 metres, he heard a rifle discharge and on turning round saw that Quinane had been shot through the left foot.

At 12th Field Ambulance, where he was initially treated, his injury was recorded as self-inflicted, but the commanding officer of 45th Battalion reported it as wounded in action. However, the 12th brigade commander directed that Quinane be tried by Field General Court Martial, while 4th Army headquarters determined in May 1918 that the casualty should be reported as 'Injured (negligently self inflicted)' with a recommendation that he be retained in France and returned to his unit as soon as possible. However, the wound was severe and by then Quinane had been evacuated to England and hospitalised at Reading War Hospital.

Injuries that were self-inflicted ranged from accidental through negligent to wilful, with the boundaries between the various causes often blurred. AIF instructions made it clear that a charge of wilful self-wounding should not lightly be brought, suggesting that unless the evidence was conclusive the charge should be 'conduct to the prejudice of good order and military discipline in wounding himself through negligently handling a rifle'.[48] Presumably, this was the charge that Private Quinane was to face on his return to France.

As officially recorded, self-harm was not widespread. The number of reported cases of self-inflicted injuries in the AIF for the years 1916–18 was 701, a figure that seems low given the difficult conditions on the Western Front and the strain the men were under. What the figures do show, though, is that the number of reported cases increased as the war progressed: 126 in 1916 (10 months only as the AIF did not arrive in France until March), 186 in 1917 and 388 in 1918. However, as it is not an area that has been the subject of detailed research, it is difficult to say what the true incidence was.[49]

Just under two months after Quinane received his injury, the wound was sufficiently healed that on 21 May 1918 he was given

Private John Quinane
(Courtesy of Frank Quinane)

14 days furlough with orders to report to No. 4 Command Depot on 4 June. When he did not report on that day, he was listed as AWL. Then, on 15 June 1918, he was admitted to Dublin's King George V Military Hospital, said to be dangerously ill. Four days later, he died of pneumonia in the hospital.

John Quinane was from a proud Tipperary family from the Thurles area and members of the family claimed his body and brought it home to Glenkeen Old Graveyard, just outside Borrisleigh, where he was laid to rest among the graves of his forebears, some of whose headstones bear inscriptions dating back more than 200 years.[50]

The speed of his demise suggests pneumonic influenza, though it is difficult to tell from the extant records. If so, he would have been an unlucky victim of the first wave of the pandemic in that it had only just reached the United Kingdom.

Private George Bardon (Grangegorman Military Cemetery, Dublin)

One whose symptoms definitely indicate Spanish flu was Private George Bardon, a 26-year-old farmer from the Atherton Tableland, who while on leave in Ireland took sick and died on 13 October 1918. Two years earlier he had followed the lead of his older brother, James, by enlisting in the AIF at Cairns. After three months training, he sailed with the 9th Reinforcements of the 47th Battalion, arriving in England on 12 April 1917, where he underwent a further three months training with the 12th Training Battalion at Codford in Wiltshire. He then proceeded to Belgium where he joined his battalion, which was in the Ypres sector waiting to play its part in the battles of Polygon Wood and Passchendaele, a shocking introduction to modern warfare for the young Queensland farmer.

As part of the 12th Brigade, the 47th Battalion shared a similar experience to Quinane's 45th Battalion during the winter of 1917–18 and again in the spring of 1918, when it helped turn back the German offensive by withstanding the enemy's attacks around Dernancourt. However, heavy casualties and a lack of reinforcements took their toll on the 47th, which was disbanded in May 1918. As a result, Bardon was transferred to the 48th Battalion, which took part in the Battle of Amiens between 8 and 10 August, and the battle to seize the Hindenburg 'outpost line' between 18 and 20 September. (The Hindenburg 'outpost line' included the old British trenches facing the Hindenburg Line, the formidable series of defences built in 1916, which the Germans incorporated into their network of defences.) This was the 48th Battalion's last battle of the war and Bardon was subsequently given leave in the UK and an opportunity to visit family in Ireland, of whom there were many. He had a grandmother living in Rathmines, a suburb of Dublin, while two of his uncles were serving with the Royal Engineers and the Irish Horse Regiment and a cousin was in the Dublin Fusiliers. What should have been a happy time, visiting relatives and relaxing before returning to Australia, soon turned to tragedy.

On 8 October 1918, Bardon was admitted to the King George V Military Hospital in Dublin suffering from pneumonia. Three days later he had a temperature of 40.6 degrees Celsius and a pulse rate of 124. He had a cough with rusty sputum and was delirious. Over the next two days, his condition rapidly deteriorated and he died at 9 pm on 13 October 1918. Like that of Quinane, his sudden demise typified the course of Spanish flu – its victims, mostly young and healthy, were quickly debilitated and their body's defences overwhelmed. Instead of returning home to Australia to resume life on the farm with his brother James, George Bardon received a funeral with full military honours at Grangegorman Military Cemetery on 18 October, in the presence of his grandmother, an aunt and a family friend. James was not present. At the time, he was being evacuated from France to England, himself a victim of the Spanish flu, which he had contracted on the day his brother died. After a month in hospital in England, James was given leave before embarking on the *Demosthenes* for return to Australia. But his troubles were not over: he had a relapse and was hospitalised for a few days on board ship before eventually arriving home on 2 March 1919. He died in 1988.

Private Charles Michael Byrne (Grangegorman Military Cemetery, Dublin)

Three weeks after George Bardon was laid to rest, Grangegorman Military Cemetery saw the interment of another Australian victim of pneumonic influenza: Private Charles Michael Byrne, a 40-year-old native of Nagambie, a small town situated at the southern end of the Goulburn Valley, 120 kilometres north of Melbourne. He had enlisted in January 1915, joining the 7th Battalion at Gallipoli as a reinforcement on 26 May 1915. Within the month, he fell sick with fever and was evacuated to a hospital in Alexandria, not rejoining his unit until September, after having spent 28 days in detention following his failure to attend an embarkation parade. It would not be the last time that Byrne was punished for breaches of military law. His record during his short military service includes a number of disciplinary offences: hesitating to obey an order; falling out of the line of march; unshaven on parade (twice); disobedience to an order; and absent without leave. He could hardly be described as a model soldier.

After the evacuation of the Gallipoli peninsula, Byrne returned to Alexandria where he transferred to the newly formed 46th Battalion, also part of the 12th Brigade. But instead of going with his new unit to France, he was admitted to hospital and evacuated to England. Not until 14 August 1916 did he eventually join the battalion, which at that time was engaged in the horrific fighting around Pozières. The battalion's next major engagement was not until April 1917, at Bullecourt, but by then Byrne was once again in hospital in England, having been evacuated there in January 1917 to have a carbuncle removed from his back. No sooner had he proceeded to France in May than he again fell sick, so that it was not until 21 June 1917 that he rejoined his unit. By then the battalion was resting after having participated in the Battle of Messines, but it was soon back in the line, taking part in the Battle of Passchendaele.

Having survived that gruelling episode, Byrne transferred for a short time to the 12th Light Trench Mortar Battery, returning to the 46th Battalion in May 1918 and taking part in the Battle of Amiens in August. It was during the battalion's final campaign in the attack on the Hindenburg 'outpost line' along the St Quentin Canal near Bellinglise that Byrne was wounded on 18 September 1918 and evacuated to England. The wound, though no doubt painful (a gun-shot wound to both buttocks), cannot have been too serious, for on 23 October he was given a fortnight's convalescent leave.

Like many wounded Australians before him, Byrne took his leave in Ireland, at a time when all the talk was of the imminent end of the war – truly something to look forward to for someone who had enlisted in January 1915 and found military discipline distasteful. But he did not live to see the peace. On 4 November 1918, one week before the armistice took effect, Private Byrne, like Privates Quinane and Bardon before him, lay dead in the King George V Military Hospital in Dublin, the cause of death given as pneumonia. When Father Loughlin buried him at Grangegorman, the priest was not alone; the funeral party included a number of Byrne's Dublin friends.

Private Robert Emmett Kinchington (Killarney New Cemetery, County Kerry)

It is not recorded whether during his convalescent leave Byrne visited Killarney, that favourite destination of Australian soldiers on leave in Ireland. But for one soldier who did, the New Cemetery at Killarney became his last resting place. Private Robert Emmett Kinchington, whose first names evoke memory of one of nationalist Ireland's greatest heroes, Robert Emmet, who led the rising of 1803, succumbed to 'septic pneumonia' (another name for pneumonic influenza) and died at the International Hotel, Killarney, on 5 February 1919.

Born in July 1893 at Longreach in Queensland, Robert moved to Sydney with his family when he was a young boy, completing his education at St Charles's School, Waverley, whereupon he became an examiner with the New South Wales Railways. He was the fourth child of Patrick Conmee and Nellie (née Scanlon), who had five boys and two girls, in that order, before Nellie was left

The Kinchingtons: left to right, Robert, James (Conmee), Thomas Neugent,
Pat, Vincent
(Courtesy of Barrie Kinchington)

widowed with a young family to raise. After her remarriage to
Thomas Kinchington in 1905, the children took their stepfather's
surname, and Nellie gave birth to another girl.

All five boys served in the AIF – four of them in the 3rd Battalion
of the 1st Division and one in the 49th Battalion, a Queensland unit of
the 4th Division. When enlisting on 27 June 1916, Robert used the
name George Emmett Kinchington, perhaps being self-conscious
of his given names. But he was not the only one of Nellie's boys to
change his name on joining up: James Timothy enlisted in the 5th
Light Horse Regiment under his father's surname Conmee, while
Thomas John signed up with the 49th Battalion as Jack Thomas
Neugent. Nellie explained the reason for the changes of name in a
letter she wrote to Major JM Lean at Base Records after being told
that Thomas had been wounded:

Two of my sons enlisted in Queensland under different names on account of me not wishing them all to go. I have 5 boys there. I was quite willing for 3 of them to go, the others promised each of them to stay at home and look after me; but I suppose the call was too strong. I felt a little annoyed that one changed his surname & the other took his cousin's name, but it was too late to make them alter it so I let it go, though I have pointed out to them it means endless troubles to their relatives if anything happen to them, but boys do not think.[51]

Nellie was a 'very remarkable little woman', according to an article in the *Catholic Press*. Apart from giving five of her sons to the nation's war effort, albeit reluctantly in the case of two of them, she devoted herself to social welfare, for which she received an MBE in 1936. As reported by the *Catholic Press* in 1915:

Mrs Kinchington ... may be found in the police courts any morning. All the magistrates, detectives and police officers are her friends, but Mrs Kinchington's friends are the poor girls who have fallen by the wayside, and whose confidence she seems to be able to win on the instant. When a woman is found guilty, the magistrate gives her the option of taking out her sentence in the home of the Sisters of the Good Shepherd, Ashfield, or some such charitable institution, or going to gaol. If she elects to go to a Catholic home, she is put under the care of Mrs Kinchington ... When their sentences have expired, many desire to remain longer in the home, but if they are leaving, Mrs Kinchington finds them respectable lodgings, and afterwards situations ... Mrs Kinchington also visits the gaols and the slums, and devotes her whole life to helping those in need. [52]

But good works did not save Nellie from the loss of two of her boys. Apart from Robert, Thomas was killed at Zonnebeke during the 4th Division's attack on Polygon Wood between 26 and 29 September 1917, being last seen on the first day of the battle in a shell hole, attempting to bandage a wound he had received from a shell splinter that had struck him behind the knee.[53] His name is engraved on the Menin Gate memorial at Ypres, which commemorates 54 896 Allied soldiers, including 6176 Australians, who fought in the Ypres salient and whose bodies were never identified.

Two of Robert's brothers were awarded the Military Medal: Patrick, who would later be commissioned, received his for gallantry during the Battle of Fromelles on 3 July 1916, becoming one of the first Australians to receive the award in France, while James, who had transferred from the Light Horse to the 3rd Battalion, won his award at Chuignes on 24 August 1918. Charles Bean wrote of Patrick's wartime activities on no fewer than five occasions in the *Official History*[54], and also mentioned James, referring to him by the surname Conmee.[55] Patrick was wounded at the Second Battle of Bullecourt in May 1917 and evacuated to England, returning to his unit two months later. But by November 1917, following Passchendaele, Patrick had become thoroughly sick of the war. In a letter to the father of a dead mate who had been with him since Gallipoli, he wrote:

> You have no idea of the troops' sufferings, summer & winter,
> rain & mud & cold. It really is a mercy for God to take us.
> I assure you at times I have asked God to take me from this
> life … It's about time this business finished, we are all sick
> of it, & I see too many come & go for my liking.[56]

He continued to soldier on and received his commission in August 1918, but the following month he was shot in the head at Hargicourt during the 3rd Battalion's last attack of the war. When Robert died on 5 February 1919, Patrick was still in hospital, embarking on the *Ascanius* three days later to return home an invalid.[57] After the war Patrick wrote of his brother's death:

> Whenever he was due for furlough it was his bad luck that
> a big stunt used be on and all leave stopped. He was in the
> firing line oftener than he should and was too run down
> when the war was over.[58]

Robert's death was a lonely affair. On 30 January 1919, he checked into Killarney's International Hotel, where he was known from a previous visit. He was already ill and the next day the management of the hotel persuaded him to go to bed and arranged for Dr Mangan to call. Despite the seriousness of his condition, the military authorities were not informed and he died at the hotel at 4.30 am on 5 February. Fearful of the spread of infection, the hotel, on the advice of the doctor, arranged his funeral for later that day, again without notifying the military authorities. Thus, Robert would not receive the military honours usually accorded a deceased member of the AIF, though, by chance, his burial was attended by five Australian soldiers on leave, who had heard of the funeral at the last minute.

Once informed of Robert's death, AIF Headquarters arranged for his brother Vincent to be given special leave to travel to Killarney to inspect the grave and to erect a wooden cross, allowing him to give some comfort to his poor mother, who no doubt had looked forward to Robert's early return once she knew he had survived the war. Her troubles did not end there. In 1922 she found herself in financial difficulties and felt the need to call on the prime minister to intervene personally on her behalf to hasten the discharge of a mortgage with the Repatriation Department, so that she could complete the sale of her house.[59] In 1939–45 Nellie's sons maintained the family's tradition of service to the nation when Australia once more found itself at war, with both James and Vincent enlisting in the 2nd AIF.[60]

Lance Sergeant William Hugh Moore (Macosquin [St Mary] Church of Ireland Churchyard, County Derry)

The military authorities were annoyed that Robert Kinchington's illness had not been reported to them, with the result that he died in a hotel without the benefit of proper medical treatment. But admission to hospital gave no guarantee of surviving the Spanish flu and, in fact, an uninfected soldier could contract the illness there. This seems to have been the case with Lance Sergeant William

Hugh Moore, who died of pneumonia at the Military Hospital in Sutton Veny, Wiltshire, England, on 21 October 1918.

Moore had been wounded on Boxing Day 1917 at Peronne in France, when he was felled by a shell explosion. At first his only symptoms were pain in the shins and knees, so he was sent down the line to No. 12 General Hospital for treatment. There the pain subsided, but his feet began to swell, he lost sensation in his legs and he was unable to stand – any attempt to move his legs caused violent spasms. He was evacuated to England and admitted to Sutton Veny hospital on 8 January 1918. At first the medical staff did not realise his symptoms were the result of trauma, attributing his debility to exposure to cold and wet. It was only later that the doctors discovered a fracture and dislocation of his lower dorsal spine, which was causing paraplegia and spasticity of his legs.

According to his attestation paper, William Moore was born in August 1888 at Greenock, Scotland, where he was apprenticed as a carpenter to his father before the family moved to Macosquin near Coleraine in County Derry.[61] Moore's family, including William, were opposed to the Irish Home Rule Bill of 1912, subscribing their names to the Ulster Covenant at the Macosquin Parochial Hall on Ulster Day, 28 September 1912.[62] From Ireland, William travelled to Australia in 1913 at age 25, taking up residence in Bundaberg, Queensland.

Moore did not enlist immediately on the outbreak of war, but joined up on 12 May 1915 in the second wave of enlistments that arose when news began arriving in Australia of the landing at Gallipoli. On 20 August 1915, a mere two years after arriving in Australia, Moore left, never to return, sailing from Sydney to Egypt with the 7th Reinforcements of the 9th Battalion on board the *Shropshire*, the same ship that carried Private Darmody, referred to above. Like Private Darmody, Moore arrived too late to participate in the fighting at Gallipoli: the 9th Battalion, which had been in the initial landing on 25 April, withdrew from the peninsula on 16–17 November 1915 for a well-earned rest at Lemnos just as the 7th Reinforcements were arriving there.[63] Because of the Anzac evacuation of the peninsula the following month, the 9th did not return to Gallipoli, transferring instead to Egypt, where in February 1916 it was split into two as part of the reorganisation and enlargement of the AIF, with one half of its strength, including Moore, forming the foundation of the 49th Battalion of the newly formed 4th Division. Moore's time with the new battalion was short-lived, however; on 16 March 1916, he transferred to the 4th Pioneer Battalion, where he remained for the rest of his service.

While in Egypt, Private Moore forfeited four days pay on 18 April 1916 for being AWL for 80 hours, but there must have been extenuating circumstances because the next month he was promoted to lance corporal. On 4 June, his battalion boarded the *Scotian* at Alexandria and a week later disembarked at Marseilles. During August and September, the 4th Pioneers were involved in the fighting at Pozières and Mouquet Farm, mainly digging trenches to protect the infantry, who were being pummelled by German artillery. It was dangerous work and Private Moore was promoted to corporal to replace another Pioneer killed in early September. The conditions were also conducive to illness and on 28 October 1916 he was admitted to the 1st Australian General Hospital with pleurisy, rejoining his unit three weeks later.

On 26 March 1917, Moore was promoted to lance sergeant after having completed a month's course at the 4th Division Infantry School and in April he was given ten days leave, which he took in Ireland, no doubt visiting his family at Macosquin. But he missed his train on the return journey and reported to AIF Headquarters in London one day late, happily with a certificate from the Railway Transport Officer at Dublin's Amiens St Station, which saved him from another fine.

From mid-1917, the 4th Division was engaged in most of the AIF's major battles in Belgium including Messines, Polygon Wood and Passchendaele. But it was on 24 June 1917, between battles, that Moore received a slight wound to the left wrist. This injury did not necessitate his evacuation to England and he rejoined his unit in mid-August in time for the battalion's involvement in the fighting at Polygon Wood and Passchendaele. Once again, it was after the major fighting was over that he received the wound at Peronne that would ultimately lead to his death ten months later at Sutton Veny.

His medical records do not disclose why a man with such serious injuries was not evacuated to Australia, but as events turned out, his remaining that long in England meant that when the second, and most deadly, wave of pneumonic influenza spread rapidly among the troops he was in one of the most dangerous places imaginable – a military hospital. After his death, his body was brought home to Ireland where he was buried in the churchyard of St Mary's Church of Ireland, Macosquin, his funeral attended by family and friends from the district. Today the distinctive CWGC headstone with its rising sun badge stands out from the other headstones around it as a reminder of this young Scots-Irishman's brief association with Australia.

Lieutenant Reginald Leopold MacLean (Belfast City Cemetery, Belfast)

Macosquin is situated in what is now Northern Ireland, though there was no such designation when Private Moore was laid to rest because the First World War preceded the partition of Ireland in 1921. Of the 25 Australian war graves in Ireland from the First World War, five are located in what is now Northern Ireland. One of these, in the Belfast City Cemetery, belongs to another victim of pneumonic influenza, Lieutenant Reginald Leopold MacLean, who, like Private Moore, fell ill after being wounded.

Born in Newcastle, New South Wales, MacLean was a 31-year-old school teacher, married for nine years to Ettie Jean Harrison, when he enlisted in the AIF in August 1916. Before the war, he had served six years in the cadets, achieving the rank of lieutenant. So, instead of being sent overseas with the next batch of reinforcements, MacLean was given a local posting before attending officer training at Royal Military College, Duntroon. It was not until February 1918, after he had been commissioned as a second lieutenant, that he embarked for overseas service aboard the *Nestor* with the 21st Reinforcements of the 19th Battalion.

Shortly after arriving in England, he was admitted to hospital for five days with broncho-pneumonia, with the result that he did not get to France until the end of July. Soon thereafter, he was posted to the 4th Army School. It was not until September that he joined in the fighting with the 19th Battalion, which was embarking on the last phase of the war, the assault on the Hindenburg Line. It was during the forcing of the Beaurevoir trench system around Montbrehain on 3 October 1918 that MacLean received a gunshot wound to the head, which resulted in his evacuation to England, where he was admitted to the 3rd London General Hospital. For MacLean, his short war was over. The battalion had fought its last battle and was disbanded on 10 October 1918, just as he began to recover from his wound. When later in October he was well enough, he was given convalescent leave and decided to spend his furlough in Ireland. But he was not there long before he was back in hospital, where the diagnosis was double pneumonia.

It is not clear from his service record what happened next. The casualty form (B103) shows his admission to Belfast Military Hospital on 28 October 1918 with the notation 'Dan Ill' (Dangerously Ill) and with a subsequent notation recording his death on 2 November 1918. Other records in his file show that he died not in the hospital but at Kilwaughter Castle, near Larne, County Antrim (about 30 kilometres north-west of Belfast). Kilwaughter Castle had been the home of the Anglo-Norman Agnew family and was at the time occupied by Mrs Bessie Galt Smith, an American, who was the widow of John Galt Smith, an Agnew descendant. During the war, many wounded officers convalesced at the castle.[64] It is difficult to understand why MacLean would have been moved from Belfast Military Hospital so soon after his admission, especially as he was reported to be dangerously ill. Was it because he had improved; or was it to isolate him from other patients? Whatever the explanation, after his death his body was brought to the Belfast City Cemetery for burial with full military honours, with his wife's brother, Lieutenant Percy Harrison of the 41st Battalion, in attendance.

Other illnesses

Although the Spanish flu had a huge impact on the health of the troops, an impact not fully acknowledged in much writing on the war, it struck only in the second half of 1918 as the war was coming to an end. Throughout the war, the soldiers were exposed to a wide range of illnesses, as is exemplified by the causes of death of the remaining Australians buried in Ireland.

Private James Carroll (Kilturra Old Graveyard, County Sligo)

Private James Carroll died in 1919, not from pneumonic influenza but of that great scourge of the Irish people for much of the 20th century – tuberculosis. An Irish native from Doocastle, County Sligo, Carroll emigrated to Australia in 1907 aged 26 and worked in the silver mines at Mareeba in North Queensland until he enlisted in December 1914. Whether his wife came to Australia is unknown. Carroll nominated her as his next-of-kin, giving her address in Ireland. In February 1915, he sailed with the 3rd Reinforcements of the 15th Battalion to Egypt, where he fell ill and was returned to Australia in May 1915 and admitted to Langwarrin Hospital, outside Melbourne. After recovering from his illness in August 1915, he was sent to Melbourne's Broadmeadows Camp, from where he officially disappeared and was struck off as a deserter in March 1916. However, it is unclear whether that was the result of an administrative error, as his military career was not over.

In July 1916, he once again embarked for overseas service, this time with the 3rd Reinforcements of the 58th Battalion, having been given a new service number. On arrival in England, he joined the 15th Training Battalion, but once again he slipped out of the system. In October 1916, he was serving at the training camp at Codford, England, when granted leave to Ireland. According to a statement Carroll made to the Australian military authorities in July 1918, he failed to return by 31 October 1916 and instead reported to the Royal Irish Constabulary a week later that he was a deserter from the AIF. He claimed that his pay allotment was not being forwarded to his wife, despite requests he had made to his officers, and that when he had arrived in Ireland he had found his wife and aged parents living in financial difficulties. As a result, he had decided to stay and work the farm and to report his situation to the police. It was not until April 1918 that the local police informed him that there was a warrant for his arrest.

When he returned to England, he signed a confession setting out the details of his desertion. He was also ill at the time and admitted to hospital. Upon his discharge, he was allowed to return to Ireland. He died at Doocastle on 20 April 1919, survived by his wife and their two-year old child, and is buried in the Kilturra Old Graveyard.

Private Philip Douglas Davis (Mount Jerome Cemetery, Dublin)

One of the most poignant aspects of visiting a war cemetery is to read the ages on the headstones. It brings home in a most compelling way the realisation that so many of the soldiers killed in the war were no more than boys. Of the Australian soldiers buried in Ireland, the youngest is Private Philip Douglas Davis of Westbury, Tasmania, who died at Fargo Hospital, Larkhill, England, on 2 May 1917, aged just 19.[65]

A commission agent when he enlisted in August 1916, he had already shown his interest in the military by rising to the rank of lieutenant in the Tasmanian citizen forces and no doubt welcomed the opportunity to take part in 'the great adventure'. On 25 October 1916, he sailed to England on board the *Ulysses*, and two months later began training on the Salisbury Plain. However, he would never get the chance to prove himself in battle; instead he succumbed to illness while in camp, and died of pneumonia following a bout of influenza – a foretaste of what would sweep through the camps the following year. A cousin, Dr FL Flood, attended him during his illness and arranged for his body to be sent to Ireland, where another cousin, Sir Lionel Carty of Dundalk, County Louth, organised his burial at Mount Jerome Cemetery, Harold's Cross, Dublin.

Private James Balfour Leathem (Lurgan New Cemetery, County Armagh)

Another young soldier who enlisted to do his bit for king and country but who died before he reached the firing line was Private James Balfour Leathem, a native of Lurgan, County Armagh, who had emigrated to Australia with his older brother George shortly before the war.[66] James, a 21-year-old carpenter, enlisted in the 42nd Battalion in November 1915, and on 5 June 1916 sailed with his battalion on the troop transport *Borda* to Egypt. Barely had he arrived when he was admitted to hospital with 'debility', which turned out to be malaria.[67] Six weeks later, he was fit enough to travel to England and he marched into Larkhill Camp on 9 September 1916. However, while on leave in Ireland with his family, he once again took sick and was admitted to Belfast Military Hospital on 4 November 1916. Again the diagnosis was 'debility'. After three days, he was transferred to Holywood Convalescent Hospital for two weeks and then to the Presbyterian Fever Hospital, before returning to the Belfast Military Hospital on 24 November 1916, where he was diagnosed with meningitis. Within 30 hours he was dead. Because the hospital was not far from his home town, he was visited by members of the family, who then took his body to Lurgan for burial at the New Cemetery.

James's father, Joseph Leathem, had married three times and James had five sisters and seven brothers. George, with whom James had come to Australia, enlisted in the 41st Battalion in May 1916 and served in France, where he was gassed in May 1918 and wounded in action three months later, necessitating his evacuation to England. After the end of the war, while awaiting transport back to Australia, George spent three months leave on full pay in Lurgan working at a linen factory. He did not survive the war long, dying in Brisbane on 3 April 1922. Another brother, Joseph, served during the war with the Canadian Army.

Gunner Ambrose Augustine Haley (Midleton Catholic [The Rosary] Churchyard, County Cork)

On 25 December 1918, when men and women across the world were celebrating the first Christmas of peace since 1913, Gunner Ambrose Augustine Haley of the 2nd Field Artillery Brigade finally succumbed to an illness that for months had been eating away at his vital organs. A 26-year-old accountant from St Helen's, Tasmania, Haley had enlisted in November 1916, sailing to England on the troop transport *Ascanius* in May 1917. After two months further training in England, he proceeded in September 1917 to France, where he was initially posted to the 1st Australian Divisional Ammunition Column and then to the 2nd Field Artillery Brigade. Three weeks after arriving in France, he was wounded in the left arm during the Third Battle of Ypres (Passchendaele). Although not evacuated to England, his injuries were severe enough for him to be in and out of a number of hospitals in France during the next six months. According to information which his father supplied to the official war historian, Haley was an exceptional musician and while convalescing in France gained a reputation as an outstanding flautist in a number of hospitals.

He eventually returned to his unit on 31 August 1918, but in less than a month he was again admitted to hospital, this time in England at Graylingwell Military Hospital, Chichester, with symptoms of deafness. This was not unusual for a gunner, but the cause of his infirmity was more insidious than the noise of the guns. On 19 November 1918, Base Records informed his father that he was now reported dangerously ill. Just over a month later he was dead, the cause being 'carcinoma of the pancreas, lungs, spleen and other organs' – a devastating diagnosis in a man so young.

Following his death, Haley's remains were taken to Midleton, County Cork, where he was buried on 30 December 1918 in the churchyard of the parish church of Our Lady of the Rosary, in the presence of his brother Warrant Officer Urban Aloysius Haley, at the time attached to AIF Headquarters in London, and of his uncles, aunts and cousins. He is buried in a family plot along with another five members of his mother's family.

Private John Michael Doyle (Cam Cemetery, County Roscommon)

Private John Michael Doyle was born at Millbrook, near Athlone in County Westmeath. He emigrated to Australia in 1911 and was working as an assistant butcher in Sydney when in January 1915, at age 29, he enlisted in the 17th Battalion, part of the 5th Brigade of the newly formed 2nd Division. On 12 May 1915, he sailed with his battalion on the troopship *Thèmistocles* to Egypt, arriving in June for further training in the summer heat. On 20 August 1915, the battalion arrived at Anzac Cove during the August offensive by means of which the Anzacs hoped to break out of their precarious foothold on the peninsula. By then, the veterans of the campaign had been worn down by months of living in appalling conditions. In the *Official History*, Charles Bean describes the arrival of the 2nd Division men: 'These troops came to the tired and somewhat haggard garrison of Anzac like a fresh breeze from the Australian bush'.[68]

But the men of A Company, which included Doyle, were soon to face the horrors of battle, being thrown into the attack on Hill 60 (see pp. 43–46). Doyle survived that ordeal but his battalion's next task was to relieve the Light Horse at Quinn's Post, 'the deadliest position on the peninsula', which they did on 3 September 1915.[69] Doyle, however, did not have to endure the trying conditions there for long. On 18 September 1915, he succumbed to dysentery, by then endemic among the troops, and was evacuated to Malta and then to England on the *Dunluce Castle*, where he was admitted to the 3rd London General Hospital a month later. He recovered from his illness and was given leave over Christmas, which he spent at home in Athlone. However, after returning to England in anticipation of rejoining his unit, he fell sick with a respiratory ailment and was admitted to Royal Herbert Hospital, Woolwich, where he had an asthma attack and died on 5 March 1916. His brother, BV Doyle, was with him when he died and arranged for the body to be taken to Ireland for burial. Private Doyle's service file includes a copy of what appears to be a newspaper obituary, which states:

The remains, enclosed in a massive oak coffin, arrived by the mid-day train at Athlone, on Thursday. They were met at the station by a guard of honour of the R.F.A. [Royal Field Artillery] and an immense crowd of the general public. They were placed on a gun carriage drawn by six horses and guarded by two mounted men. A firing party of 12 preceded the remains and a company of 25, under the command of a lieutenant, followed the gun carriage.

As the sad procession proceeded through Castle Street, Barrack Street, King Street, and Connaught the shops were closely shuttered and business was suspended. In private houses the blinds were closely drawn. He was interred in the family burial ground, Cam, with full military honours.[70]

Private Arthur Andrew Murphy (Grangegorman Military Cemetery, Dublin)

Born at Gulargambone, New South Wales, Arthur Andrew Murphy was a 32-year-old forest guard when he enlisted in the AIF in January 1916. He was a tall man, over six feet in height. On 22 August 1916, he sailed from Sydney with the 14th Reinforcements of the 19th Battalion to England on the troop transport *Wiltshire*, arriving in October 1916. After further training he proceeded to France, where he joined the battalion on 24 February 1917, just as it was being discovered that the Germans had covertly withdrawn from their forward positions to the strongly fortified Hindenburg Line. The 19th Battalion took part in the pursuit of the retreating Germans as well as in three major battles in France and Belgium before the year was out: second Bullecourt (3–4 May), Menin Road (20–22 September) and Poelcappelle (9–10 October).

Early in the new year, Murphy was granted leave to the United Kingdom and decided to visit Ireland. However, while in Dublin he took sick and was admitted to the King George V Military Hospital with enteritis. His condition did not improve and he was kept at the hospital. His situation was made worse by contracting pleurisy. In early April, an exploratory operation failed to reveal the cause of his illness and he became depressed. Later, however, an abscess of the liver was discovered and drained. But his condition worsened and further intervention failed to reverse his deterioration. He continued to weaken and he died on 2 June 1918, just after midnight. His body was buried with full military honours at Grangegorman Military Cemetery, Dublin. Although a long way from home, Murphy was not alone during his long, slow decline. A local woman, Mrs OEH Beatty, visited him regularly and wrote each week to his mother so that she would know he had a friend by him during his illness. Mrs Beatty also kept the Australian Red Cross in London informed of his situation.

Sergeant Thomas Robert Reid (Boho Church of Ireland Churchyard, County Fermanagh)

Thomas Robert Reid was born on 18 May 1880 at Boho, County Fermanagh, a little village in the hills above Lough Erne.[71] On 21 March 1901, shortly before his 21st birthday, while working as a shop assistant at Omagh, County Tyrone, Reid applied to join the South African Constabulary. It had been formed the previous October by Colonel Robert Baden-Powell at the request of Field Marshal Lord Roberts, the Anglo-Irish commander of British forces in South Africa, who wanted a force of ten thousand mounted men prepared by the middle of 1901 to take over the police duties of the country, which at the time was in the middle of the Boer War. Their task was to assist in the pacification of the Boer rebels.

Reid had had no prior military experience, but Captain Williams, a recruiting officer in Ireland acting on behalf of the governments of the Transvaal and Orange River Colony, adjudged him to be a good rider and a fair shot. For more than six years, during and after the Boer War, Reid served in the South African Constabulary, rising to the rank of sergeant second class and taking responsibility for a number of outposts. On 3 October 1907, he took his discharge and left South Africa for Canada and subsequently Australia, where he married a Victorian girl, Alice Lillian Robertson, in 1910. They had three children. In Australia, Reid worked as a horse breaker and trainer.

The parish church in Boho. The memorial plaque to Sergeant Thomas Reid and his brother George is on the wall between the two flags.
(Jeff Kildea)

He and Alice were living in Victoria when the war broke out in August 1914 and he enlisted before the end of the month, serving in the 2nd Field Artillery Brigade and the 1st Divisional Ammunition Column. He saw action at Gallipoli and on the Western Front, rising to the rank of sergeant, but he was only in France a few months before he fell ill and was admitted to hospital suffering from malaria. Evacuated to England in June 1916, Reid remained there until November 1917, before returning to his unit. In August 1918, he again fell ill, and this time the diagnosis was influenza, which may well have been the case as this was during the first wave of the Spanish flu epidemic. However, in reality he was suffering from an even more deadly illness than pneumonic influenza. Upon admission to Essex County Hospital in Colchester, England he was diagnosed with diabetes mellitus, then an incurable and untreatable disease. (It would be another three years before Dr Frederick Grant Banting and Dr Charles Herbert Best at the University of Toronto discovered insulin.) Doctors could only watch their diabetic patients waste away before their eyes and that is what Sergeant Reid did, losing 15 kilograms in a month. He was transferred to the 1st Australian Auxiliary Hospital at Harefield, where it was reported in September that his condition was improving with treatment. However, he died there on 3 October 1918.

Reid's body was taken to Ireland by his brother Fred, who paid £21.2.0 to do so.[72] He was buried next to his father in the Church of Ireland churchyard at Boho, his funeral being attended by his Irish relations, including his mother, his brother and his sisters, as well as friends of the family. Today, a marble tablet flanked by an Australian Red Ensign and the Union flag hangs on the wall inside the church, commemorating Sergeant Reid and his brother George, who was killed in action on 26 October 1917 fighting with the Royal Irish Fusiliers. Their names also appear on the Enniskillen war memorial.

Caring for the graves

The graves of all 25 of the Australian servicemen of the First World War buried in Ireland – the 'wattle among the shamrocks' – are under the care of the Commonwealth War Graves Commission (CWGC). Established by Royal Charter in May 1917 as the Imperial War Graves Commission, the CWGC was set up to locate and register the remains of all the soldiers who died during or in the immediate aftermath of the war. Once hostilities ended, the commission was able to devote itself to the consolidation, design and construction of war cemeteries and memorials. It took 20 years from the end of the war to complete the building program. A year after finishing the last of the cemeteries of the First World War, the Second World War broke out; as a result, the commission's construction program was extended into the 1960s.

From its earliest days, the CWGC had a policy of banning the repatriation of remains, partly for practical reasons but also because it felt that repatriation would conflict with the sense of brotherhood that had developed between all ranks serving in the war. But as we have seen, Irish families could take the remains of loved ones who died in England to Ireland, because it was then still part of the United Kingdom, for burial, though at considerable cost, if Sergeant Reid was a typical case.

Today, the CWGC continues its work, preserving the cemeteries and memorials in its care and encouraging the act of remembrance. Partner governments of the Commonwealth nations (Australia, Canada, India, New Zealand, South Africa and the United Kingdom) share the cost of the CWGC's operations in proportion to the number of their graves, while other nations contribute by absorbing the cost of maintaining Commonwealth war graves in their own country. The Republic of Ireland has almost 3000 Commonwealth war graves, including 2500 from the First World War, that are maintained by the Office of Public Works and regularly inspected by officers of the CWGC.[73]

CHAPTER 6

WHO FEARS TO SPEAK OF '14-'18?

REMEMBRANCE IN AUSTRALIA AND IRELAND

The war of 1914–18 had a profound effect on Ireland and Australia.[1] In his major work, *Modern Ireland*, Roy Foster claimed, 'The First World War should be seen as one of the most decisive events in modern Irish history'[2], while Joan Beaumont in *Australia's War 1914–18* wrote, 'Clearly it was a towering experience in the national history, and the course of Australia's development would have been different had it not occurred'.[3]

Both countries suffered huge losses, killed and wounded; so much so that few families or communities were unaffected. Consequently, it is a period that is etched into the social psyche of each country.[4] In Australia this is evidenced physically by the profusion of war memorials across the landscape and conceptually by the vitality of the Anzac tradition, which more than 90 years after the landing at Gallipoli, as Beaumont puts it, 'retains significant emotional power and political utility'.[5] But in Ireland attitudes to the soldiers of the First World War have been deeply divided, more or less along the border that divides north from south. In the north, remembrance is observed with diligence and emotion, much as it is in Australia, though with a sectarian edge, while in the south it has been noteworthy for its near-complete absence, both physically and conceptually.

This chapter explores how the First World War has been commemorated over the years in Ireland and Australia. In particular, it will examine the interrelationship between remembrance and the expression of national identity in each country. Although for the most part remembrance in Australia has been a unifying national influence, it has at times and for a variety of reasons been contentious. Relevantly, in the context of this book, there were divisions along sectarian lines lasting into the 1960s. In Ireland, on the other hand, remembrance became a battleground upon which unionists and nationalists, each in their own way, continued the national struggle, particularly in Northern Ireland, long after the guns fell silent.

Remembrance in Australia

In 2002, eighty-seven years after the Gallipoli campaign, Alec Campbell became the focus of national attention in the final months of his life simply because he was the last of the Anzacs who had fought at Gallipoli. In the words of *Sydney Morning Herald* journalist Tony Stephens, he 'had become national property'.[6] His passing on 16 May 2002 at age 103, described by Prime Minister John Howard as 'an important moment in the history of our nation', was marked by a state funeral, an honour the federal government accords significant national leaders and national legends such as Sir Donald Bradman, but few others. The prime minister went on to say, 'Of all the traditions that Australians hold dear, none is held more dearly than the ANZAC tradition. It is a story of great valour under fire, unity of purpose and a willingness to fight against the odds that has helped to define what it means to be an Australian'.[7]

Some commentators were less effusive. Shortly after Campbell's death historian David Day told ABC Radio that as a country we should move on and leave behind us the Anzac legend, which he regards as a simplistic myth that is fast becoming the single foundational story of the nation to the exclusion of other episodes in Australian history, such as 1788, Eureka, Federation and Kokoda.[8] But such concerns were not often heard in the days following Campbell's death. And although interest in Kokoda increased during 2002 with the celebration of the 60th anniversary of the New Guinea campaign – a campaign far more critical to Australia's defence than Gallipoli – the remote Turkish battlefield continues to hold the interest of Australians, even though none of its participants is alive today.

While most of Australia's First World War allies set aside 11 November to commemorate those who fought and died in that war[9], Australians have chosen to commemorate not the day the killing stopped, but the day on which for them it began – the day widely regarded as the anniversary of their national baptism of fire, the day of the landing at Gallipoli, 25 April 1915. Throughout the country, in cities, towns and suburbs, tens of thousands of Australians turn out to attend commemoration services and to march, or watch others march, in honour of those who fell in all the wars in which Australia has participated. Many Australians take the commemoration one step further and travel more than ten thousand kilometres to Turkey, to be on the spot at Gallipoli where the Anzacs landed, as dawn breaks on Anzac Day.

To enthusiasts of the Anzac legend, it matters not that the campaign was a disastrous defeat – for that was the fault of Winston Churchill and the British generals, not of the raw but willing young men who clambered across the beach at Anzac Cove, scaled Ari Burnu and, against the odds, held onto their tenuous positions on the heights for eight months until the evacuation in December. Our soldiers, so it is said, were tested in the most appalling conditions and not found wanting. Their actions allowed Australia to proudly take its place among the nations of the world.[10]

But Anzac Day has not always enjoyed the popularity it does today. In the 1950s, Anzac Cove was almost deserted on 25 April, while on the 50th anniversary in 1965 the question being asked in the media was whether it would continue to be observed for much longer.[11] In the late 1960s, the anti-Vietnam War movement challenged the assumptions underlying the Anzac tradition, as did the feminist movement in the 1980s: members of the Women Against Rape campaign attempted to join in Anzac Day marches to protest against male violence and rape in war and to criticise the 'male glorification of war' they regarded as inherent in the Anzac legend.[12] When Anzac Day was first celebrated in 1916, a march of Australian soldiers took place in London, while spontaneous unofficial activities occurred in Egypt, where there were concentrations of Australian soldiers. In Australia, a variety of small-scale events was organised by state governments and community groups. These ceremonies were the product of popular enthusiasm, with a local rather than a national focus, a pattern that continued for some years. Yet, from the outset there were high hopes that Anzac Day would become a symbol of national unity.

When the idea of Anzac Day was first promoted, Catholics enthusiastically endorsed it, seeing it as a portent of a new Australia in which they might find acceptance. Catholic newspaper the *Freeman's Journal*, in an editorial subtitled 'The Birth of a Nation', opined effusively:

> We were Australian in name, and we had a flag, but we had been taught by our politicians not to trust ourselves – we were constantly admonished by our daily journals to remember that we were nothing better than a joint in the tail of a great Empire … The Empire Day orators had a better hearing than the faithful souls who clung to Australia Day and gave special honour to their own starry banner.
>
> Anzac Day has changed all that. The Australian flag has been brought from the garret and has been hoisted on a lofty tower in the full sight of its own people. No matter how the war may end – and it can only end one way – we are at last a nation, with one heart, one soul, and one thrilling aspiration … Anzac Day and Australia Day, honoured by hundreds of thousands of deeply-stirred people – what a great change this is![13]

But as the editor was penning those words, news of the Easter

Rising was beginning to reach Australia. Irish–Australian Catholics initially deplored the rising as misguided and a threat to the promised implementation of Irish home rule. However, following the execution of the leaders and the imposition of martial law, they became quite critical of British rule in Ireland, in turn provoking a Protestant backlash that saw sectarianism in Australia, dormant since the outbreak of war, flare up and intensify, particularly during the conscription debates of 1916 and 1917 (see p. 85). By 1920, interdenominational relations in Australia were at flashpoint, even infecting relations between soldiers who a few years before had been serving shoulder to shoulder in the trenches. In November that year, Catholic returned soldiers formed a separate ex-servicemen's organisation because of perceived anti–Catholic bigotry of the Returned Sailors' and Soldiers' Imperial League of Australia (RSSILA).[14]

For years after the war, Catholic ex-servicemen refused to participate in some Anzac Day ceremonies.[15] This was not because they disapproved of remembrance as such, but rather because as Catholics they were forbidden by church teaching of the time from attending interdenominational religious services of any kind, and the main Anzac Day ceremonies included such a service. In the case of Sydney, for instance, this meant that Catholic ex-servicemen would start out marching with their units but would then proceed to St Mary's Cathedral to attend mass while their Protestant comrades continued to Hyde Park or the Domain for the official ceremony there.[16] The withdrawal of Catholic ex-servicemen from such ceremonies reinforced Protestant impressions of Catholic exclusiveness and raised suspicions as to the reasons for their reservation, while Catholics felt excluded because the organisers' insisted on including a combined religious service as part of the commemoration.

Finding an acceptable solution to the problem was not easy. In 1938 Catholic ex-servicemen in Melbourne persuaded the RSSILA to substitute a civic service for the combined religious service. Archbishop Mannix applauded the initiative, but Protestant clergy boycotted the new service, protesting that it was no longer a Christian ceremony. In Sydney, it was not until 1962 that the issue was resolved by a compromise which, though simple, illustrated the absurdity of the stand-off. The ceremony was to include a religious service, but the prayers would be said by leaders of the armed services and the RSSILA, while a religious leader would give the Anzac address, which would be patriotic and not religious.[17]

But in the decade after the war, provincialism rather than sectarianism posed the greatest threat to Anzac Day's becoming a symbol of national unity. Not until 1921 did Prime Minister William Hughes express interest in a national celebration, a suggestion the RSSILA took up and promoted among the states. It was another two years before the states agreed at the 1923 Premiers' Conference that Anzac Day should be Australia's national day of remembrance and that it should be celebrated on 25 April. They also decided that each state should take its own steps to implement the day's observance. In 1919, Western Australia had been the first state to declare Anzac Day a public holiday. In 1923, the Commonwealth government made it a holiday, but only for federal public servants. Not until the end of the decade did all the states pass the necessary legislation to make it a public holiday across the country.

The emerging national focus of Anzac Day was boosted by the inauguration of the Australian War Memorial at Canberra on Anzac Day 1929. However, the project progressed slowly, with the building not being completed and open to the public until 1941. The inauguration ceremony itself sent a mixed message. Prime Minister Stanley Bruce said that the memorial was 'destined to stand as a symbol of Australia's nationhood'. However, Governor-General Lord Stonehaven 'spoke of the spirit of sacrifice displayed by "more than 60 000 Australian soldiers [who] had died to save the institutions and the birthright of all those who inhabited British soil"'.[18] In some people's minds, the link between the nation and the Empire was still strong. The Catholic Church was not represented at the ceremony, a fact that historian Joan Beaumont attributes to the legacy of the divisive conscription debates.[19] However, the absence was more likely to have been due to the order of the ceremony, which included prayers and bible readings by Protestant ministers of religion.[20]

In the meantime, local communities had demonstrated their desire to remember those who had fought and died in the Great War by erecting war memorials. The popularity of the movement to erect memorials is evidenced by the presence in almost every city, town and suburb across the country of a memorial as a 'community's statement of bereavement, pride and thanksgiving'.[21] Although there were divisions in Australian society, those divisions related not so much to remembrance itself, but rather to the manner in which people of different ethno-religious backgrounds might participate in the forms of remembrance. Ken Inglis has written: 'The making of the Great War memorials in Australia was a quest for the right way, materially and spiritually, to honour the soldiers'.[22]

Inglis, whose detailed study of Australian war memorials is itself a monumental work, cites many instances where divisiveness impacted on the movement. For instance, in Boorowa, in western New South Wales, where there was a large Irish Catholic population, it was not until 1933 that a memorial was erected because Protestants and Catholics could not find common cause about its meaning. Eventually, the RSSILA stepped in and built a memorial clock tower.[23] In Moruya, on the New South Wales South Coast, in a district with a high proportion of Irish Catholics, no standalone public memorial was ever erected, though in 1992 a small memorial was built as part of the memorial hall of the Returned and Services League (the name by which the RSSILA is known today). The town had voted two to one against conscription, and the 1917 referendum campaign had witnessed local violence. Private memorials were erected in the state school and in the Protestant churches, but not the Catholic church. Inglis has written: 'Moruya's missing memorial is itself a kind of monument, to wartime division so painful that people unwilling to risk a recurrence tacitly agree not to put the matter on their civic agenda'.[24]

Some towns ended up with two memorials. One example is Wagga Wagga, in south-western New South Wales. Two committees were established, one Protestant and the other Catholic. One committee erected a pillar, the other an arch. The pillar was erected in 1922 and

Wagga Wagga's two war memorials
(Jeff Kildea)

the arch five years later. But by the time of the later ceremony, the rupture had been healed and the chairman of the pillar committee spoke as mayor at the unveiling of the arch.[25]

There were, however, some individuals who disapproved of the remembrance movement itself, and either stayed away from commemorations or remained silent if they were obliged to attend as part of their official duties. An example of the latter is Joseph Lyons, son of Irish-born Catholic parents, who had led the Tasmanian anti-conscription campaign in 1916 and who as premier of his state sat on platforms at the unveiling of monuments but did not speak.[26] Lyons later became prime minister in a non-Labor government during the 1930s. Jack Bailey, Labor MLA for Goulburn and a wartime anti-conscriptionist, absented himself from remembrance ceremonies[27]. But opposition of this kind was not united and motives were mixed: some were pacifists, some socialists, some Irish nationalists, while some simply believed the money would be better spent on those who had returned and were now in need.

Such examples are the exceptions that made the rule that Australians tended to look positively on the sacrifice of the soldiers of the Great War. Partly this was because both Empire loyalists and Australian nationalists could interpret the war to suit their own preconceptions: it was either a wonderful victory for the British Empire or it was an experience out of which the Australian nation emerged. Either way, it was something to be remembered.

Remembrance in Ireland

While the Irish share with Australians a self-irony that often elevates defeat into victory, nationalist Ireland, unlike Australia, does not commemorate Gallipoli, even though its soldiers were slaughtered in their thousands in much the same needless fashion as the Anzacs. In *The Irish at the Front*, an exaltation of the Irish contribution to the war effort published in 1916, Michael MacDonagh made the following prediction (wrongly as it turned out): 'Because of those [Irish] dead Gallipoli will ever be to the Irish race a place of glorious pride and sorrow'.[28]

In fact, prior to the mid-1980s, when Irish historians rediscovered the Great War, the popular understanding in the south was that Ireland had played only a minor part in the war. Most people in the 26 counties were infinitely more acquainted with the rising in Easter week, in which 64 rebels and 254 Irish civilians were killed, than with the four years of the Great War that claimed the lives of over 35 000 Irishmen. The harsh treatment of the leaders of the rising 'created an atmosphere in which the achievements of Irish soldiers in the Great War was [*sic*] never glorified'.[29] Furthermore, in seeking to establish its own sense of nationhood during the postwar years, a nationhood which, unlike Australia's, claims an ancient heritage predating English occupation, 'the Irish Free State had little use for the memory of Irishmen who served in the British army'.[30] As historian Charles Townshend put it:

> Far from being honored as returning heroes of the 'war
> for civilization', they were a distinct embarrassment to the
> governments of the independent Irish state, whose credentials
> rested on resistance to recruitment and, indeed, outright
> rebellion against British rule.[31]

It is this point that so clearly distinguishes the Irish and Australian experiences.

After federation had united the six Australian colonies the people of this self-governing dominion began searching for a sense of nationhood to go with their new country, and they believed they had found it in the blood sacrifice of Gallipoli and the Western Front. Although they had fought in the Empire's cause, they did so for Australia as members of the *Australian* Imperial Force, a force which through the digger legend had developed a sense of identity that was unique and superior. Although Irish soldiers also developed a sense of their superiority as warriors, not unlike that of the Australians, the three Irish divisions did not possess or maintain a distinctive national identity in the same way as did the five Australian divisions. From the start, the 36th (Ulster) Division saw itself as exclusively Protestant and unionist, while the 16th (Irish) Division was 'nationalist and catholic Ireland's most distinctive contribution to the British war effort'.[32] Moreover, both the 16th and the 10th (Irish) Division included British units and individuals. As the war progressed, the Irishness of these divisions declined even further as English and Indian reinforcements replaced Irish casualties. After its near-destruction at Gallipoli, the 10th (Irish) Division spent the rest of the war in the backwater of the eastern theatre, eventually becoming an Indian formation in May 1918, while the 16th (Irish) Division suffered the ignominy of annihilation during the German offensive of March 1918.[33] By contrast, the Australian divisions ended the war on a high note with a series of brilliant victories, the most outstanding being the Battle of Hamel on 4 July 1918, which diverted attention from the symptoms of decline, such as mutinies, that were beginning to manifest themselves due to the lack of adequate reinforcements.

Nevertheless, in Ireland, collective amnesia of the war, which historian FX Martin called 'the Great Oblivion', did not set in immediately.[34] Some public memorials were erected and, although not as ubiquitous as in the north or in Australia, they can be seen in towns such as Bray, Cahir, Drogheda, Longford, Sligo, Tullamore, Whitegate and Cork City, as well as Dublin. But often they were dedicated in a manner that emphasised imperial over national sentiment, thus alienating Irish nationalists, who objected to having the Union Jack waved in their faces.[35]

Between the wars, Armistice Day was commemorated in the south, with masses being offered up for the war dead and poppies being sold openly in Dublin, the money usually going to ex-servicemen's charities. Throughout the 1920s, Armistice Day services in Dublin drew large crowds, including an estimated 70 000 in 1924, though a sour note was struck in 1919, when students from Trinity College, singing 'God Save the King', clashed with students from University College, singing the 'Soldier's Song', a nationalist song soon to become the Irish national anthem. Ordinary citizens often found themselves harassed from both sides by aggressive poppy sellers or poppy-snatchers.

Construction of the National War Memorial at Islandbridge near Phoenix Park, designed by Sir Edwin Lutyens, an Englishman who had designed the cenotaph in London, began in 1931. Even so, the project was not without controversy. The site was deliberately located on the outskirts of the city rather than in a prominent position nearer the city centre. A bill introduced in the Senate in 1927, proposing to erect it at Merrion Square, had been withdrawn in the face of nationalist opposition. The memorial was completed by ex-servicemen in 1938, but the opening ceremony was postponed indefinitely and did not occur until more than half a century later.

In its efforts to create a national identity, the new Irish state enshrined the Easter Rising as the country's defining historical moment. Public acknowledgement of Ireland's participation in 'England's war' was discouraged, with the result that Armistice Day services in Dublin came to be regarded as an outmoded celebration of Ireland's imperial past. From 1933, no government representative attended the ceremonies. Ireland's part in the Great War was no longer seen as its contribution to the defence of small nations as John Redmond had envisaged; rather it was 'a great mistake, a profound betrayal'.[36] Even in 1992, Terence Denman wrote:

> The fate of tens of thousands of patriotic Irishmen who, in response to the granting of home rule, chose to follow a different path to Irish nationhood by volunteering to serve with the British armed forces rarely attracts more than a passing reference, and that often pejorative.[37]

What might have served as a bridge between Ireland and the Empire, even while the fetters on Irish independence were being loosened, was gradually obliterated from public memory. As if to symbolise the dominant mood, after the Second World War the National War Memorial was allowed to fall into a state of dilapidation. In 1986, Jane Leonard described it in these terms:

> Today the Irish National War Memorial is in a sorry state. The memorial records have long since been destroyed by vandals, the fountains are dry, the graffiti seem ineradicable. The most constant visitors are horses grazing and dogs being exercised … In a sense the bleak granite, decapitated columns, broken-down hedges, rotted pergolas, damaged fountains and empty pavilions are aptly evocative of a long-abandoned battlefield. Neglect verging upon desecration symbolises the persistent indifference to the War and its legacy of successive administrations, anxious to guard the people from historical awareness lest they remember too much.[38]

It was as if the Irish war dead had once again found themselves in no-man's-land – this time a political no-man's-land. Stephen Gwynn, a poet and Irish Nationalist MP who had fought in the war, wrote:

> We trod our way to the end;
> We were part of victory:
> And in the face of the world
> Ireland disowned us.[39]

In Northern Ireland 'memory of the war soon became an ideological football kicked around for the sake of political expediency'.[40] The Great War was appropriated as another sacred chapter in unionist mythography, with Ulster Protestants commemorating their war dead as defenders of the Empire, where 'death on the battlefield is commemorated as some sort of ritualistic act reaffirming Ulster Protestants' covenant with the Union and faith in their preordained political destiny'.[41] This manifest destiny was irreparably linked with the sacrifice of the 36th (Ulster) Division on the first day of the Somme, an event whose significance for unionists is akin to that of Gallipoli for Australians, being remembered not as a disastrous British failure but as a glorious chapter in the quest for communal identity.[42]

Memorial services in the north took on an imperial and sectarian tone, with the Somme becoming as emblematic as the Boyne. Protestant churches installed memorials, while Catholic churches in the main did not. Remembrance Day services employed imperialistic ritual and were often organised by the local Orange lodge, deterring attendance by nationalists fearful that their participation might be construed as an act of solidarity with unionism. Catholic ex-servicemen formed the Irish Nationalist Veterans Association separate from the Royal British Legion and organised their own church services. The poppy became synonymous with the Orange lily, seen by nationalists as a supremacist emblem commemorating 'their' sacrifices but not 'ours'. It was also regarded, both north and south, as an imperial icon. The identification of remembrance with Protestantism, imperialism and unionism served to reinforce northern nationalists' indifference by deterring their participation, effectively hijacking Irish memory of the war for the unionist cause.[43]

Of the war years, it is 1916 that holds a special place in the memory of the people of Ireland, much as 1915 does for Australians. But, whereas Australians look back to 1915, with its evocation of Gallipoli and the Anzacs, as a source of unity, remembrance of 1916 for the people of Ireland is a source of division. Two major events of that year in Irish history, the Easter Rising and the Battle of the Somme, have become exclusively iconic for nationalists and unionists, respectively.

As David Fitzpatrick has pointed out in *The Two Irelands 1912–1939*[44], both events share a sense of fighting against overwhelming odds, an acceptance of defeat with dignity, the suffering of appalling losses, and the sense of martyrdom for a just cause. According to Fran Brearton in *The Great War in Irish Poetry*:

> The Battle of the Somme and the Easter Rising functioned, in their different ways, as part of the origin myths of Northern Ireland and the Irish Free State respectively. They became events which were held to encapsulate the inherent qualities of the true Ulster Protestant (proud, reticent, unimaginative) or true Irish Catholic (spiritual, voluble, imaginative), oppositional stereotypes used and abused on both sides. But they have this in common: they simplify interpretations of history, and in doing so leave completely out of the equation those Irish soldiers who fought in the Great War and yet were committed to an independent Ireland, or indeed those who fought for no complex political reason at all – those, in other words, whose actions cannot be easily explained in one or other version of events.[45]

By viewing the Easter Rising as part of the Irish experience of the Great War, rather than as an event independent of it, we can begin to understand how it came to displace the memory of the 10th and 16th Divisions, in much the same way as northern remembrance of the Somme has displaced memory of the 36th Division's other battles and obliterated memory of the 10th and 16th Divisions, in which many northerners fought and died. A similar phenomenon has occurred in Australia, where Gallipoli has displaced other battles in which the AIF fought. How many Australians have heard, for instance, of the Battle of Hamel, arguably the finest Australian military achievement of the war? The Easter Rising, as it came to be imagined with all the overlays of heroic romanticism and blood sacrifice, provided a memory that was both compelling and effective in bolstering a sense of national identity. Thirty-five thousand Irishmen might have died at Gallipoli and in Flanders and Picardy, but as far as most nationalists were concerned they had been simply in the wrong place at the wrong time.

A loyalist mural in Belfast
(Jeff Kildea)

As he prepared to leave Ireland for the front, Tom Kettle, an Irish Nationalist MP who had been in Dublin during Easter week 1916, referred to the rebels and lamented: 'These men will go down in history as heroes and martyrs, and I will go down – if I go down at all – as a bloody British officer'.[46] He was killed a few weeks later during the 16th Division's attack on Ginchy on 9 September. A memorial to him in St Stephen's Green was erected only after controversy, including objections to the words, 'Killed in France'

from the Commissioners of Public Works, who, according to historian Keith Jeffery, feared 'possible political repercussions'.[47] Francis Ledwidge, another nationalist soldier-poet, was recovering from wounds received while fighting with the 10th Division when he penned his famous 'Lament for Thomas McDonagh', one of the executed leaders of the rising. Ledwidge was killed in July 1917 during the Third Battle of Ypres (Passchendaele).

Today, in Northern Ireland, the powerful symbolism of the Easter Rising and the Somme is exploited by the propagandists. Loyalist murals in Belfast depicting scenes of battle during the First World War seek to reinforce tribal identity. Jim Haughey in *The First World War in Irish Poetry* points out that 'Memory of the war has been submerged by the subsequent mythmaking industry of unionism and nationalism ... Surely these divergent memories of the Great War have played their part ... in maintaining current political divisions in Ireland'.[48]

A Remembrance Sunday ceremony was the occasion for one of the worst atrocities of the recent Troubles. Shortly before 11 am on 8 November 1987, as the citizens of Enniskillen in County Fermanagh were assembling at the cenotaph for the remembrance service, a bomb exploded, killing 11 people and injuring 63. The bombing drew immediate condemnation from around the world. Apart from deploring the number killed and injured and the fact that the victims were mostly civilians – men, women and children – many critics of the IRA's tactics on that day, including Irish nationalists, singled out for particular abhorrence the fact that the victims had come to the cenotaph to commemorate their war dead.

The rhetoric of remembrance

But remembrance is not simply about honouring the dead. It forms 'a potent element in the endorsement of a particular political culture or the creation of an alternative one'.[49] Its power derives from the fact that it evokes a sense of duty owed by the survivors to those who died 'for us'. But it is a duty without legal or moral force, imagined rather than real. And in the same way that nations derive their power as imagined communities, it is the imagined duty to the dead which empowers remembrance.[50] While the community is exhorted to further the cause for which 'they' died, so that their sacrifice is not in vain, it is those who control the rituals of remembrance who define the cause for which the remembered were 'faithful until death'. And it is they who are in a position to deploy its power to further the interests of a section of the community.

James Loughlin illustrates the phenomenon with the following extract from the *Belfast News-Letter* published in 1920:

> The war is now, happily, a thing of the past, but we can profit by its lessons, and one of the most important of these is that no community can be deprived of its birthright if it is sufficiently firm in its determination to defend and maintain it. The two minutes of silence was an act of solemn remembrance – remembrance of the men who were faithful until death and recollection of the duty laid upon us, for whom they died, to see that their sacrifice was not in vain.[51]

Because the unionists controlled the rituals of remembrance in Ulster, they were able to use remembrance of the war dead to further the interests of unionism during the critical post war period when various forms of constitutional arrangement were being considered by the British government, including an all-Ireland parliament. The subtext of the above quotation is that these men died to defend and maintain Ulster as an integral part of the United Kingdom, free from the tyranny that would inevitably flow from the grant of Irish self-government to an all-Ireland parliament. In other words, the duty laid upon 'us', the survivors, is to see that their sacrifice was not in vain, by mobilising to defeat home rule. The political quality of remembrance in postwar Ulster can be seen in stark relief when one considers the thousands of Irishmen from that province who enlisted to further the cause of home rule, as John Redmond and Belfast Nationalist MP Joe Devlin had urged them to do. Is there no duty laid upon the survivors to see that their sacrifice was not in vain? And what of those who enlisted without regard to a cause, but did so out of a sense of adventure or for economic reasons. Are they less worthy of remembrance?

Remembrance in Northern Ireland is not so much unique as polarised: its spectrum of public discourse lacking the shades of grey that moderate differences in most other communities. In Australia too, remembrance serves a political purpose, but one that accommodates a broader cross-section of the community.

In Ireland in recent years, however, the rituals and rhetoric of remembrance have been changing. This transformation has coincided with a revolution in Irish historiography in which traditional interpretations have given way to a more complex, varied and inclusive narrative of Ireland's past. The change in attitudes to remembrance has been symbolised in the south by the condition of the National War Memorial, which underwent a major restoration in the 1990s. Attempts have been made in the north to bridge the gap between unionist and nationalist attitudes to remembrance and in the south to dispel ignorance of Ireland's part in the First World War. In the 1990s, a spate of publications, some by journalist-historians whose work is accessible to a mass readership, raised the awareness of the Irish people to the significant contribution which nationalist Ireland made during the war. These included books by Tom Johnstone, Terence Denman, Tom Dooley and Myles Dungan.[52]

In 1996, plans were announced to build a memorial to commemorate Irish war dead in the form of an Irish round tower at Mesen (formerly Messines) in Belgium, where in June 1917 the 16th (Irish) Division and 36th (Ulster) Division had fought alongside each other. As far back as 1921, a monument had been erected to the 36th Division at Thiepval, where the Ulstermen had suffered so terribly on the first day of the Battle of the Somme. Memorials had also been erected in 1923 to the 10th (Irish) Division at Salonika and in 1926 to the 16th (Irish) Division at Guillemont in France and at Wytschaete in Belgium. But the round tower was to be a memorial to *all* Irishmen who had served, regardless of politics or religion. On 11 November 1998, the Irish Peace Park at Mesen was dedicated in a ceremony in which the Irish President Mary McAleese stood beside Queen Elizabeth. Just a few days earlier, President McAleese had been seen wearing a poppy while laying a wreath at London's Cenotaph.[53]

On both sides of the border there have been attempts to find common ground. At Newtownards, a unionist stronghold east of Belfast, the Somme Heritage Museum tells the story not only of the 36th (Ulster) Division, but of the 10th and the 16th Divisions as well. At the 1996 West Belfast Festival, an annual cultural festival organised by the nationalist community, one of the topics discussed was 'on the lessons of 1916 – both the Easter Rising and the Battle of the Somme'. Seamus Breslin, from a nationalist area of Derry, has written numerous articles in the press on the contribution of Derry nationalists in the First World War.[54] However, as yet, he does not participate in the official Remembrance Day ceremony as he considers it totally British in nature; instead, after the service, he and others lay a wreath for 'everybody'.[55]

There is still a long way to go, and, in this highly contested aspect of Irish political and cultural life, mutual ground can be hard to find. In 2002, the Sinn Féin Lord Mayor of Belfast, Alex Maskey, laid a wreath at the cenotaph on the anniversary of the Somme – a gesture that would have been unimaginable a few years before. However, Maskey performed the ritual two hours before the official ceremony. While some unionists accepted the gesture as a step forward, others took it as an insult, arguing he should have attended the main ceremony, to which Maskey's supporters replied that nationalists might consider doing so if the ceremony were made inclusive. At the same time, many diehard republicans remain opposed to honouring Irishmen killed in the Empire's war in the same manner as those who died fighting for Ireland's liberation.[56]

In the south, a number of groups have been formed to promote the memory of the Irish war dead, such as the Royal Dublin Fusiliers Association and the Fame of Tipperary Group. In recent years, war memorials have been erected: at Bandon, County Cork, in 1996; at Leighlinbridge, County Carlow, in 2002; and at Tipperary town in 2005. In October 2006, Taoiseach Bertie Ahern unveiled a new war memorial at Fermoy, County Cork, saying in the course of his speech:

> As a country, we owe it to the many Irish men who fought and died in [the First World War] to remember the part that they played … Those that survived came back to a very changed Ireland that did not value their sacrifice. Those that died in the battlefield came close to being completely forgotten by the following generations. It is right and proper that in more recent times the memory of these men has been resurrected and proper tribute has been paid to them.[57]

Philip Lecane of Dún Laoghaire has been instrumental in having a memorial erected to remember those who perished in October 1918 on the RMS *Leinster* (see p. 151). There are museums with exhibits on the First World War at the Waterford County Museum, Dungarvan, and at the Athy Heritage Centre in County Kildare. In October 2006 the National Museum of Ireland opened an exhibition at the Collins Barracks museum in Dublin, which includes displays on Irish soldiers in the First World War.

Remembrance Day is commemorated each year in St Patrick's Church of Ireland Cathedral, Dublin, under the auspices of the Royal British Legion, though it has not enjoyed popular support, despite the presence in recent years of President McAleese. However, a number of cities and towns have recently revived remembrance services: in 1999, a remembrance ceremony was held at the Drogheda War Memorial for the first time in 30 years[58]; in 2003, the Sinn Féin mayor of Sligo attended the remembrance service at the town's war memorial[59]; in 2005, Cork's Lord Mayor attended that city's wreath-laying ceremony.[60]

In a gesture of inclusiveness, Belvedere College, the Jesuit school in Dublin, unveiled a memorial plaque in 2003, which lists the names of old Belvederians who died in all Irish wars and civil strife. These included those who fought and died on opposing sides in the Easter Rising, the Civil War, as well as those from the two world wars.

At a popular level, Sebastian Barry's *A Long Long Way*, a best-selling novel about the Dublin Fusiliers during the war, is informing a new Irish generation of their long-forgotten past.[61] But perhaps the most significant recent development was the Irish government's commemoration of the 90th anniversary of the Battle of the Somme, which involved a ceremony in Dublin attended by the President and the Taoiseach, as well as ministerial representation at commemorations in France. It was the first time the Irish state has commemorated that battle, so long the exclusive preserve of unionists.[62] As yet there is no official commemoration in the Republic of Ireland of the Gallipoli campaign in which thousands of Irishmen died. Nevertheless, there is an Anzac Day service in Dublin, organised alternately by the Australian embassy and the New Zealand Irish

Association. The ceremony involves a church service and reception. In 2006, the Irish government was represented for the first time by a minister of state, while senior Irish military officers have attended for a number of years, as have members of Irish ex-service associations.

These are but a few examples of the many initiatives currently being undertaken in Ireland as part of the new enterprise of remembrance of the First World War and Ireland's part in it. In her speech at the opening of the Irish Peace Park at Mesen, President McAleese put that enterprise into the broader context of recent Irish history:

> The Peace Park does not invite us to forget the past but to remember it differently. We are asked to look with sorrow and respect on the memory of our countrymen who died with such courage far from the common homeland they loved deeply. Their vitality, genius, youth and commitment was lost to Ireland. In this generation we redeem their memory, acknowledging their sacrifice and the pain of those who loved them. We pray that just as this Park has changed the landscape of Belgium, so too it will help to change the landscape of our memory. These too are Ireland's children as those who fought for her independence are her children, and those who fought against each other in our country's civil war – and of course the dead of recent decades – their children's children – who have not known the peace for which they yearned. To each let us give his or her acknowledged place among our island's cherished dead.[63]

As the Irish increasingly come to recall and recognise the part that Irish men and women serving in the First World War played in the evolution of modern Ireland, the time is surely ripe to revive memories of the links between Australia's soldiers and Ireland – links forged in battle at Gallipoli and nurtured by the hospitality extended to Australian soldiers on leave; links that remain visible today in the Irish landscape in the form of headstones over the graves of Australian servicemen who lie buried in Irish soil and of memorials on which are inscribed the names of the Irish Anzacs who died fighting for their new country.

Appendix 1

Australian soldiers recorded on Irish war memorials

Ballycastle, County Antrim (7)

1619 Private David Rennie, 2nd Battalion, killed in action 9 April 1917, 34 years
70 Sergeant Arthur Bernard, 2nd Battalion, Served
3614 Private Charles Darragh, 47th Battalion, Served
209 Private Alec Gillan-Murphy, MM and bar, 1st Field Ambulance, Served[1]
16997 Private William John McConaghie, 2nd Light Horse Field Amublance, Served
3790 Private William Quigg, 31st Battalion, Served
1334 Private William Boyd White, 18th Battalion, Served

Ballymoney, County Antrim (9)[2]

5999 Lance Corporal John Craig, 14th Battalion, died of wounds 9 August 1918, 28 years
3414 Private Frank McBride, 11th Battalion, killed in action 30 May 1916, 26 years
877 Corporal Andrew Curry McBride, 42nd Battalion, died of wounds 5 April 1918, 28 years
1997a Sergeant Michael McFerran, 10th Field Artillery Brigade, died of wounds 5 April 1918, 25 years
2842 Private Robert Shannon, 4th Battalion, killed in action 6 May 1917, 36 years
3638 Private Edward James Thompson, 60th Battalion, killed in action 19 July 1916, 19 years
1842 Corporal Robert Turner, 54th Battalion, killed in action 25 September 1917, 26 years
2938 Private Alexander Walker, 48th Battalion, killed in action 6 August 1916, 29 years

5444 Sapper John Wallace, 1st Tunnelling Company, killed in action 25 April 1917, 45 years

Ballywalter, County Down (1)

6769 Private Alexander Boyle, 20th Battalion, killed in action 11 August 1918, 29 years

Bray, County Wicklow (4)

379 Private John Cooling, 2nd Battalion, killed in action 6 August 1915, 24 years

4396 Private Harry Donegan, 29th Battalion, killed in action 29 July 1918, 26 years[3]

1500 Private Arthur Cecil Edwards, 34th Battalion, died of wounds 7 June 1917, 26 years

4202 Private Robert McGregor Gow, 7th Battalion, died of wounds 11 October 1917, 30 years

Cahir, County Tipperary (3)[4]

599 Lance Corporal David Clohessy, 9th Battalion, killed in action 20 September 1918, 40 years

Staff Sergeant Thomas Patrick Holloway, Base Depot, died of illness 27 March 1917, 34 years

1693 Private James Lonergan, 48th Battalion, killed in action 12 October 1917, 27 years

Carlow War Memorial, Leighlinbridge, County Carlow (11)

1509A Private David Gibson Alexander, 13th Battalion, died of wounds 15 August 1915, 24 years

2552 Private William Atkinson, 53rd Battalion, killed in action 27 April 1918, 24 years

1635 Private Rupert William Burgess, 47th Battalion, killed in action 7 June 1917, 21 years

116 Private James Byrne, 15th Battalion, killed in action 27 April 1915, 32 years

880 Private Peter Fraser, 24th Battalion, killed in action 19 November 1916, 23 years

5086 Private Charles George Fryer, 49th Battalion, killed in action 5 April 1917, 27 years[5]

2646 Sergeant Edward Meaney, 3rd Battalion, killed in action 4 October 1917, 29 years

6183 Private Thomas Henry O'Donnell, 50th Battalion, killed in action 28 September 1917, 27 years

6542 Private Matthew O'Mara, 15th Battalion, killed in action 15 October 1917, 41 years

1983 Private Michael Ryan, 58th Battalion, killed in action 27 March 1918, 24 years

3775 Private Peter Joseph Ryan, 57th Battalion, died of wounds 1 October 1918, 32 years

Castlebellingham, County Louth (1)

6950 Gunner Thomas Joseph Greenan, 22nd Field Artillery Brigade, killed in action 31 July 1916, 25 years[6]

Coleraine, County Derry (4)[7]

6954 Private John Alfred Rudolph Bell, 49th Battalion, died of wounds 10 April 1918, 25 years[8]

4765A Private William J Campbell, 22nd Battalion, killed in action 10 April 1918, 30 years

686 Sergeant Charles Alfred Jewell, 16th Battalion, died of wounds 10 August 1916, 43 years

877 Corporal Andrew Curry McBride, 42nd Battalion, died of wounds 5 April 1918, 28 years

Derry, County Derry (7)[9]

1063 Private Norman Ross Anderson, 5th Battalion, killed in action 20 September 1917, 24 years

265 Corporal Charles Friell, 2nd Battalion Australian Machine Gun Corps, died of wounds 6 November 1916, 26 years[10]

6328 Corporal Robert Finlay, 23rd Battalion, killed in action 1 September 1918, 23 years

30 Private James Holmes Hazlett, 3rd Field Ambulance, killed in action 9 August 1915, 26 years[11]

1232 Driver Thomas Kelly, 17th Battalion, killed in action 16 April 1917, 42 years

735 Trooper Henry George McNeill, 10th Light Horse Regiment, killed in action 7 August 1915, 19 years

2428 Private John Watkins, 21st Battalion, killed in action 29 July 1916, 39 years

Drogheda, County Louth (3)

4396 Private Harry Donegan, 29th Battalion, killed in action 29 July 1918, 26 years

1805 Private Thomas McCarthy, 27th Battalion, died of wounds 21 October 1915, 28 years

14 Able Seaman Thomas McDonnell, 1st Naval Bridging Train, Died of sickness 27 August 1915, 28 years[12]

Enniskillen, County Fermanagh (8)

1412 Private William Ethelbert Abbott, 2nd Machine Gun Battalion, killed in action 3 October 1918, 35 years

798 Private Andrew George Atkinson, 25th Battalion, died of wounds 27 November 1915, 24 years

Lieutenant Thomas Henry Britton, MC, 34th Battalion, died of wounds 21 June 1918, 28 years

1341 Private John Johnston, 15th Battalion, killed in action 7 May 1915, 28 years

Second Lieutenant Cornwallis Charles Wyndham Maude, 9th Australian Light Horse Regiment, killed in action 13 August 1915, 39 years

652 Sergeant James Arthur Moffitt, 2nd Battalion, died of wounds 3 September 1916, 24 years

1304 Sergeant Thomas Robert Reid, 2nd Field Artillery Brigade, 3 October 1918, 38 years

6379 Private William John Stinson, 50th Battalion, killed in action 28 September 1917, 30 years

Fermoy, County Cork (1) [13]

7971 Private Clair Patrick Couche, 51st Battalion, died of wounds 8 June 1918, 26 years

Kilrea, County Derry (7) [14]

2457 Private Robert Armstrong, 24th Battalion, killed in action 14 August 1916, 29 years

3347 Private Stewart Faulkner, 49th Battalion, killed in action 14 August 1916, 23 years

Lieutenant George Kirkland, 4th Machine Gun Company, died of wounds 13 April 1917, 27 years

1961 Lance Corporal John McCotter, 11th Australian Light Trench Mortar Battery, died of wounds 26 March 1917, 24 years

832 Private Alexander Michael, 34th Battalion, killed in action 13 October 1917, 26 years

165 Sergeant William James Richmond, 34th Battalion, killed in action 28 January 1917, 26 years

63 Private Jack Stewart, 4th Battalion, killed in action 1 May 1915, 25 years

Newcastle, County Down (1)

2nd Lieutenant Everard Digges La Touche, 2nd Battalion, killed in action 6 August 1915, 32 years

Portadown, County Armagh (6) [15]

2345 Private William Allen, 2nd Battalion, killed in action 27 October 1917, 28 years

631 Trooper John Boseman, 1st Light Horse Regiment, killed in action 7 August 1915, 24 years

3549 Private Robert H Cooper, 1st Battalion, died of accidental injuries 28 August 1916, 31 years

3973 Private John Matthews, 26th Battalion, died of wounds 21 June 1916, 23 years

2174 Private Patrick Morgan, 3rd Battalion, killed in action 7 August 1915, 40 years

6107A Private Joseph Weir, 3rd Pioneer Battalion, died of wounds 7 October 1918, 20 years

Portrush, County Antrim (1)

1845 Private Samuel James MacFarlane, 13th Battalion, killed in action 20 August 1915, 21 years

APPENDIX 2

AUSTRALIAN WAR GRAVES OF THE FIRST WORLD WAR IN IRELAND

Republic of Ireland

Dublin

In Dublin two cemeteries contain a total of nine Australian war graves of the First World War: Grangegorman Military Cemetery, Blackhorse Avenue, Phoenix Park, with seven graves; and Mount Jerome Cemetery, Lower Harold's Cross Road, Harold's Cross, with two graves.

Grangegorman Military Cemetery
5365 Private Arthur Andrew Murphy, died 2 June 1918 (Grave RC 1)
3446 Private George Bardon, died 13 October 1918 (Grave RC 2)
4530 Private Michael Ernest Smith, 19th Battalion, died 10 October 1918 (Grave RC 3)
1853A Private Charles Michael Byrne, 46th Battalion, died 4 November 1918 (Grave RC 4)
2872 Private Joseph Gratton, died 10 October 1918 (Grave CE 1)
2880 Private Edwin Johnson Carter, died 10 October 1918 (Grave CE 2)
6784 Private Joseph Thomas Barnes, died 10 October 1918 (Grave CE 3)

To reach the graves, walk past the administration building and work shed into the burial ground and continue along the bitumen path to a roundabout, 20 metres beyond which is a large yew tree. On the left, are the headstones of three New Zealanders, including the Australian-born 14/191A Lance Corporal Peter Freitas of the New Zealand Army Service Corps, who died in the sinking of the *Leinster*. About another ten metres beyond are four Australian graves in a row. Ten metres behind those headstones is a row of three Australian graves, two of which are obscured by a large flax bush.

Mount Jerome Cemetery
Lieutenant George Gilmour Allardyce, died 18 May 1918 (Grave C16 13587)
6864 Private Philip Douglas Davis, died 2 May 1917 (Grave 290 A8)

The two Australian war graves in Mount Jerome Cemetery are located amid civilian graves and are not easy to find. Lieutenant Allardyce is buried in a family plot with a marble headstone in the shape of a scroll, on which his name is inscribed along with the names of other family members, while Private Davis's grave has a distinctive CWGC headstone. Walk from the main gate along the Avenue to the church and then follow the path around to the right of the church, continuing along the East Walk to a roundabout. Turn right at the roundabout and walk along the North Walk to the maintenance/plant room shed. At the far end of the shed and before the trees, take the first walkway on the right, which runs past the grave of Mary Maud. Turn left into the fourth row of graves. The Allardyce grave is the seventh plot in that row. Return to the roundabout and continue along the main path (the West Walk) on the other side of the roundabout from the East Walk. About 20 metres short of where the West Walk veers to the left (at an intersection with another path that runs off to the right), a cluster of three headstones (George Oglesby, Brian Wilkes and Eileen Waddock) stands on the right of the path. The Davis headstone is located about 15–20 metres behind those graves.

County Clare

Bridgetown Catholic Churchyard
1699 Private John Joseph Hickey, 60th Battalion, died 27 January 1918

From Limerick, take the R463 north for 16 kilometres to O'Briensbridge, then turn left onto the R466 and drive 1.5 kilometres to Bridgetown. The spot where Private Hickey is buried is to the east of the church, but his grave is not separately marked and, according to his nephew, Chris Mannix, is indicated by three headstones belonging to Jack (John) Hickey, Mary Hickey and Michael Hickey.

County Cork

Blackrock (St Michael) Church of Ireland Churchyard
252 Private Thomas Paget Sudlow, 11th Battalion, died 12 August 1916

Blackrock is a suburb of Cork City, lying to the east of the city centre on a peninsula that is bounded on the north and east by the River Lee and on the south by the Douglas River. St Michael's Church of Ireland is situated on the eastern side of Church Road about 150 metres south of Blackrock Road. The grave, marked by a headstone made of sandstone in the shape of an open book standing at an angle of 45 degrees, is in the first row of graves on the southern side of the church's transept.

Midleton (The Rosary) Catholic Churchyard
34423 Gunner Ambrose Augustine Haley, 2nd Field Artillery Brigade, died
    25 December 1918

Midleton lies 27 kilometres to the east of Cork City, just off the N25, which is the main route between Cork City and Waterford. To the south of the church towards the school, a large cross stands at the centre of a four-way intersection. Continue south along the footway past the cross. The grave is located on the right about halfway to the end of the footway and is marked by a large Latin cross on a stone bearing Haley's name and the names of members of the O'Sullivan family.

Mitchelstown Catholic Churchyard
4069 Private John Joseph Cahill, 23rd Battalion, died 17 June 1917

Mitchelstown lies 32 kilometres north of Cork City on the N8. Just to the south-west of the church is a large plot with a high sandstone headstone without a cross. Eight members of the Cahill family are listed on it, including John J Cahill.

County Donegal

Upper Fahan (St Mura's) Church of Ireland Churchyard
2426 Able Seaman Frederick Allen Sheedy, HMS *Laurentic*, died 25 January 1917

The church is on the Derry–Buncrana road, 5 kilometres south of Buncrana. Sheedy is buried in a mass grave marked by a memorial in the form of a Celtic High Cross on a red granite plinth. Also buried in that grave is the Australian-born Sailmaker Francis Leonard Royle of the Mercantile Marine Reserve.

County Kerry

Killarney New Cemetery
2875B Private Robert Emmett Kinchington, 3rd Battalion, died 5 February 1919

From Killarney take the Tralee Road (N22) and about 2 kilometres north of Killarney turn right onto the road to Kilcummin. The cemetery is located on the right, about 250 metres from the intersection, just over the bridge. The CWGC headstone is close to the back wall in the centre of the graveyard.

County Limerick

Limerick (King's Island) Military Cemetery
167 Corporal John Taylor Anderson, 3rd Field Company, Royal Australian
Engineers, died 17 December 1915

Located not far from King John's Castle on Kings Island, the cemetery is in Island View Terrace opposite a triangular park in which there is a shrine to the Blessed Virgin Mary. There is no sign and you must pass through an outer gate and a second gate, which might be locked. In the centre of the graveyard is a row of CWGC headstones. Anderson's grave is in the middle of that row.

County Roscommon

Cam Cemetery
191 Private John Michael Doyle, 17th Battalion, died 5 March 1916

The Cam Cemetery is on the R363 about 15 kilometres west of Athlone. It is a large cemetery on ground that rises on the southern side of the road towards the ruin of an old stone church. Doyle's grave, which is marked by a CWGC headstone, is located behind the church ruin.

County Sligo

Kilturra Old Graveyard
2036 Private James Carroll, 57th Battalion, died 20 April 1919

Turn off the R294 just south of Bunnanaddan along a narrow road leading through Doocastle to Charlestown, and travel south for about 300 metres to where there is a road running off to the left. Follow that road for about 1 kilometre to where there is another road off to the left. Follow that road for about 550 metres, keeping to the right at the fork about halfway along.

At the graveyard, pass through the gate and turn to the left. The CWGC headstone is on the top of the slight rise in the ground.

County Tipperary

Powerstown (St John) Catholic Churchyard
1673 Private John Parnell Darmody, 26th Battalion, died 24 August 1916

The church is at Powerstown, 3 kilometres east of Clonmel. The grave is located to the east of the church near the fence, in a plot with three large white headstones marking graves of members of the Darmody family. Private Darmody's grave is marked by the middle headstone.

Glenkeen Old Graveyard
2225 Private John Quinane, 45th Battalion, died 19 June 1918

From Borrisleigh, about 900 metres west of the intersection of the R498 and R501, take the road that comes off to the right, veer left at the fork and drive about 1 kilometre along a narrow lane. The cemetery is marked by a large crucifix at a gate on the road. Pass through the gate and walk about 50 metres to the entrance to the graveyard. Turn right and follow the wall. The Quinane grave is marked by a CWGC headstone located among a number of Quinane and Kinane graves.

Northern Ireland
Belfast

Belfast (Balmoral) Cemetery
3139 Private James Cowan, 48th Battalion, died 24 November 1917

The graveyard is in Stockmans Lane, near the intersection with Lisburn Road. Pass through the gates and walk to the end of the graveyard and turn right. The CWGC headstone is located in a family plot.

Belfast (Belfast City Cemetery)
Lieutenant Reginald Leopold MacLean, 19th Battalion, died 2 November 1918
(Grave J 133)

The cemetery is off the Falls Road, at the corner of Whitechapel Road. Once inside the cemetery, drive or walk to the Cross of Sacrifice, located along the road which runs east–west through the centre of the cemetery. Continue on that centre road in a westerly direction. The grave is located in the second section on the left. At the time of writing, the headstone was missing but due to be replaced.

County Armagh

Lurgan New Cemetery
410 Private James Balfour Leathem, 42nd Battalion, died 26 November 1916
   (Grave F 111)

The graveyard is on Tandragee Road, about 4 kilometres south-west of
Lurgan town centre. The grave is in the north-west quarter of the cemetery.
Private Leathem's grave is also occupied by James and Lily Uprichard. Lily
Uprichard (née Leathem) was Private Leathem's half-sister.

County Derry

Macosquin (St Mary) Church of Ireland Churchyard
2418 Lance Sergeant William Hugh Moore, 4th Australian Pioneers, died 21 October
   1918

The church is located on the south-west of the town, which is about
4 kilometres south-west of Coleraine on the A37. The grave, marked by a
CWGC headstone, is 20 metres east of the church.

County Fermanagh

Boho Church of Ireland Churchyard
1304 Sergeant Thomas Robert Reid, 2nd Field Artillery Brigade, died 3 October
   1918

Boho is situated about 10 kilometres west of Enniskillen. Just after leaving
Enniskillen on the A46, turn left at the B81 and pass by Springfield up
into the hills, following the signs to Boho. The Church of Ireland church
is on the side of the road. The grave is in the south-eastern corner of the
graveyard.

NOTES

INTRODUCTION

1 Estimates of Australians claiming Irish descent vary from 25 to 40 per cent (Tim Pat Coogan, *Wherever Green is Worn: The Story of the Irish Diaspora*, Hutchinson, London, 2001, p. 431).

2 In addition, two Australians serving with the forces of other nations are buried in Ireland, while four serving with the forces of other nations drowned in the seas off Ireland and their bodies were not recovered. See chapter 5.

3 The War of Independence is outside the period of this study, but after the First World War a small number of Australian ex-servicemen joined the Royal Irish Constabulary when the British government was recruiting for what came to be called the 'Black and Tans' and the Auxiliary Division. See, for example, TNA: HO 184/50, Register No. 1, Numbers 1243, 1244; HO 184/51, Register No. 2, Numbers 72314, 72115. In addition, Flying Officer FC Penny of Tasmania served with the RAF in Ireland at this time. For an account of his service, see IWM: 7223 76/16/1, reproduced in William Sheehan, *British Voices from the Irish War of Independence 1918–1921*, Collins Press, Cork, 2005, pp. 58–73.

4 See, for example, EM Andrews, *The Anzac Illusion: Anglo-Australian Relations during World War I*, Cambridge University Press, Cambridge, 1993; Alistair Thomson, *Anzac Memories: Living with the Legend*, Oxford University Press, Oxford, 1995; Graham Seal, *Inventing Anzac: The Digger and National Mythology*, University of Queensland Press (UQP), St Lucia, Qld, 2004.

5 Seal, *Inventing Anzac*, pp. 10–18.

CHAPTER 1
SHARED EXPERIENCE

1 Address by New Zealand Deputy Prime Minister Don McKinnon, ANZAC Day 1996 <http://www.executive.govt.nz/93-96/minister/dpm/dmks250496.htm>. At the 90th anniversary commemoration at Gallipoli, Australian Prime Minister John Howard said, 'They bequeathed Australia a lasting sense of national identity'. <http://www.pm.gov.au/News/speeches/speech1353.html>.

2 See Keith Jeffery, 'Gallipoli and Ireland', a paper delivered at a symposium, 'Ireland, Australia and the Imperial War Effort, 1914–18', held at the National University of Ireland, Galway, 12 March 2004, which discusses how Gallipoli has been remembered (and not remembered) in Ireland over the years. I am grateful to Keith Jeffery for providing me with a copy of his paper.

3 Figures taken from the Australian Department of Veterans Affairs website: <http://www.dva.gov.au/commem/commac/studies/anzacsk/aday4.htm>. For Turkish casualties, see also Kevin Fewster, *A Turkish View of Gallipoli*, Hodja Educational Resources Cooperative, Melbourne, 1985, p. 20.

4 Myles Dungan, *Irish Voices from the Great War*, Irish Academic Press, Dublin, 1995, p. 80. Dungan states there were 28 000 British dead, of whom ten per cent were Irish. Tom Johnstone in *Orange, Green and Khaki: The Story of the Irish Regiments in the Great War, 1914–18*, Gill and Macmillan, Dublin, 1992, p. 152, gives a figure of 3411 Irish dead, not including officers.

5 Peter Stanley, *Quinn's Post, Anzac, Gallipoli*, Allen & Unwin, Sydney, 2005, pp. 142–43 mentions the presence of English and Welsh troops at Quinn's Post, but not the Irish. However, Major General Sir Alexander Godley congratulated Brigadier General RS Vandeleur on the work of the Leinster Regiment there (TNA: WO 79/49, Material for History of the Connaught Rangers). See also TNA: WO 95/4296, War Diary of the 6th Battalion Leinster Regiment.

6 In recent years, the New Zealand-Ireland Association and the Australian Embassy have organised a commemoration ceremony at St Ann's Church in Dawson Street, attended by the Turkish ambassador, senior Irish military personnel and members of Irish ex-service associations. In 2006, a service was held at Grangegorman Military Cemetery. In 2003, the newly opened Outback Bar in Parnell Street held an Anzac tribute that was preceded by the screening of *Gallipoli* and a game of two-up.

7 From the October 1914 edition of *Irish Freedom*, the newspaper of the Irish Republican Brotherhood, quoted in John S Ellis, 'The Degenerate and the Martyr: Nationalist Propaganda and the Contestation of Irishness, 1914–1918', *Éire-Ireland*, Vol. 35, Fall/Winter 2000–2002, pp. 7–33, at p. 18.

8 Denis Winter, *25 April 1915: The Inevitable Tragedy*, UQP, St Lucia, Qld, 1994. Stanley, *Quinn's Post*, p. 16, supports Winter, and Robert Rhodes James, *Gallipoli*, Pimlico, London, 1999, pp. 104–107, after reviewing a number of possible explanations for the change in landing place, expresses the opinion that a last-minute change of orders cannot be lightly dismissed. However, Tim Travers, *Gallipoli 1915*, Tempus, Stroud, 2002, pp. 68–70, supports the traditional view, while Les Carlyon, *Gallipoli*, Macmillan, Sydney, 2001, pp. 142–44, describes as speculation the explanation of a late change of plans. Nigel Steel and Peter Hart, *Defeat at Gallipoli*, Papermac, London, 1995, pp. 53–58, accept that the shift in location was deliberate, but attribute it to the decision of a midshipman commanding one of the steamboats to alter course to avoid enfilade fire from Gaba Tepe.

9 Martin Middlebrook, *Your Country Needs You: From Six to Sixty-Five Divisions*, Pen

& Sword, Barnsley, 2000; Johnstone, *Orange, Green and Khaki*, pp. 1–8. They also included some English battalions to make up the required number.

10 He died of wounds on 29 June 1915 (Richard Doherty and David Truesdale, *Irish Winners of the Victoria Cross*, Four Courts Press, Dublin, 2000, pp. 110–111).

11 Johnstone, *Orange, Green and Khaki*, p. 107.

12 Commander Edward Unwin and four other naval men were awarded Victoria Crosses for their gallantry in restoring the landing bridge.

13 TNA: WO 95/4310, War Diary of the Royal Munster Fusiliers, Report of Captain GW Geddes.

14 TNA: PRO 30/71/5, Capt. Guy Nightingale's diary.

15 On 30 April 1915, when the 29th Division was temporarily reorganised, the 1st Battalion Royal Dublin Fusiliers comprised 1 officer and 374 men and the 1st Battalion Royal Munster Fusiliers comprised 12 officers and 596 men (CEW Bean, *The Official History of Australia in the War of 1914–1918: The Story of Anzac*, UQP, St Lucia, Qld, 1981, Vol. 2, p. 8).

16 TNA: WO 95/4310, War Diaries of the 86th Infantry Brigade of the 29th Division.

17 Myles Dungan, *They Shall Grow Not Old: Irish Soldiers and the Great War*, Four Courts Press, Dublin, 1997, p. 65.

18 TNA: WO 95/4310, War Diary of the Royal Munster Fusiliers, Report of Captain GW Geddes.

19 Sir Ian Hamilton, *Gallipoli Diary*, Edward Arnold, London, 1920, Vol. 1, p. 138.

20 For further information on McCay, see chapter 3.

21 AWM: PR91/015, entry for 7 May 1915.

22 Hamilton, *Gallipoli Diary*, Vol. 1, p. 201.

23 Rhodes James, *Gallipoli*, p. 153.

24 Chris Pugsley, *Gallipoli: The New Zealand Story*, Reed Books, Auckland, 1998, chapter 7, gives an account of the New Zealanders' part in the battle.

25 CF Aspinall-Oglander, *History of the Great War: Military Operations: Gallipoli*, William Heinemann Ltd, London, 1929, Vol. 1, p. 346.

26 Rhodes James, *Gallipoli*, p. 154.

27 Bean, *Official History*, Vol. 2, p. 36.

28 Aspinall-Oglander, *Military Operations: Gallipoli*, Vol. 1, p. 346.

29 Aspinall-Oglander, *Military Operations: Gallipoli*, Vol. 1, p. 347.

30 Although born and educated in England, Godley was of Anglo-Irish stock, from County Leitrim, and regarded himself as an Irishman. His autobiography is entitled *Life of an Irish Soldier*. He was commissioned in the Royal Dublin Fusiliers and, among his many postings, served in the Irish Guards.

31 Recruiting in Ireland had yielded insufficient recruits to form the required 12 infantry battalions and 1 pioneer battalion of the division, so an English unit had been added.

32 TNA: WO 95/4296, War Diary of the 5th Battalion Connaught Rangers, 6 August 1915; Bryan Cooper, *The Tenth (Irish) Division in Gallipoli*, Irish Academic Press, Dublin, 1993 (originally published by Herbert Jenkins, London, 1918), p. 53.

33 AWM: PR91/015, entry for 9 August 1915.

34 TNA: WO 95/4296, War Diary of the 6th Leinster Regiment; Cooper, *Tenth (Irish) Division in Gallipoli*, p. 56; Dungan, *Irish Voices from the Great War*, p. 54.

35 TNA: WO 79/49, Material for History of the Connaught Rangers.

36 CEW Bean, *Anzac to Amiens*, Australian War Memorial, Canberra, 1983, pp. 156–7.

37 It is likely that Malone was killed by a shell fired by the New Zealand artillery. See Pugsley, *Gallipoli: The New Zealand Story*, pp. 300–301.

38 Bean, *Official History*, Vol. 2, p. 699.

39 TNA: WO 95/4296, 6th Royal Irish Rifles file, letter dated 7 February 1931 from Eastwood to the Director of the Historical Section (Military Branch). His helmet would have been a pith helmet as steel helmets were not issued in the British Army until 1916.

40 Bean, *Official History*, Vol. 2, pp. 711–12.

41 Cooper, *Tenth (Irish) Division in Gallipoli*, p. 58.

42 Pugsley, *Gallipoli: The New Zealand Story*, p. 309. But he cites no source. Cf. Bean, *Official History*, Vol. 2, pp. 707–11 and CF Aspinall-Oglander, *Military Operations: Gallipoli*, William Heinemann Ltd, London, 1932, Vol. 2, pp. 304–306. See also TNA: WO 95/4296, War Diary of the 6th Leinster Regiment.

43 Bean, *Official History*, Vol. 2, p. 713. Cyril Falls, *The History of the Royal Irish Rifles*, Gale and Polden, Aldershot, 1925, p. 52.

44 Falls, *Royal Irish Rifles*, p. 52.

45 TNA: WO 95/4296, War Diary of the 6th Leinster Regiment; Cooper, *Tenth (Irish) Division in Gallipoli*, p. 119.

46 TNA: PRO 30/57/63.

47 Quoted in Michael MacDonagh *The Irish at the Front*, Hodder and Stoughton, London, 1916, pp. 9–10. MacDonagh's book is a laudatory account of the Irish in the first two years of the war, with an obvious propaganda purpose to encourage enlistment, as evidenced by John Redmond's introduction: 'Those brave sons in the field need not fear for the honour they have won for their country. Their brothers are coming to them. Ireland's armies will be maintained'.

48 For accounts of the Irish at Suvla Bay, see Philip Orr, *Field of Bones: An Irish Division at Gallipoli*, Lilliput Press, Dublin, 2006; Dungan, *Irish Voices from the Great War*, chapter 3; Johnstone, *Orange, Green and Khaki*, chapter 12; Cooper, *Tenth (Irish) Division in Gallipoli*, chapters 5 and 6.

49 Cooper, *Tenth (Irish) Division in Gallipoli*, p. 102.

50 AWM: PR91/015, entry for 9 August 1915.

51 TNA: WO 79/49, Material for History of the Connaught Rangers, 1915–1916.

52 Bean, *Official History*, Vol. 2, p. 732.

53 TNA: WO 95/4296, War Diary of the 5th Battalion Connaught Rangers.

54 Carlyon, *Gallipoli*, p. 485.

55 TNA: WO 95/4296, War Diary of the 5th Battalion Connaught Rangers.

56 Cooper, *Tenth (Irish) Division in Gallipoli*, p. 131.

57 HFN Jourdain, *Record of the 5th (Service) Battalion, The Connaught Rangers from 19th August 1914 to 17th January 1916*, privately published, 1916, p. 72.

58 TNA: WO 95/4296, letter dated 11 February 1931 to CF Aspinall-Oglander.

59 Hansard, 5 Jan. 1916, 77 HC Deb. 5s, col. 1050.

60 Thomas Hennessey, *Dividing Ireland: World War I and Partition*, Routledge, London, 1998, p. 119.

61 Ben Novick, *Conceiving Revolution: Irish Nationalist Propaganda during the First World War*, Four Courts Press, Dublin, 2001, pp. 17, 56–64, 196.

62 Katharine Tynan, *The Years of the Shadow*, Constable, London, 1919, pp. 178, 186.

CHAPTER 2
CALLED TO ARMS

1 PJ Hally, 'The Easter 1916 Rising in Dublin: The Military Aspects', *The Irish Sword*, Vol. 7, pp. 313–26.

2 The article is republished as 'Inside Trinity Colege' in Roger McHugh (ed.), *Dublin 1916*, Arlington Books, London, 1966, pp. 158–74. The author was later

identified as John Joly, FRS, Professor of Geology (TCDLMD: MS 4874/2). The anthology also includes, at pp. 63–78, the diary of Miss Lilly Stokes, written during the rising and originally published in *Nonplus* in 1916, in which she refers to Anzacs at Trinity College.

3   Warre B Wells and N Marlowe, *A History of the Irish Rebellion of* 1916, Maunsell & Co., Dublin, 1916, p. 154.

4   Max Caulfield, *The Easter Rebellion*, Gill & Macmillan, Dublin, 1995 (2nd edition; original edition 1963), pp. 94–95. See also pp. 156, 215–16 and 250. See also Michael Foy and Brian Barton, *The Easter Rising*, Sutton Publishing, Stroud, Gloucestershire, 2000, p. 180. Many of the standard accounts of the rising do not mention Anzacs or Australians at all. For a list, see Jeff Kildea, 'Called to Arms: Australians in the Irish Easter Rising 1916', *Journal of the Australian War Memorial*, No. 39 (October 2003).

5   Caulfield, *The Easter Rebellion*, p. 250. The episode is probably based on Brennan-Whitmore's own account of the event, which appears in his memoir *Dublin Burning: The Easter Rising from Behind the Barricades*, Gill & Macmillan, Dublin, 1996, pp. 116–18. Another account is in Peter de Rosa's *Rebels: The Irish Rising of 1916*, Ballantine Books, New York, 1992, p. 330.

6   It was originally published in 1916 as the *Sinn Féin Rebellion Handbook: Easter 1916*, with an augmented edition appearing in 1917. It is a comprehensive reference source on many aspects of the rising, providing, inter alia, extracts from official reports and lists of names under various categories. It was republished by Mourne River Press, Dublin, in 1998, with the title *1916 Rebellion Handbook*.

7   *1916 Rebellion Handbook*, pp. 260–61. Some eyewitness accounts suggest more than one Australian was at Trinity College but, written long afterwards, they may not be reliable. James A Glen in 1967 referred to 'half a dozen soldiers (Australians and I think one or two South Africans)' (TCDLMD: MS 4456), while Lieutenant Arthur Aston Luce in 1965 referred to 'one or two Australians' (TCDLMD: MS 4874/2).

8   AWM 1DRL/0197: Diary of Lieutenant John Joseph Chapman of the 9th Battalion, entry for 26 April 1916. For an account of the engagement, see Foy and Barton, *The Easter Rising*, p. 116.

9   Neither Chapman's nor McHugh's service in Dublin is mentioned in the 9th Battalion histories (Norman K. Harvey, *From Anzac to the Hindenburg Line: the History of the 9th Battalion*, AIF, 9th Battalion AIF Association, Brisbane, 1941, and CM Wrench, *Campaigning with the Fighting 9th (In and Out of the Line with the 9BN AIF) 1914–1919*, Boolarong Publications for the 9th Battalion Association, Brisbane, 1985).

10 AWM: PR88/203, pp. 27–33. For the provenance of this source, see Kildea, 'Called to Arms', footnote 29.

11 CEW Bean, *The Official History of Australia in the War of 1914–1918: The Story of Anzac*, UQP, St Lucia, Qld, 1981, Vol. 2, pp. 301–306.

12 TCDLMD: MS 2783, Dublin University Officer Training Corps: Reports on the Defence of the College in 1916 and Correspondence Relating to the Distribution of Silver Cups to the Defenders, Item 19, Report of Joseph Marshall, Chief Steward, to Major GW Harris, Adjt, DUOTC.

13 TCDLMD: MS 2783, item 58, DUOTC Men Attached to Contingent during Rebellion 1916.

14 TCDLMD: MS 4456, Glen, James A: His Account of Trinity College Dublin in Easter Week 1916, pp. 1–2.

15 TCDLMD: MS 4456, p. 2. Glen's reference to 'motor dispatch rider' differs from Joly's and from other accounts that refer to the messengers being on bicycles.

16   *1916 Rebellion Handbook*, p. 276.
17   TCDLMD: MS 11107/1, Fitzgibbon, Gerard, Letters to William Hume Blake 1916–1923, letter dated 10 May 1916, pp. 3-7.
18   TCDLMD: MS 2783, item 20, George Crawford Acting Porter report to Chief Steward 26 April 1916.
19   TCDLMD: MS 2074, Mahaffy, Elsie, 'Ireland in 1916, an Account of the Rising in Dublin, illustrated with printed items, letters and photographs', pp. 11–12.
20   Brian Barton, *From Behind a Closed Door: Secret Court Martial Records of the 1916 Easter Rising*, Blackstaff Press, Belfast, 2002, pp. 316–18.
21   DP Russell, *Sinn Féin and the Irish Rebellion*, Fraser & Jenkinson, Melbourne, 1916, pp. 70–71.
22   Barton, *From Behind a Closed Door*, pp. 316–18.
23   CEW Bean, *The Official History of Australia in the War of 1914–1918: The AIF in France*, Vol. 3, UQP, St Lucia, Qld, 1982, p. 593n.
24   Bean, *Official History*, Vol. 3, p. 802n.
25   The correspondence concerning the presentation of McHugh's cup is in TCDLMD: MS 2783, items 92, 93, 93c, 93d, 93e and 93f. In an article entitled 'A Sideshow in Dublin', in *Wartime*, Issue 14, Winter 2001, pp. 48–49, Georgina Fitzpatrick wrote that the correspondence was written in 1916, that McHugh, 'desperate to escape the hell of the Somme trenches', was seeking to attend the presentation ceremony in the Provost's garden on 5 August 1916, and that the cup was sent to him in France. However, the correspondence is dated 12 months later and McHugh received the cup in England.
26   His account generally coincides with the evidence given by witnesses at Bowen-Colthurst's court martial and at the royal commission set up to inquire into the murders of the three journalists. See *1916 Rebellion Handbook*, pp. 109–114 (court martial), 213–22 (royal commission report), 223–31 (royal commission evidence). For a more detailed examination of the case and a reconciliation of the discrepancies in the various accounts, see Kildea, 'Called to Arms'.
27   *1916 Rebellion Handbook*, p. 227.
28   Mary Louisa and Arthur Hamilton Norway, *The Sinn Fein Rebellion As They Saw It*, Irish Academic Press, Dublin, 1999, p. 54. She was the mother of Nevil Shute, the novelist, who emigrated to Australia in 1945, and who was in Dublin at the time on school holidays. During the rising, he served with an ambulance unit. See Nevil Shute, *Slide Rule: The Autobiography of an Engineer*, W. Morrow, 1954, pp. 22ff.
29   TCDLMD: MS 2074, Mahaffy, Ireland in 1916, pp. 97–98.
30   TNA: WO 374/14934, Bowen-Colthurst, Capt JC 1914–1920, 1966; HO 144/21349, Ireland, Captain John Bowen-Colthurst.
31   See *1916 Rebellion Handbook*, pp. 213–31.
32   Anne Haverty, *Constance Markievicz: Irish Revolutionary*, Pandora, London, 1988; Anne Marreco, *The Rebel Countess: The Life and Times of Constance Markievicz*, Phoenix Press, London, 2000.
33   The list is in a War Office file covering the inquiry into the deaths of the three journalists (TNA: WO 35/67).
34   TNA: PRO: PIN 26/21245, Bowen-Colthurst, John C Capt. RI Rifles.
35   Monk Gibbon, *Inglorious Soldier*, Hutchinson, London, 1968, p. 40.
36   Republished in *Catholic Press*, 13 July 1916, p. 17. See also *Advocate,* 8 July 1916, p. 23.
37   Russell, *Sinn Féin and the Irish Rebellion*, pp. 69–71.
38   'Experiences of a VAD at Dublin Castle during the Rebellion', December 1916, p. 830.

39 *Sydney Morning Herald,* 16 May 1916, p. 5.

40 Bill Gammage, *The Broken Years: Australian Soldiers in the Great War*, Penguin, Ringwood, Victoria, 1975, pp. 75–81.

41 John Ellis, *Eye-deep in Hell: The Western Front 1914–18*, Penguin Books, London, 2002, p. 190.

42 AWM: PR88/203.

43 Members of his family, who still live in North Queensland, were unaware of 'Uncle Mick's' adventure until I told them about it in 2002, during research for this book.

44 Hally, 'Easter 1916 Rising', pp. 313–15.

45 Quoted in Barton, *From Behind a Closed Door*, p. 101.

46 Keith Jeffery, *Ireland and the Great War*, Cambridge University Press, Cambridge, 2000, p. 55. Timothy Bowman, in his study of discipline in the Irish regiments during the war, wrote that his research confirmed the view of historians that 'the Rising had no detrimental impact on Irish troops'. See Timothy Bowman, *Irish Regiments in the Great War: Discipline and Morale*, Manchester University Press, Manchester, 2003, pp. 127–29.

47 The attitude of Dubliners to the rising is complex. See, for example, Jeffery, *Ireland and the Great War*, pp. 44–47 and Ben Novick, *Conceiving Revolution: Irish Nationalist Propaganda during the First World War*, Dublin, Four Courts, 2001, for a discussion of some of the perceptions. Joseph Lee cautions against making any generalisation as to the weight of public opinion, criticising historians who do so for basing their assessment on inadequate evidence. (JJ Lee, *Ireland 1912–1985: Politics and Society*, Cambridge University Press, Cambridge, 1989, pp. 28–36).

48 *Advocate,* 6 May 1916, p. 25.

49 AWM: 1DRL/0474, letter dated 29 April 1916.

50 A copy of the intelligence summary (No. 13) is in AWM: 3DRL/2316 (Monash Papers Series 3, Folder 39). I am grateful to Geoff Barr, a researcher from Canberra, who drew this item to my attention.

51 Quoted in the *Sydney Morning Herald,* 9 May 1916, p. 9. Before the war, both the nationalist Irish Volunteers and the unionist Ulster Volunteer Force had imported weapons from Germany.

52 AWM: 1DRL/0474, letter dated 1 May 1916.

53 I explore this theme in '1916 and All That: The Irish Struggle for Independence and Australian Nationalism' in Peter Gray (ed.), *Passing the Torch*, The Aisling Society of Sydney, Sydney, 2005, pp. 277–301.

54 AWM: 1DRL/0045.

55 From the oath taken by persons enlisting in the AIF in 1914.

CHAPTER 3
THE IRISH ANZACS

1 For details of these and other members of the AIF recorded on Irish public war memorials see Appendix 1.

2 According to the AWM website <http://www.awm.gov.au/atwar/statistics/1885_1973.htm>, 421 809 enlisted in the AIF. This figure includes soldiers and nurses, of whom there were over 2500. As at January 2006, the National Archives of Australia Record Search included in series B2455 First Australian Imperial Force Personnel Dossiers, 1914–1920, the names of 375 867 members of the AIF or 89.10 per cent of the total enlistments. A search of the NAA database using the keyword 'Ireland' returned 5863 entries for the B2455 series. Of these, 83 persons had the surname Ireland, none of whom has Ireland as the place of birth. (Some entries include an Irish county for the place of birth without the word 'Ireland', and there

may be other Irish-born soldiers whose place of birth is not stated in the title, but the number is not knowable without searching each file.) Therefore, I found approximately 5818 persons with a disclosed place of birth in Ireland. Of the 375 867 persons whose names have been entered into the database, 5435 have 'N/A' for place of birth. Deducting that number gives 370 432 as the number of entries that do disclose a place of birth, of which the 5818 Irish-born represent 1.57 per cent. Applying that percentage to the total enlistments of 421 809 gives a figure of 6622. The number of deaths is derived by applying the fatality rate of 14.63 per cent (that is, 61 720 deaths out of 421 809 enlistments), as per the AWM website, to the estimate of 6622 Irish-born enlistments giving 969.

3   The reasons for enlistment are many and varied. See Richard White, 'Motives for Joining Up: Self-sacrifice, Self-interest and Social Class', *Journal of the Australian War Memorial*, Vol. 9, 1986, pp. 3–16; John McQuilton, 'Enlistment for the First World War in Rural Australia: The Case of North-eastern Victoria, 1914–1918', *Journal of the Australian War Memorial*, Issue 33, 2000.

4   AWM Commemorative Roll. This records the names of those Australians who died during or as a result of wars in which Australians served, but who were not serving in the Australian Armed Forces and therefore not eligible for inclusion on the Roll of Honour.

5   I am grateful to Anne Stevens, who is researching a book on the Hughes family and who gave me a copy of the paper she delivered to the Australian Catholic Historical Society at Sydney on 10 September 2006 entitled 'The Hughes Family and the Great War'.

6   Richard Doherty and David Truesdale, *Irish Winners of the Victoria Cross*, Four Courts Press, Dublin, 2000, p. 11.

7   In 1916 'there were over 22,000 Irish-born people living in Sydney and its suburbs and around 150,000 of Irish descent' (John O'Brien, 'The Irish Revolutionary Movement and WM Hughes, 1916–1922' in Anne E O'Brien, *Studies in Irish, British and Australian Relations 1916–1963: Trade, Diplomacy and Politics*, Four Courts Press, Dublin, 2005, p. 35).

8   *Census of the Commonwealth of Australia for 1911*, Vol. 2, p. 135.

9   James Jupp, *The Australian People: An Encyclopedia of the Nation, Its People and Their Origins*, Cambridge University Press, Cambridge, 2001, p. 51.

10   The subject is examined in detail in Jeff Kildea, *Tearing the Fabric: Sectarianism in Australia 1910–1925*, Citadel Books, Sydney, 2002.

11   Oliver MacDonagh, 'The Irish in Australia: A General View' in Oliver MacDonagh and WF Mandle, *Ireland and Irish-Australia: Studies in Cultural and Political History*, Croom Helm, London, 1986, pp. 155–74 at p. 169.

12   David Fitzpatrick, 'Irish Immigrants in Australia: Patterns of Settlement and Paths of Mobility', *Australia* 1888, Bulletin No. 2, 1979, pages 48–54 at p. 49; GM Tobin, 'The Sea-Divided Gael: A Study of the Irish Home Rule Movement in Victoria and New South Wales, 1880–1916', Australian National University, MA thesis, 1969, pp. 15–16.

13   *Census 1911*, Vol. 2, pp. 242–43.

14   These figures are as quoted in the *Catholic Press,* 28 June 1917, pages 26–27. See also the *Freeman's Journal,* 12 July 1917, p. 39.

15   LL Robson 'The Origin and Character of the First AIF, 1914–18: Some Statistical Evidence', *Historical Studies*, Vol. 15, No. 61, 1973, pp. 737–48 at p. 748. Unfortunately, Robson does not indicate the numbers of Irish-born, referring to the geographical entity 'Great Britain', within which, presumably, he includes Ireland.

16   Patrick O'Farrell, *The Irish in Australia*, New South Wales University Press, Sydney, 1993, p. 256.

17 *Catholic Press,* 8 October 1914, p. 26. Although the Home Rule Bill was enacted on 18 September 1914, it was suspended for twelve months or the duration of the war, whichever was the longer. Even so, the Australian Irish generally regarded the home rule issue as resolved in Ireland's favour.

18 John Connor, 'Irish Soldiers in the 1st Australian Imperial Force' in Rebecca Pelan (ed.), *Papers Delivered at the Seventh Irish-Australian Conference July 1993,* Crossing Press, Sydney, 1993. See also John Connor, 'Some Examples of Irish Enlistment in the Australian Imperial Force, 1914', *Irish Sword,* Vol. 21, No. 83, pp. 85–94.

19 I am grateful to Dr Peter Dennis, formerly of the Australian Defence Force Academy (ADFA), for supplying the data for this survey from the AIF Database. Dr John Connor has informed me that his sample of 350 Irish-born was not totally random and might have included a bias towards Catholic Irish, which could account for the difference.

20 Andrews, *The Anzac Illusion: Anglo-Irish Relations during World War I,* Cambridge University Press, Cambridge, 1993, p. 44.

21 Robson, 'Origin and Character of the First AIF', pp. 740–41.

22 The spike in March 1915 among the Irish-born is attributable to a dramatic increase in enlistments in Western Australia, where enlistments in that month were twice the average enlistments for the first six months of 1915. Throughout the war, Western Australia contributed just under 8 per cent of the AIF, but in March 1915 the figure was almost 11.5 per cent. Among the Irish-born sample, enlistments across Australia averaged 18 for the first six months of 1915, while in March there were 26 enlistments, of which the data indicate a place of enlistment for 25. Nine of those 25 (36 per cent) were from Western Australia. The reason why the number of Irish-born in Western Australia rose more sharply than the general population of that state is not apparent. But because the sample is so small, a random event, such as a group of Irish-born mates deciding to enlist, could influence the data. The spike in July 1915 for the AIF is due to an anomaly in Victoria where enlistments were more than six times higher than June and August, with the state contributing almost 60 per cent of the AIF's recruits that month, more than double its average for the war. The traditional explanation for the spike is an intensive recruiting drive in Victoria in July 1915 – See, for example, Ernest Scott, *The Official History of Australia in the War of 1914–1918: Australia During the War,* Vol. 11, UQP, St Lucia, Qld, 1989, p. 292. While acknowledging the positive effect of the recruitment drive, Robson, 'Origin and Character of the First AIF', p. 740, speculates that recruiting officials may have made an upward adjustment of the true figure for that month so as to correct clerical errors that had resulted in Victorian enlistments for previous months being understated. For 1917–18, Irish-born enlistments from the sample are generally at a lower level than the AIF as a whole. However, the numbers in the sample for each month after November 1916 are in single digits and after April 1917 are less than five, so it is difficult to draw hard and fast conclusions.

23 Lionel Wigmore, *They Dared Mightily,* Australian War Memorial, Canberra, 1986.

24 Information on parents is derived from articles on each soldier in the Australian Dictionary of Biography (ADB): Buckley, Vol. 7, p. 475; Carroll, Vol. 7, p. 572; Sadlier, Vol. 11, p. 507.

25 ADB Vol. 11, p. 86.

26 CEW Bean, *The Official History of Australia in the War of 1914–1918: The AIF in France,* Vol. 3, UQP, St Lucia, Qld, 1982, p. 750.

27 Doherty and Truesdale, *Irish Winners of the Victoria Cross,* p. 121. The money proved insufficient and was used to repair the local parish church at Lorrha.

28 AWM Information sheets: Researching Australian military service: First World War nurses. <http://www.awm.gov.au/research/infosheets/nurses/ww1.asp>. The information sheet states that 29 AANS nurses died, but I have only been able to confirm the names of 25. The *British Journal of Nursing* of April 1925 lists only 21 (p. 84).

29 AM Kellett interview (No. 55) of Nurse JVM Kennedy, as quoted in Ruth Rae, 'Jessie Tomlins: An Australian Army Nurse – World War One', unpublished PhD thesis, Department of Clinical Nursing, University of Sydney, 2000.

30 <http://www.unsw.adfa.edu.au/%7Ermallett/Generals/index.html>. In Mallett's list, the birthplaces of two generals are not identified: Brigadier General SM Anderson and Brigadier General CS Davies. The AIF personnel dossier for Anderson gives his place of birth as Melbourne, while Charles Bean states that Davies was born in Dunedin, New Zealand (CEW Bean, *The Official History of Australia in the War of 1914–1918: The AIF in France*, Vol. 5, UQP, St Lucia, Qld, 1983, p. 15). It should be understood that more generals served with the Australian forces than the 68 in Mallett's list. The extras were British generals who were not members of the AIF and accordingly not included (Bean, *Official History*, Vol. 5, p. 14–16).

31 Quoted by Geoffrey Searle in his ADB article on McCay in Vol. 10, pp. 224–27, from which much of the biographical information has been drawn. See also Christopher Wray, *Sir James Whiteside McCay: A Turbulent Life*, Oxford University Press, Melbourne, 2002.

32 HS Gullett, *The Official History of Australia in the War of 1914–1918: The Australian Imperial Force in Sinai and Palestine, 1914–1918*, Vol. 7, UQP, St Lucia, Qld, 1983, p. 379.

33 See Elyne Mitchell's ADB article on Meredith in Vol. 10, pp. 485–86, from which much of the biographical information has been drawn.

34 A number of chaplains received multiple awards. Of these, the Irish-born Father Francis Clune, MC MID, Father William Devine, MC CdG, Father John Fahey, DSO MID, and Father John Joseph Kennedy, DSO MID, received two awards, while Father Thomas Mullins, MC MID (twice), received three awards.

35 NAA B2455 Shannon William Floyd. His service record shows his birthplace as Ireland and that he was a graduate of the Royal University of Ireland, but does not identify his town or county of birth.

36 Myles Dungan, *They Shall Grow Not Old: Irish Soldiers and the Great War*, Four Courts Press, Dublin, 1997, p. 74.

37 Extract from a letter dated 22 June 1915 to a fellow priest in Mellaray, Western Australia, the text of which was published in the *Catholic Press*, 23 October 1915, p. 7. A letter from Father Fahey to his bishop, Archbishop Clune, along similar lines was published in the *Advocate* on 31 July and 7 August 1915 and is reproduced in Michael McKernan, *Padre: Australian Chaplains in Gallipoli and France*, Allen & Unwin, Sydney, 1986, pp. 46–52.

38 Michael McKernan, *Australian Churches at War: Attitudes and Activities of the Major Churches 1914–1918*, Catholic Theological Faculty, Sydney and AWM, Canberra, 1980, p. 50.

39 Article republished in the *Catholic Press*, 6 January 1916, p. 17. The story was repeated in MacDonagh's *The Irish at the Front*, Hodder and Stoughton, London, 1916, pp. 115–16.

40 Dungan, *They Shall Grow Not Old*, p. 75; McKernan, *Padre*, p. 54.

41 *Catholic Press*, 23 October 1915, p. 7.

42 *Catholic Press*, 23 October 1915, p. 7.

43 Extract from a letter dated 13 June 1915 to Archbishop Clune and published in the

Catholic Press, 5 August 1915, p. 18.

44 *Catholic Press,* 23 October 1915, p. 7.

45 Quoted in Tom Johnstone, *The Cross of Anzac: Australian Catholic Service Chaplains,* Church Archivists Press, Virginia, Qld, 2000, p. 51.

46 For an account of Father Fahey's life and chaplaincy, see the ADB entry by Michael McKernan at Vol. 8, p. 456; McKernan, *Australian Churches at War,* pp. 50–51; and Dungan, *They Shall Grow Not Old,* pp. 73–76.

47 AWM28 1/212P2, p. 62.

48 Biographical details are taken from Father Bergin's service record (NAA: B2455 Bergin M) and a biographical note in the AWM written by Father JP Gorman SJ (AWM: 3DRL/7359). For a published account of Father Bergin's service as a chaplain, see Dungan, *They Shall Grow Not Old,* pp. 76–77.

49 Alan Stephens, *The Australian Centenary History of Defence, Vol. 2: The Royal Australian Air Force,* Oxford University Press, Oxford, 2001. Information on the Half Flight is derived from this source and FM Cutlack, *The Official History of Australia in the War of 1914–1918: The Australian Flying Corps,* Vol. 8, UQP, St Lucia, Qld, 1984. More general information on the Mesopotamia campaign and the siege of Kut is drawn from Martin Gilbert, *First World War,* HarperCollins, London, 1995, and Russell Braddon, *The Siege,* Jonathan Cape, London, 1969, while details of the fate of David Curran are drawn from Dungan, *They Shall Grow Not Old,* pp. 145–49.

50 The Germans used both the Dublin rising and the fall of Kut in a crude attempt to persuade Irish troops on the Western Front to defect. See chapter 2, p. 75.

51 Gilbert, *First World War,* p. 247.

52 Cutlack, *The Australian Flying Corps,* p. 26.

53 AWM30 B3.1, Prisoner of war statements – Mesopotamia 1916, Statement of Acting Flight Sergeant JM Sloss.

54 AWM: 1DRL/0428, Australian Red Cross Society (ARCS) Wounded and Missing Enquiry Bureau files, 1914–18 War, 45 Air Mechanic David Curran, Australian Flying Corps.

55 AWM: 1DRL/0428, ARCS Wounded and Missing Enquiry Bureau files, 1914–18 War, 10 Corporal Thomas Montague Newey Soley, Australian Flying Corps. White described his own experiences as a prisoner of the Turks in TW White, *Guests of the Unspeakable: An Australian Airman's Escape from Turkey in the First World War,* Little Hills Press, Sydney, 1990 (originally published 1928).

56 AWM 1DRL/0428, ARCS Prisoner of War Dept 1914–1918, Box 47/7, letter dated 9 July 1917 from Samuel Curran to ARCS; letter dated 30 January 1917 from AIF Headquarters to Samuel Curran; letter dated 12 March 1917 from ARCS to Samuel Curran; letter dated 26 May 1917 from ARCS to Mr Curran.

57 NAA: B2455, Curran D, copy of letter dated 23 April 1917 from Captain Thomas White to Miss Chomley of ARCS. Curran's AIF personnel file, the AWM Roll of Honour and the CWGC record his date of death as 16 June 1917, which is clearly incorrect given the date of White's letter.

58 AWM 1DRL/0428, ARCS Prisoner of War Dept 1914–1918, Box 47/7, letter dated 31 July 1917 from ARCS to Maggie Malone.

59 AWM 1DRL/0428, ARCS Prisoner of War Dept 1914–1918, Box 47/7, letter dated 3 August 1917 from Esther Curran to ARCS.

60 NAA: B2455, Curran D, postcard dated 18 November 1917 from Captain Thomas White to Mrs Curran.

61 NAA: B2455, Curran D, copy of letter dated 26 November 1927 from Imperial War Graves Commission to Australian Graves Section.

62 His personnel file at the NAA is filed under B2455 McBarren M. It was only after

the war when his mother was trying to prove his death to finalise his estate that she disclosed his name as Lomesney (see correspondence in his B2455 file). The surname, more usually spelt Lomasney, is an old Munster family name originally from southern Tipperary. Not much is known of Private Lomesney's personal life. Although he informed the Red Cross that he had a child, he nominated his mother rather than a wife as his next of kin.

63 CEW Bean, *The Official History of Australia in the War of 1914–1918: The AIF in France*, Vol. 4, UQP, St Lucia, Qld, 1982, p. 349.

64 Bean, *Official History*, Vol. 4, pp. 342–43.

65 Bean, *Official History*, Vol. 4, p. 342.

66 PM Regan, 'Neglected Australians: Prisoners of War from the Western Front, 1916 to 1918', MA (Hons) thesis, ADFA, UNSW, 2005, p. 84.

67 AWM: 1DRL/0428 ARCS Wounded and Missing Enquiry Bureau files, 1914–18 War, 6287 Private Michael Lomesney (Michael McBarren) 13th Battalion.

68 AWM: 1DRL/0428, ARCS Prisoner of War Dept 1914–18 War, 6287 McBarren M, 13th Battalion. Correspondence in this and Lomesney's B2455 file indicates that at least five Australians at Schneidemuhl prison camp died of the Spanish flu at about this time.

69 Fred and Elizabeth Brenchley, *Stoker's Submarine*, HarperCollins, Sydney, 2001.

70 The list is far from comprehensive and is a work in progress. Michael Pegum of Dublin is compiling an inventory of Irish war memorials and making the information available on his website at <http://www.irishwarmemorials.ie>. The Imperial War Museum is endeavouring to list the estimated 70000 war memorials throughout the United Kingdom, which includes those in Northern Ireland, but not the Republic of Ireland. The UK National Inventory of War Memorials can be accessed at <http://www.ukniwm.org.uk>, but as yet it does not permit searching by names of soldiers.

71 Robert Thompson, *Ballymoney Heroes 1914–1918*, self-published, Bushmills, 1999. Some of the stories can be read on the Stories of the Fallen website at <http://www.ballymoneyheroes.co.uk/Stories.htm>.

72 In 2005, a CD-ROM version was published by Eneclann Ltd (an enterprise company of Trinity College Dublin), which makes the memorial more accessible to the wider public and allows the records to be searched. The images on the CD-ROM display facsimiles of the original pages complete with Harry Clarke's artwork.

73 Colin Moffett, *Newry's War Dead*, Newry and Mourne District Council, Newry, 2002. The Australians are 643 Corporal John Scott Rowan of the 15th Battalion, who was killed in action at Lone Pine on 8 August 1915; 376 Sergeant Albert Hamilton Livingston of the 4th Battalion, who was killed in action at Pozières on 23 July 1916; and 73 Private John Durkin of the 31st Battalion, who was killed in action at Bellicourt on 29 September 1918.

74 I am grateful to Philip Lecane for providing me with death notices from the *Irish Times*.

75 <http://www.freewebs.com/snake43/index.htm>.

76 <http://homepage.tinet.ie/~tipperaryfame/cahirmem.htm>.

77 Robert Thompson, *Portrush Heroes 1914–1918*, self-published, Bushmills, 2001, pp. 19–20. Signed pages of the Ulster Covenant can be searched by name and viewed on the website of the Public Record Office of Northern Ireland <http://www.proni.gov.uk/ulstercovenant>. Information on Macfarlane's UVF service was provided by his mother in a completed circular sent to the Official Historian, which may be viewed at the Roll of Honour Database page for Private Macfarlane on the AWM website <http://www.awm.gov.au>.

78 It was either for varicose veins or for an ear complaint (Connor, 'Some Examples of Irish Enlistment in the Australian Imperial Force, 1914', p. 90; Dungan, *They Shall Grow Not Old*, p. 104).

79 Information on Digges La Touche is derived from Dungan, *They Shall Grow Not Old*, pp. 103–105; Robert D Linder, *The Long Tragedy: Australian Evangelical Christians and the Great War, 1914–1918*, Openbook Publishers, Adelaide, 2000, pp. 145–46; Connor, 'Some Examples of Irish Enlistment in the Australian Imperial Force, 1914'.

80 AWM28, Honours and Awards (Recommendations: First World War)

CHAPTER 4
SIX-BOB-A-DAY TOURISTS

1 Charles Bean wrote of the origin of the term in *Letters from France*, Cassell, London, 1917: 'The sort of Australian who used to talk about our "tinpot navy" labelled the Australians who rushed at the chance of adventure the moment the recruiting lists were opened "the six bob a day tourists". Well – the "Tourists" made a name for Australia such as no other Australians can ever have the privilege of making'. (p. 224).

2 New Zealanders received five shillings, Americans the equivalent of four shillings and seven pence, while the British Tommy received only one shilling (CEW Bean, *The Official History of Australia in the War of 1914–1918: The Story of Anzac*, Vol. 1, UQP, St Lucia, Qld, 1981, p. 42).

3 Richard White, 'The Soldier as Tourist: The Australian Experience of the Great War', *War & Society*, Vol. 5, No. 1, 1987, pp. 63–77. Robin Gerster and Peter Pierce, who seem to have missed the irony, consider 'six-bob-a-day tourists' to be a disparaging term, 'one of the more ill-conceived idioms of the First World War' (*On the Warpath: An Anthology of Australian Military Travel*, Melbourne University Press, Carlton, 2004).

4 White, 'The Soldier as Tourist', p. 65.

5 AWM: RC02289 (Leaflet call number: 5/5/3)

6 Richard White, 'Europe and the Six-bob-a-day Tourist: the Great War as a Grand Tour, or Getting Civilised', *Australian Studies*, No. 5, April 1991, pp. 122–39 at p. 125.

7 On wartime postcards, see John Laffin, *World War I in Postcards*, Alan Sutton, Gloucester, 1988; James Wieland, "What Do You Think of This Card?" Postcards to and from Australia during the First World War' in Anna Rutherford and James Wieland, *War: Australia's Creative Response*, Allen & Unwin, Sydney, 1997.

8 AWM: PR00142, diary of Lance Corporal Leonard Clyde Bryant.

9 White, 'The Soldier as Tourist', p. 71.

10 White, 'Europe and the Six-Bob-a-Day Tourist', p. 122.

11 See also his 'Sun, Sand and Syphilis: Australian Soldiers and the Orient, Egypt 1914', *Australian Cultural History*, No. 9, 1990.

12 James Wieland, 'There and Back with the Anzacs: More Than Touring', *Journal of the Australian War Memorial*, No. 18, April 1991, pp. 49–56. Wieland described the article as 'a corrective to White's theses', arguing that the soldier's lived experience of the absurd world of the frontline 'involved an experience quite as compelling and more realistic than the notion of the soldier-as-tourist' (p. 49).

13 James Curran, '"Bonjoor Paree!" The First AIF in Paris, 1916–1918', *Journal of Australian Studies*, No. 60, 1999.

14 Peter Cochrane, 'Sergeant Donald E MacDonald and the Soldier-Photographers of World War One', *ozhistorybytes,* Issue 4, 2004 (On-line journal: <http://www.

hyperhistory.org/index.php?option=displaypage&Itemid=681&op=page>).

15 Gerster and Pierce, *On the Warpath*, p. 5.

16 John Ellis, *Eye-deep in Hell: The Western Front 1914–18*, Penguin Books, London, 2002, chapter 10.

17 Suzanne Brugger, *Australians and Egypt, 1914–1919*, Melbourne University Press, Carlton, 1980; Bill Gammage, *The Broken Years: Australian Soldiers in the Great War*, Penguin, Ringwood, 1975, pp. 205–207; Michael McKernan, *The Australian People and the Great War*, Nelson, Melbourne, 1980, chapter 6.

18 McKernan, *The Australian People and the Great War*, p. 116.

19 AWM: PR00561.

20 AWM: PR00142, diary entry for 29 August 1917.

21 From February 1915 to 31 December 1917, a soldier overseas forfeited all pay for any absence from duty on account of venereal disease. In 1918, the forfeit was reduced to 2s 6d. AG Butler, *Official History of the Australian Army Medical Services, 1914–1918: Special Problems and Services*, Vol. 3, Australian War Memorial, Canberra, 1943, p. 152–54.

22 Butler, *Official History of the Australian Army Medical Services*, Vol. 3, p. 180.

23 Butler, *Official History of the Australian Army Medical Services*, Vol. 3, pp. 154, 156. See also Philippa Levine, *Prostitution, Race, and Politics: Policing Venereal Disease in the British Empire*, Routledge, New York, 2003, chapter 6.

24 Butler, *Official History of the Australian Army Medical Services*, Vol. 3, pp. 172, 161.

25 AWM: PR00513, letter dated 25 August 1917 (folder 6). For the meaning of 'chatty', see JM Arthur and WS Ramson, *WH Downing's Digger Dialects*, Oxford University Press, Melbourne, 1990 (original edition 1919), pp. 42–43.

26 AWM: AWM27 366/57. Routine orders mandated that a soldier going on leave to the United Kingdom must be in possession of his rifle but not ammunition (AWM27 366/51). The rifle would have been among the items of equipment the soldier checked in at the kit store at Horseferry Road.

27 In the week ending 9 March 1918, 6828 men of the AIF were in hospital in the United Kingdom, with 1688 being discharged (AWM: 1DRL/0631).

28 Diary of JP Byrne (original held by his granddaughter Jane Keneally).

29 After the AIF moved from the Mediterranean to Europe, about 50000 members of the AIF were in the United Kingdom at any given time (Graham Wilson, 'The Relevance of Miscellany Administrative, Support and Logistic Units of the AIF', *Sabretache*, Vol. 44, March 2003, p. 59). In addition, London played host to thousands more soldiers from Britain and Ireland as well as the other dominions.

30 AWM: Entertainment for the Troops Collection, Souvenirs 4.

31 McKernan, *The Australian People and the Great War*, p. 129.

32 AWM: PR00733, letter dated 19 January 1918.

33 Letter dated 13 December 1917 (original held by Margaret McKenna).

34 AWM: 2DRL/0234, personal account of service based on diary, p. 25.

35 AWM: PR03137, letter dated 17 March 1918.

36 AWM: PR00264, p. 174.

37 AWM: PR00733, letter dated 1 September 1918.

38 AWM: PR00513 (folder 6), letter dated 2 January 1918,.

39 AWM: PR00264, Diary of Colonel JL Beeston, pp. 175–76.

40 AWM: PR90/105, letters dated 21 and 27 December 1916.

41 Letter dated 13 December 1917 (original held by Margaret McKenna).

42 AWM: PR00513 (folder 5), letter dated 2 February 1916 [*sic*: 1917].

43 AWM: PR00513 (folder 6), letter dated 14 December 1917.

44 AWM: PR00513 (folder 8), letters dated 22 February 1919 and 5 March 1919.

45 A jaunting car is a light, one-horse, two-wheeled vehicle with road springs,

used in Ireland for the carriage of passengers. Its seats run longitudinally and the passengers' feet are placed on a footboard outside each wheel.

46 AWM: 2DRL/0234, p. 26.
47 AWM: PR00513 (folder 6), letter dated 22 December 1917.
48 AWM: PR00513 (folder 8), letter dated 5 March 1919. Emphasis in original.
49 AWM: PR03137, letter dated 25 March 1918 to his sister Violet.
50 AWM: PR00733, letter dated 1 September 1918.
51 AWM: 2DRL/0234, p. 26.
52 AWM: PR88/203, p. 27.
53 AWM: PR88/203, p. 27.
54 AWM: PR00733, letter dated 1 September 1918.
55 AWM: PR00561.
56 AWM: PR00142.
57 AWM: PR00187.
58 I am grateful to John Gallagher for information on Corporal Nelson.
59 AWM: PR88/088, letter dated 12 May 1919.
60 AWM: PR88/088, letters dated 20 and 25 May 1919.
61 AWM: 2DRL/0234, p. 53.
62 AWM: PR00733, letter dated 19 January 1918.
63 AWM: PR88/088, letter dated 20 May 1919.
64 AWM: PR83/222.
65 AWM: 2DRL/0234, p. 53.
66 AWM: PR00142, diary entries for 6 and 7 September 1917.
67 AWM: PR88/088, letter dated 20 May 1919.
68 AWM: PR88/088, letter dated 20 May 1919.
69 AWM: PR83/222.
70 AWM: PR00142, diary entry for 3 September 1917.
71 The scheme is referred to in AG Butler, *Official History of the Australian Army Medical Services*, Vol. 3, p. 646, though without reference to its operation in Ireland.
72 AWM: PR00513 (folder 6), letter dated 22 December 1917.
73 AWM: PR00513 (folder 6), letter dated 14 December 1917.
74 CEW Bean, *The Official History of Australia in the War of 1914–1918: The AIF in France*, Vol. 5, UQP, St Lucia, Qld, 1983, pp. 25–33. In fact, the AIF had the highest rate of desertion. See EM Andrews, *The Anzac Illusion: Anglo-Australian Relations during World War I*, Cambridge University Press, Cambridge, 1993, pp. 103–108 and Peter A Pedersen, 'The Australian Experience', a paper given at the 'Unquiet Graves' International Conference on Executions held in Flanders in May 2000, a summary of which appears on the *Shot at Dawn* website at <http://www.shotatdawn.org.uk/page38.html>.
75 Bean, *Official History*, Vol. 5, p. 25.
76 AWM: PR88/203, entry for 1 March 1916. The quoted figure seems too high for March 1916, but Davis's memoir tends to include retrospective details.
77 AWM: AWM10 4332/3/94.
78 AWM: AWM4 War Diaries, Australian Provost Corps, 1918, Police Report for Week Ended 6th July 1918.
79 NAA: A402 W294.
80 Stuart Macintyre, *The Reds*, Allen & Unwin, Sydney, 1998.
81 Geoffrey Barr, *Beyond the Myth: Australian Military Police 1914–1920*, HJ Publications, Canberra, 2005, p. 151.
82 AWM: PR00513 (folder 5), letter dated 2 February 1916 [*sic*: 1917].
83 AWM: PR00513 (folder 6), letter dated 22 December 1917.
84 AWM: PR00594, letter started 17 Mar 1918 at Belfast but completed on return to

West Farm Camp Fovant.
85 AWM: 1DRL/0197.
86 AWM: PR88/203, p. 32.
87 AWM: PR00142.
88 Letter dated 13 December 1917 (original held by Margaret McKenna).
89 AWM: PR00733, letter dated 19 January 1918.
90 AWM: PR83/222.
91 AWM: PR00561.
92 NAA: A471 2829.
93 *Junee Southern Cross,* 7 September 1949.
94 Accounts of this saga are to be found in LL Robson, '"Mad Ireland Made Me": the Arrest and General Court-martial of Captain the Reverend Father TJ O'Donnell, AIF 1919', *Tasmanian Historical Research Association Papers and Proceedings*, Vol. 34, No. 4, 1987, pp. 100–17 and Tom Johnstone, 'The Court Martial of an AIF Catholic Chaplain', *Australian Catholic Historical Society Journal*, Vol. 22, 2001, pp. 71–80. The trial proceedings and Father O'Donnell's service record contain further information. They are held at the NAA as two separate items, both designated as B2455 O'Donnell Thomas Joseph.
95 Quoted in Gammage, *Broken Years*, p. 229.
96 AWM: PR00513 (folder 6), letter dated 22 December 1917.

CHAPTER 5
WATTLE AMONG THE SHAMROCKS

1 After the disaster, the Army Council designated all on board the *Leinster* as having been 'on duty'. See AWM18 9953/1/1, letter dated 5 December 1918 from the Commandant of AIF Headquarters to the Secretary of the Department of Defence.
2 See appendix 2 for the locations of all the Australian war graves in Ireland.
3 See AWM18 9953/1/1, letter dated 1 November 1918 from the Commandant of AIF Headquarters to the Secretary of the Department of Defence.
4 In this section I have relied on Philip Lecane, *Torpedoed!: The RMS Leinster Disaster*, Periscope Publishing, Cornwall, 2005, and Roy Stokes, *Death in the Irish Sea: The Sinking of the RMS Leinster*, Collins Press, Cork, 1998, for background information concerning the sinking of the *Leinster*. I am grateful to Philip Lecane for providing in discussion and email correspondence additional information and insights into this tragic event. Although this chapter concentrates on the *Leinster*'s Australian passengers, it needs to be understood that in the overall context their involvement was slight. My failure to address the broader context, which Philip covers so well, is not intended in any way to diminish the significance of the event or the immeasurable loss suffered by the families of the more than 500 passengers, crew and postal workers killed in the tragedy.
5 The information concerning Sergeant Coleman is taken from statements he made and letters he wrote that are in AWM18 9953/1/1.
6 Lecane, *Torpedoed!*, p. 52.
7 Letter dated 13 January 1919 from Captain Parker to the Secretary of the Wounded and Missing Enquiry Bureau in Australian Red Cross Society (ARCS) Wounded and Missing Enquiry Bureau files, 1914–18 War, AWM: 1DRL/0428, File 0700610 2880 Private Edwin Johnson Carter 29th Battalion (hereafter ARC, Carter file). This file contains documentation relating to all the missing, while their individual files contain copies of documents pertaining to each of them. At the time of the sinking, Parker was a second lieutenant. See Lecane, *Torpedoed!*,

pp. 139–41, which reproduces Parker's official report on the sinking.

8   AWM18 9953/1/1, handwritten statement of Pte Meigan dated 16 October 1918.

9   AWM18 9953/1/1, typed statement of Pte Meigan dated 24 October 1918.

10 Note in ARC, Carter file.

11 CEW Bean, *The Official History of Australia in the War of 1914–1918: The AIF in France*, Vol. 6, UQP, St Lucia, Qld, 1983, p. 357.

12 For an account of that fighting and Lieutenant Laracy's part in it, see Bean, *Official History*, Vol. 6, pp. 411–22.

13 NAA: B2455, Knuckey, Frederick William, Service and Casualty Form Part II B103.

14 Information from *Ruvigney's Roll of Honour*, quoted in Lecane, *Torpedoed!*, p. 238.

15 Letter dated 13 January 1919 from W Bousden of the New Zealand High Commission to Vera Deakin of the ARCS in ARC, Carter file. A typescript of the text of the letter is reproduced in the ARC file 2610108 Nurse Winifred Starling.

16 *The Times,* 31 January 1917, p. 7; 1 February 1917, p. 5.

17 *The Times,* 31 January 1917, p. 7.

18 NAA: A6770, Sheedy FA.

19 I am grateful to Peter Threlfall for this information. It is difficult to understand how these errors on the memorial came to be made, as the report in *The Times* of 3 February 1917, p. 6, lists their names and details correctly.

20 Leigh Bishop, 'Golden Dreams in an Emerald World', *Diver*, June 2003, <http://www.divernet.com/cgi-bin/articles.pl?id=3351&section=&action=display&show=laurentic>.

21 NAA: A6769, Biddlecombe TW; B168 1905/8839 Sub. Lt. TW Biddlecombe appln. for appt. to Aust. Naval Forces.

22 NAA: MP1049/1 1916/098, Cdr Biddlecombe RAN – supersession in command of 'Pioneer'.

23 AWM45 1/77 (Naval Records, 1914–1918), Commander Thomas W Biddlecombe RAN [report on].

24 NAA: MP1049/1 1917/051, Act Commdr TW Biddlecombe Appt to Command HMAS 'Warner' on special service.

25 NAA: MP1049/1 1917/051.

26 Tony Bridgland, *Sea Killers in Disguise: The Story of the Q-ships and Decoy Ships in the First World War*, Leo Cooper, South Yorkshire, 1999; Gordon Campbell, *My Mystery Ships*, Hodder and Stoughton, London, [1928]; E Keble Chatterton, *Q-ships and Their Story*, Sidgwick and Jackson, London, 1922; Patrick Stearns, *Q ships, Commerce Raiders and Convoys*, Spellmount, Staplehurst, 2004.

27 Harold Auten, *Q Boat Adventures: The Exploits of the Famous Mystery Ship by a Q Boat Commander*, Herbert Jenkins Limited, London, 1918, p. 23.

28 AWM: 1DRL/0120, Biddlecombe, Thomas Wyburn (Acting Commander, HMS Warner, RN, b: 1880 d: 1917).

29 NAA: MP1049/1 1917/051.

30 NAA: A6769, Biddlecombe TW. Zeebrugge is also recorded as his place of death in a typed note at the front of the file containing the abovementioned correspondence (AWM: 1DRL/0120) and on the 'Particulars required for the Roll of Honour completed by the Official Historian's staff in 1927' (AWM: AWM131), though not in the Roll of Honour database itself, which gives the location as the west coast of Ireland.

31 <http://www.maritimequest.com/daily_event_archive/2006/jan/13_hms_viknor.htm>.

32 G Mosse, 'Shell-shock as Social Disease', *Journal of Contemporary History*, Vol. 35, No. 1, 2000, pp. 101–108, at p. 101.

33 See AG Butler, *Official History of the Australian Army Medical Services, 1914–1918: Special Problems and Services*, Vol. 3, Australian War Memorial, Canberra, 1943, chapter 2, revealingly entitled 'Moral and Mental Disorders'; Joanna Bourke, 'Shell Shock and Australian Soldiers in the Great War', *Sabretache*, Vol. 36, No. 3 1995, pp. 3–10; Cathryn Corns and John Hughes-Wilson, *Blindfold and Alone: British Military Executions in the Great War*, Cassell, London, 2001, chapters 6, 7, 25 and 26; and Michael Tyquin, *Madness and the Military: Australia's Experience of the Great War*, Australian Military History Publications, Sydney, 2006. The *Journal of Contemporary History* devotes an issue to shell shock in Vol. 35, No. 1, 2000. For a discussion of PTSD during the wars of the 20th century, see Joanna Bourke, *An Intimate History of Killing: Face to Face Killing in Twentieth Century Warfare*, Granta Books, London, 2000, chapter 8.

34 *Limerick Chronicle*, 18 December 1915, p. 1; 21 December 1915, p. 2.

35 The coronial finding is included in Hickey's personnel file: B2455, Hickey JJ, 1699.

36 Letter dated 20 February 1918 from Matron, Birmingham General Hospital, to Vera Deakin (ARCS Wounded and Missing Enquiry Bureau files 1914–18 War, AWM: 1DRL/0428, File 08204131 3139 Private James Cowan 48th Battalion).

37 George Newbury, 'Ex-AIF Members of the Royal Flying Corps', *Sabretache*, Vol. 37, No. 4, 1996, pp. 12–13.

38 AWM 1DRL/0024, Allardyce, George Gilmon [*sic*] (Lieutenant), being typed copies of a diary and letters.

39 According to medical historian Rod Daniels, 'The given name "Spanish" is a twist of history that occurred because Spain, not being involved in the war, had a free press which could report on the ravages of the pandemic in their country. In turn, when Russia reported on the situation in Moscow, Pravda printed "*Ispanka* (The Spanish Lady) is in town" and the name has stuck'. Rod Daniels, 'In Search of an Enigma: The "Spanish Lady"', *Mill Hill Essays*, National Institute for Medical Research, 1988 <http://www.nimr.mrc.ac.uk/MillHillEssays/1998/influenza1918.htm>.

40 Niall Johnson and Juergen Mueller, 'Updating the Accounts: Global Mortality of the 1918–1920 "Spanish" Influenza Pandemic', *Bulletin of the History of Medicine*, Vol. 76, No. 1, 2002, pp. 105–15, p. 115.

41 Martin Gilbert, *First World War*, HarperCollins, London, 1995, p. xv.

42 Geoffrey W Rice and Edwina Palmer, 'Pandemic Influenza in Japan, 1918–19: Mortality Patterns and Official Responses', *Journal of Japanese Studies*, Vol. 19, No. 2, 1993, pp. 389–420, p. 410; John M Barry, *The Great Influenza: The Story of the Deadliest Pandemic in History*, Penguin Books, London, 2005, pp. 375–77.

43 Anthea Hyslop, 'A Question of Identity: JHL Cumpston and Spanish Influenza, 1918–1919', *Australian Cultural History*, Vol. 16, 1997–98, pages 60–76; McQueen, Humphrey, 'The "Spanish" Influenza Pandemic in Australia 1918–1919', in Jill Roe (ed.), *Social Policy in Australia: Some Perspectives 1901–1975*, Cassell, Stanmore, 1976, pages 131–47. Johnson and Mueller, 'Updating the Accounts', p. 114, puts the figure at 14 528.

44 Rice and Palmer, 'Pandemic Influenza in Japan', p. 411. The Australian figure is for its European population. According to Humphrey McQueen, 'Mortality was higher amongst non-Europeans and some Aboriginal tribes were almost entirely wiped out' ('"Spanish" Influenza Pandemic', p. 141). Johnson and Mueller, in 'Updating the Accounts', p. 114, give a mortality rate of 2.7 for Australia.

45 AWM: 2DRL/0234.

46 Barry, *The Great Influenza*, p. 35. The link is such that 'it is customary for statistical bureaux to merge influenza and pneumonia in published vital statistics' (Andrew

Noymer, 'Testing the Influenza-Tuberculosis Selective Mortality Hypothesis in Australia', Population Association of America Extended Abstract, 2005, p. 2. <http://paa2006.princeton.edu/download.aspx?submissionId=61313>). See also K David Patterson and Gerald F Pyle, 'The Geography and Mortality of the 1918 Influenza Pandemic', *Bulletin of the History of Medicine*, Vol. 65, No. 1, 1991, pp. 4–21 at p. 13.

47 CEW Bean, *The Official History of Australia in the War of 1914–1918: The AIF in France*, Vol. 5, UQP, St Lucia, Qld, 1983, pp. 193–211.
48 NAA: B2455, Quinane John, Army Form 3428.
49 Butler, *Official History of the Australian Army Medical Services*, Vol. 3, p. 897 (Table 27). For monthly figures, see <http://www.unsw.adfa.edu.au/~rmallett/AIFCasualties.html>. There is a discussion of malingering in the AIF, including self-inflicted injuries, in Tyquin, *Madness and the Military*, pp. 33–37. See also Dale Blair, *Dinkum Diggers: An Australian Battalion at War*, Melbourne University Press, Melbourne, 2001, pp. 178–83.
50 There is a family website which includes details of Private John Quinane, at <http://www.quinane.id.au/hist.html>.
51 NAA: B2455, Neugent Jack Thomas, letter dated 17 July 1917.
52 *Catholic Press,* 9 September 1915, p. 21.
53 ARCS Wounded and Missing Enquiry Bureau files, 1914–18 War, AWM: 1DRL/0428, File: 1990711 2707A Private Thomas John Kinchington (Jack Thomas Neugent) 49th Battalion.
54 CEW Bean, *The Official History of Australia in the War of 1914–1918: The AIF in France*, Vol. 4, UQP, St Lucia, Qld, 1982, pp. 245, 492–93; Bean, *Official History*, Vol. 6, pp. 54–55, 401, 900.
55 Bean, *Official History*, Vol. 6, pp. 749–50.
56 Letter reproduced in John Laffin, *We Will Remember Them: AIF Epitaphs of World War I*, Kangaroo Press, Sydney, 1995, p. 130.
57 He was active in the returned servicemen's organisations and contributed articles to *Reveille*. He followed his mother's lead in devoting himself to charitable work, visiting ex-servicemen in hospital and through the St Vincent de Paul Society. Also, he became an alderman on Waterloo Municipal Council (AWM: AWM43 A452).
58 AWM131, AWM Roll of Honour Database Circular Information.
59 NAA: A2487 1922/3827.
60 Members of the family in Australia continue to visit Robert's grave. In 2005, while researching this book, I discovered a floral arrangement, a religious statue and a note left there by his nephew, Barrie Kinchington of Sydney.
61 NAA: B2455, Moore WH, attestation form. The Roll of Honour particulars form, completed by his father, gives his birthplace as Ardverness, Macosquin (AWM: AWM131 Moore, WH). However, on the attestation form Lance Sergeant Moore nominated his father as next-of-kin, writing his address as Eastbourne Street, Greenock, Scotland. The address was altered to Macosquin following notification of a change of next-of-kin in August 1917.
62 <http://www.proni.gov.uk/ulstercovenant/index.html>.
63 CM Wrench, *Campaigning with the Fighting 9th (In and Out of the Line with the 9th AIF) 1914–1919*, Boolarong Publications, Brisbane, 1985, p. 82.
64 <http://www.larne.gov.uk/print_heritage_rail.html>; <http://www.bbc.co.uk/northernireland/yourplaceandmine/antrim/A1098713_replies.shtml>.
65 Davis was three months short of his 20th birthday when he died. He is not the youngest Australian serviceman of World War I buried in Ireland. Able Seaman Sheedy was 19 years and 3 months old.

66 Information additional to that in the service records was provided by Christine Armstrong of Lurgan, Co. Armagh, a great niece of James and George Leathem.
67 According to a death notice in the *Lurgan Mail,* 2 December 1916.
68 CEW Bean, *The Official History of Australia in the War of 1914–1918: The Story of Anzac,* Vol. 2, UQP, St Lucia, Qld, 1981, p. 739.
69 The 17th's period as occupiers of Quinn's Post is described in Peter Stanley, *Quinn's Post, Anzac, Gallipoli,* Allen & Unwin, Sydney, 2005, pp. 150ff.
70 NAA: B2455, Doyle JM.
71 Information in addition to that contained in Sergeant Reid's service record at the NAA was obtained from his service record in the South African Constabulary, held at the National Archives and Record Service of South Africa and from his granddaughter Yvonne Bell.
72 Bearing in mind that a private in the AIF was paid 6 shillings a day, or £2.2.0 a week, for a seven-day week, this represents 10 weeks pay.
73 Information supplied by the CWGC.

CHAPTER 6
WHO FEARS TO SPEAK OF '14–'18?

1 The chapter title is a reference to 'Who Fears to Speak of '98?', the popular name of John Kells Ingram's poem 'The Memory of the Dead', written in 1843 to commemorate those who died in the rising of 1798. It became a popular nationalist ballad.
2 RF Foster, *Modern Ireland 1600–1972,* Penguin, 1988, p. 471.
3 Joan Beaumont, *Australia's War 1914–18,* Allen & Unwin, Sydney, 1995, p. xviii.
4 In relation to remembrance of the war generally, see, for example, Paul Fussell, *The Great War and Modern Memory,* Oxford University Press, Oxford, 1977; Jay Winter and Emmanuel Sivan (eds), *War and Remembrance in the Twentieth Century,* Cambridge University Press, Cambridge, 2000; TG Ashplant, Graham Dawson, Michael Roper (eds), *The Politics of War Memory and Commemorations,* Routledge, London, 2000.
5 Beaumont, *Australia's War,* p. xvii.
6 Tony Stephens in the *Sydney Morning Herald,* 17 May 1916. See Jonathon King, *Gallipoli: Our Last Man Standing: The Extraordinary Life of Alec Campbell,* John Wiley & Sons, Brisbane, 2003.
7 Prime Minister's Media Release, 16 May 2002. A copy is available at <http://www.pm.gov.au/news/media_releases/2002/media_release1651.htm>.
8 Audio files of the interviews of David Day on 20 and 24 May 2002 are available at <http://www.abc.net.au/wa/stories/s559359.htm> and <http://www.abc.net.au/worldtoday/ TWTChronoidx_Friday24May2002.htm> (accessed 14 May 2005).
9 This day, variously known as Armistice Day or Remembrance Day, marks the armistice that ended the fighting in 1918. In some places it is observed on the nearest Sunday and referred to as Remembrance Sunday.
10 This desire of Australians to prove themselves was demonstrated by contemporary commentators. For example, in 1915, EC Buley wrote: 'Now they were to prove themselves in the eyes of the world, for they were fighting side by side with men drawn from four continents'. (*Glorious Deeds of Australasians in the Great War,* Andrew Melrose, London, 1915, p. 104).
11 Jenny Macleod, 'The Fall and Rise of Anzac Day: 1965 and 1990 Compared', *War and Society,* Vol. 20, May 2002.
12 Alistair Thomson, *Anzac Memories: Living with the Legend,* Oxford University Press, Oxford, 1995, pp. 189–90, 200.

13 *Freeman's Journal,* 27 April 1916, p. 22.
14 Letter from the General Secretary of the Catholic Returned Soldiers and Sailors Association, published in the *Sydney Morning Herald* and republished in the *Catholic Press,* 22 June 1922, p. 15.
15 Joan Beaumont, 'The Politics of a Divided Society' in Beaumont, *Australia's War,* p. 56.
16 John Luttrell, 'Cardinal Gilroy's Anzac Day Problem', *Journal of the Royal Australian Historical Society,* Vol. 85, June 1999, pp. 1–19.
17 Luttrell, 'Cardinal Gilroy's Anzac Day Problem'.
18 Graham Seal, *Inventing Anzac: the Digger and National Mythology,* UQP, St Lucia, Qld, 2004, p. 119.
19 Beaumont, 'Politics of a Divided Society', p. 56.
20 KS Inglis, 'A Sacred Place: The Making of the Australian War Memorial', *War & Society,* Vol. 3, No. 2, 1985, pp. 99–126 at p. 109.
21 KS Inglis, *Sacred Places: War Memorials in the Australian Landscape,* Melbourne University Press, Carlton, 2001, p. 124.
22 Inglis, *Sacred Places,* p. 128.
23 Inglis, *Sacred Places,* p. 227.
24 Inglis, *Sacred Places,* p. 227–228, 384–385.
25 Inglis, *Sacred Places,* p. 128.
26 Inglis, *Sacred Places,* p. 224.
27 Inglis, *Sacred Places,* p. 226.
28 Hodder and Stoughton, London, 1916, p. 102.
29 Mark McCarthy (ed.), *Ireland's Heritages: Critical Perspectives on Memory and Identity,* Ashgate Publishing Ltd, Aldershot, 2005, p. 22.
30 Jim Haughey, *The First World War in Irish Poetry,* Bucknell University Press, Lewisburg, 2002, p. 37.
31 Charles Townshend, 'Religion, War, and Identity in Ireland', *The Journal of Modern History,* Vol. 76, No. 4, December 2004, pp. 882–902.
32 Terence Denman, *Ireland's Unknown Soldiers: The 16th (Irish) Division in the Great War, 1914–1918,* Irish Academic Press, Dublin, 1992, p. 17.
33 For a history of the changing national identity of the Irish divisions during the war, see Nicholas Perry, 'Nationality in the Irish Infantry Regiments in the First World War', *War & Society,* Vol. 12, No. 1, May 1994, pp. 65-95.
34 FX Martin, '1916 – Myth, Fact and Mystery', *Studia Hibernica,* No. 7, pp. 7–124 at p. 68.
35 Keith Jeffery, *Ireland and the Great War,* Cambridge University Press, Cambridge, 2000, chapter 4, and David Fitzpatrick, 'Commemoration in the Irish Free State: A Chronicle of Embarrassment' in Ian McBride, *History and Memory in Modern Ireland,* Cambridge University Press, Cambridge, 2001, pp. 184–203, discuss forms of remembrance of World War I in the south. See also Ewan Morris, *Our Own Devices: National Symbols and Political Conflict in Twentieth-Century Ireland,* Irish Academic Press, Dublin, 2005, pp. 153–66.
36 DG Boyce, '"That Party Politics Should Divide Our Tents": Nationalism, Unionism and the First World War', in Adrian Gregory and Senia Paseta (eds), *Ireland and the Great War: 'A War to Unite Us All'?,* Manchester University Press, Manchester, 2002, pp. 190–216, p. 202.
37 Denman, *Ireland's Unknown Soldiers,* p. 16
38 Jane Leonard, 'Lest We Forget' in David Fitzpatrick, *Ireland and the First World War,* Trinity History Workshop Publications, Dublin, 1986, p.67.
39 Quoted in Haughey, *The First World War in Irish Poetry,* p. 206.
40 Haughey, *The First World War in Irish Poetry,* p. 37.

41 Haughey, *The First World War in Irish Poetry*, p. 42.
42 See David Officer, "For God and for Ulster": The Ulsterman on the Somme', in McBride, *History and Memory in Modern Ireland*, pp. 160–83.
43 James Loughlin, 'Mobilising the Sacred Dead: Ulster Unionism, the Great War and the Politics of Remembrance' in Gregory and Paseta (eds), *Ireland and the Great War*, pp. 133–54.
44 Oxford University Press, Oxford, 1998, p. 61.
45 Fran Brearton, *The Great War in Irish Poetry: WB Yeats to Michael Longley*, OUP, Oxford, 2003, pp. 37–38.
46 Quoted in Boyce, 'That Party Politics Should Divide Our Tents', p. 201.
47 Jeffery, *Ireland and the Great War*, p. 128.
48 Haughey, *The First World War in Irish Poetry*, p. 61.
49 P Travers, 'Our Fenian Dead: Glasnevin Cemetery and the Genesis of the Republican Funeral' in J Kelly and U MacGearailt (eds), *Dublin and Dubliners* (Dublin 1990), p. 52, quoted in Nuala C Johnson, 'The Spectacle of Memory: Ireland's Remembrance of the Great War, 1919', *Journal of Historical Geography*, Vol. 25, No. 1, 1999, pp. 36–56 at p. 37.
50 See Benedict Anderson, *Imagined Communities: Reflections on the Origin and Spread of Nationalism*, Verso, London, 1991.
51 Loughlin, 'Mobilising the Sacred Dead', pp. 142–43.
52 Tom Johnstone, *Orange, Green and Khaki: The Story of the Irish Regiments in the Great War, 1914–18*, Gill and Macmillan, Dublin, 1992; Denman, *Ireland's Unknown Soldiers*, 1992; Thomas P Dooley, *Irishmen or English Soldiers?: The Times and World of a Southern Irish Man (1876–1916) Enlisting in the British Army During the First World War*, Liverpool University Press, Liverpool, 1995; Myles Dungan, *Irish Voices from the Great War*, Irish Academic Press, Dublin, 1995; Myles Dungan, *They Shall Grow Not Old: Irish Soldiers and the Great War*, Four Courts Press, Dublin, 1997.
53 Haughey, *The First World War in Irish Poetry*, p. 38.
54 See, for example, *Derry Journal*, 12 January 1996, p. 17; 23 January 1998, p. 22; 3 August 2004, p. 17; *Andersontown News*, 30 October 1999, p. 32.
55 Email communications with the author.
56 See reports in the BBC News Archive at <http://news.bbc.co.uk>.
57 <http://www.taoiseach.gov.ie/index.asp?locID=200&docID=2920> (Accessed 29/11/06).
58 <http://community.channel4.com/eve/ubb.x/a/tpc/f/8896096411/m/683608464/p/18>.
59 *Sligo Weekender*, 18 November 2003. <http://archives.tcm.ie/sligoweekender/2003/11/8/story15300.asp>.
60 <http://www.corkcorp.ie/news/archive/2005/remembrance_day.shtml>
61 Faber & Faber, London, 2005. It was shortlisted for the Man Booker Prize for 2005.
62 In 2006, the Taoiseach's website added a page entitled 'Irish Soldiers in the First World War', which includes a reasonably detailed narrative of Ireland's role in the war <http://www.taoiseach.gov.ie/eng/index.asp?docID=2517>.
63 <http://www.president.ie/index.php?section=5&speech=172&lang=eng>

APPENDIX 1
AUSTRALIAN SOLDIERS
RECORDED ON IRISH WAR
MEMORIALS

1 The inscription on the memorial is 'Gillen A Pte'. Records at the NAA and AWM Nominal Roll do not include the name 'A Gillen'. There is a service record for a John Gillen of Greencastle, Ireland, but that is in County Donegal some distance from Ballycastle. There is also a record for Anthony Gillan, but he was born in Australia. There is, however, a record for Alexander Gillan Murphy of Armoy, County Antrim, near Ballycastle, who signed his name on his attestation form as 'Alec Gillan-Murphy'. He survived the war, so the designation 'Served' on the memorial fits and I have assumed him to be the one commemorated.

2 Detailed information on those whose names appear on the Ballymoney War Memorial can be found in Robert Thompson, *Ballymoney Heroes 1914–1918*, self-published, Bushmills, 1999.

3 Inscribed on the memorial as 'Donegan, Henry'.

4 Details of those whose names appear on the Cahir War Memorial can be found at <http://homepage.tinet.ie/~tipperaryfame/cahirmem.htm>.

5 There is doubt as to the accuracy of this entry. The war memorial lists 'Pte. Charles George Fryer Australian Infantry Force 4-5-17 age 27'. The AWM Roll of Honour database, which gives the names of all Australians who died during the First World War, shows only one Charles George Fryer, who was killed on 5 April 1917. The National Archives of Australia Record Search also has only one person of that name. He is shown as killed in action on 5 April 1917, aged 27. His enlistment papers, however, give his place of birth as Rockhampton, Queensland.

6 Although born in Omagh, County Tyrone, Gunner Greenan was educated at Dundalk, ten kilometres north of Castlebellingham.

7 Detailed information on those whose names appear on the Coleraine War Memorial can be found in Robert Thompson, *Coleraine Heroes 1914–1918*, self-published, Bushmills, 2004.

8 Inscribed on the memorial as 'Alfred Bell'.

9 I am grateful to Seamus Breslin for providing details of the Derry War Memorial.

10 Inscribed on the memorial as 'Friel'.

11 Inscribed on the memorial as 'Haslett'.

12 Inscribed on the memorial as 'Pte T McDonnell AIF'.

13 I am grateful to Paudie McGrath for providing information on the Fermoy War Memorial.

14 I am grateful to Robert Thompson for informing me of the Australian names recorded on the Kilrea War Memorial.

15 I am grateful to Robert Thompson for informing me of the Australian names recorded on the Portadown War Memorial.

BIBLIOGRAPHY

Primary sources

Australian War Memorial

AWM4 War Diaries, Australian Provost Corps, 1918

AWM10 4332/3/94, Revisit of APM, AIF depots in UK to Ireland (18 April 1918)

AWM18 9953/1/1, Casualties on 'Leinster' [torpedoed October 1918] (October 1918–March 1919)

AWM18 9955/6/3, Percentage of Men in the AIF Who Are Not Colonial Born (November)

AWM25 273/10, [Disposal of Sick and Wounded] Report by OC Australian and New Zealand Forces in England, regarding strength distribution and training of convalescent troops in UK, 18 November 1915

AWM27 366/51, Regulations regarding leave to the United Kingdom (August 1917)

AWM27 366/57, AIF in Great Britain, official statement – 'Treatment of the Sick and Wounded'

AWM28 Honours and Awards (Recommendations: First World War)

AWM30 B3.1, Prisoner of war statements – Mesopotamia 1916

AWM43 A452 [Official History, 1914–18 War: biographical files and other research files], Kilby T … Kindon FJ

Private Papers Collection

1DRL/0024, Allardyce, George Gilmon (Lieutenant)

1DRL/0045, Letters of Private John Collingwood Angus of the 28th Battalion

1DRL/0120, Biddlecombe, Thomas Wyburn (Acting Commander, HMS Warner, RN, b: 1880, d: 1917)

1DRL/0197, Diary of Lieutenant John Joseph Chapman of the 9th Battalion

1DRL/0428, Australian Red Cross Wounded and Missing Enquiry Bureau files, 1914–18 War

1DRL/0428, Australian Red Cross Prisoner of War Dept files, 1914–1918 War

1DRL/0474, Letters of Sergeant James Joseph Makin of the 21st Battalion and AIF HQ

1DRL/0631, Green, N James (Methodist Chaplain)

2DRL/0234, Schwinghammer, Verdi G (Private, 42nd Battalion)

2DRL/2316, Papers of General Sir John Monash

3DRL/7359, Bergin, Michael H (Chaplain, MC, 51st Battalion)

PR83/222, Tulloch, Robert A (Private)

PR88/088, Stichnoth, Ferdinand August (Lance Sergeant)

PR88/203, Diary of Driver George Edward Davis of the 2nd Australian Motor Transport Company

PR90/105, Scanlon, Daniel Joseph (Sergeant, 49th Battalion)

PR91/015, Diary of Private John Turnbull of the 8th Battalion

PR00142, Bryant, Leonard Clyde, MM (Lance Corporal)

PR00187, Dick, Arthur Morrison, MM (Sergeant)

PR00264, Beeston, Joseph Livesley, CMG MID (Colonel)

PR00513, Carleton, Charles Richard, MC (Lieutenant [Captain])

PR00561, Keating, Noel Michael (Corporal)

PR00594, Murray, Ken (Private) 1899–1937

PR00733, Simpson, Ronald Henry (Private)

PR03137, Heming, Frederick Thomas (Private)

RC02289 [Leaflet call number: 5/5/3]

Entertainment for the Troops Collection, Souvenirs 4

National Archives of Australia

Series

A6769, Service Cards for Navy Officers, 1911–1970

A6770, Service Cards for Petty Officers and Men, 1911–1970

B2455, First Australian Imperial Force Personnel Dossiers, 1914–1920

Items

A402 W294, Baker, Clarence Wilbur – 5th Pioneer Battalion AIF – Deserter, socialist, pacifist, etc

A471 2829, District Court Martial proceedings – 1 August 1919 – Sergeant John H Clark, regimental number 188, AIF

A2487 1922/3827, Request for assistance in expediting settlement on sale of property – Mrs E Kinchington

B168 1905/8839, Sub. Lt. TW Biddlecombe appln. for appt. to Aust. Naval Forces

MP1049/1 1916/098, Cdr Biddlecombe RAN – supersession in command of 'Pioneer'

MP1049/1 1917/051, Act Commdr TW Biddlecombe Appt to Command HMAS 'Warner' on special service

National Library of Ireland

MS 34,236, Notes of Inquiry into the Killing of Francis Sheehy-Skeffington and Two Others

The National Archives (UK)

HO 144/21349, Ireland: Captain John Bowen-Colthurst
HO 184/50, Irish constabulary records: Auxiliary Division Register No. 1
HO 184/51, Irish constabulary records: Auxiliary Division Register No. 2
PIN 26/21245, Bowen-Colthurst, John C Capt. RI Rifles
PRO 30/57/63, Hamilton to Kitchener. Description of battles of Suvla Bay and Sari Bair. Disaster of General Stopford's failure to advance after Suvla landing 1915 Aug. 11–12 GHQ, MEF
PRO 30/71/5, Capt. Guy Nightingale's Diary 1915 Jan–Dec
WO 35/67, Easter Rising 1916–1918
WO 79/49, Material for History of the Connaught Rangers 1915–1916
WO 95/4296, War Diary of the 5th Battalion Connaught Rangers
WO 95/4296, War Diary of the 6th Battalion Leinster Regiment
WO 95/4296, 6th Battalion Royal Irish Rifles file
WO 95/4310, War Diary of the 86th Infantry Brigade of the 29th Division
WO 95/4310, War Diary of the Royal Munster Fusiliers
WO 141/21–23, Shooting of civilians by troops 1916
WO 374/14934, File CO 6663, Capt J Bowen-Colthurst/R Irish Rifles/Complaint
WO 374/14934, Bowen-Colthurst: Capt J C 1914–1920; 1966

National Archives and Record Service of South Africa

South African Constabulary Record of Conduct and Service of Thomas Robert Reid

Trinity College Dublin Library Manuscripts Department

MS 2074, Mahaffy, Elsie: Ireland in 1916, an Account of the Rising in Dublin, illustrated with printed items, letters and photographs
MS 2783, Dublin University Officer Training Corps: Reports on the Defence of the College in 1916 and Correspondence Relating to the Distribution of Silver Cups to the Defenders
MS 4456, Glen, James A: His Account of Trinity College Dublin in Easter Week 1916
MS 4874/2, Luce, Rev Prof A Aston, Lieutenant, 12th Royal Irish Rifles: Recollections of Easter 1916: memoirs of the defence of Trinity College Dublin during the Sinn Féin rebellion, 14 October 1965
MS 11107/1, Fitzgibbon, Gerard: Letters to William Hume Blake 1916–1923

Newspapers and magazines

Advocate
The Age
Andersontown News
British Journal of Nursing

Catholic Press
Derry Journal
Freemans Journal
Junee Southern Cross
Limerick Chronicle
Lurgan Mail
Reveille
Sydney Morning Herald
The Times

Secondary sources

Official histories and publications

Aspinall-Oglander, CF, *History of the Great War: Military Operations: Gallipoli*, Vol. 1, William Heinemann Ltd, London, 1929

—— *History of the Great War: Military Operations: Gallipoli*, Vol. 2, William Heinemann Ltd, London, 1932

Bean, CEW, *The Official History of Australia in the War of 1914–1918: The Story of Anzac*, Vol. 1, University of Queensland Press, St Lucia, Qld, 1981 (first published 1921)

—— *The Official History of Australia in the War of 1914–1918: The Story of Anzac*, Vol. 2, University of Queensland Press, St Lucia, Qld, 1981 (first published 1924)

—— *The Official History of Australia in the War of 1914–1918: The AIF in France*, Vol. 3, University of Queensland Press, St Lucia, Qld, 1982 (first published 1929)

—— *The Official History of Australia in the War of 1914–1918: The AIF in France*, Vol. 4, University of Queensland Press, St Lucia, Qld, 1982 (first published 1933)

—— *The Official History of Australia in the War of 1914–1918: The AIF in France*, Vol. 5, University of Queensland Press, St Lucia, Qld, 1983 (first published 1937)

—— *The Official History of Australia in the War of 1914–1918: The AIF in France*, Vol. 6, University of Queensland Press, St Lucia, Qld, 1983 (first published 1942)

Butler, AG, *Official History of the Australian Army Medical Services, 1914–1918: Special Problems and Services*, Vol. 3, Australian War Memorial, Canberra, 1943

Cutlack, FM, *The Official History of Australia in the War of 1914–1918: The Australian Flying Corps*, Vol. 8, University of Queensland Press, St Lucia, Qld, 1984 (first published 1923)

Gullett, HS, *The Official History of Australia in the War of 1914–1918: The Australian Imperial Force in Sinai and Palestine, 1914–1918*, Vol. 7, University of Queensland Press, St Lucia, Qld, 1983 (first published 1923)

Jose, AW, *The Official History of Australia in the War of 1914–1918: The Royal Australian Navy*, Vol. 9, University of Queensland Press, St Lucia, Qld, 1987 (first published 1928)

Scott, Ernest, *The Official History of Australia in the War of 1914–1918: Australia During the War*, Vol. 11, University of Queensland Press, St Lucia, Qld, 1989 (first published 1936)

Census of the Commonwealth of Australia for 1911
Ireland's Memorial Records, CD-ROM, Eneclann Ltd, Dublin, 2005

Memoirs and accounts by contemporary commentators

Anon., 'Experiences of a VAD at Dublin Castle during the Rebellion', *Blackwood's Magazine*, December 1916, pp. 814–40; republished as 'A Nurse in Dublin Castle' in Roger McHugh (ed.), *Dublin 1916*, Arlington Books, London, 1966

—— 'Inside Trinity College' in Roger McHugh (ed.), *Dublin 1916*, Arlington Books, London, 1966

Arthur, JM and Ramson, WS, *WH Downing's Digger Dialects*, Oxford University Press, Melbourne, 1990 (original edition 1919)

Auten, Harold, *Q boat Adventures: The Exploits of the Famous Mystery Ship by a Q Boat Commander*, Herbert Jenkins Limited, London [1918]

Bean, CEW, *Letters from France*, Cassell, London, 1917

Brennan-Whitmore, WJ, *Dublin Burning: The Easter Rising from Behind the Barricades*, Gill & Macmillan, Dublin, 1996

Buley, EC, *Glorious Deeds of Australasians in the Great War*, Andrew Melrose, London, 1915

Cooper, Bryan, *The Tenth (Irish) Division in Gallipoli*, Irish Academic Press, Dublin, 1993 (originally published by Herbert Jenkins, London, 1918)

Dooley, Thomas P, *Irishmen or English Soldiers?: The Times and World of a Southern Irish Man (1876–1916) Enlisting in the British Army During the First World War*, Liverpool University Press, Liverpool, 1995

Falls, Cyril, *The History of the Royal Irish Rifles*, Gale and Polden, Aldershot, 1925

Gibbon, Monk, *Inglorious Soldier*, Hutchinson, London, 1968

Hamilton, Sir Ian, *Gallipoli Diary*, Edward Arnold, London, 1920

Jourdain, HFN, *Record of the 5th (Service) Battalion, The Connaught Rangers from 19th August 1914 to 17th January 1916*, privately published, 1916

MacDonagh, Michael, *The Irish at the Front*, Hodder and Stoughton, London, 1916

Norway, Mary Louisa, and Norway, Arthur Hamilton, *The Sinn Fein Rebellion As They Saw It*, Irish Academic Press, Dublin, 1999

Russell, DP, *Sinn Féin and the Irish Rebellion*, Fraser & Jenkinson, Melbourne, 1916

Ryan, Desmond, *The Rising: the Complete Story of Easter Week*, 3rd ed., Golden Eagle Books, Dublin, 1957

Shute, Nevil, *Slide Rule: The Autobiography of an Engineer*, W Morrow, 1954

Sinn Féin Rebellion Handbook, Mourne River Press, Dublin, 1998 (Originally published in 1916 by the *Weekly Irish Times* as the *Sinn Féin Rebellion Handbook: Easter 1916*, with an augmented edition appearing in 1917)

Stephens, James, *The Insurrection in Dublin*, 3rd ed., Scepter Books, Chicago, 1965

Stokes, Lilly, 'Easter Week Diary of Miss Lilly Stokes' in Roger McHugh (ed.), *Dublin 1916*, Arlington Books, London, 1966

Taaffe, Michael, *Those Days are Gone Away*, Hutchinson, London, 1959

Tynan, Katharine, *The Years of the Shadow*, London, 1919

Wells, Warre B, and Marlowe, N, *A History of the Irish Rebellion of 1916*, Maunsell & Co., Dublin, 1916

White, TW, *Guests of the Unspeakable: An Australian Airman's Escape from Turkey in the First World War*, Little Hills Press, Sydney, 1990 (originally published 1928)

Books and monographs

Alliston, John, *The African River Wars, 1914–1916*, Garden Island, NSW : The Naval Historical Society of Australia, 1996

Anderson, Benedict, *Imagined Communities: Reflections on the Origin and Spread of Nationalism*, Verso, London, 1991

Andrews, EM, *The Anzac Illusion: Anglo-Australian Relations during World War I*, Cambridge University Press, Cambridge, 1993

Ashplant, TG, Dawson, Graham, and Roper, Michael (eds), *The Politics of War Memory and Commemorations*, Routledge, London, 2000

Barr, Geoffrey, *Beyond the Myth: Australian Military Police 1914–1920*, HJ Publications, Canberra, 2005

Barry, John M, *The Great Influenza: The Story of the Deadliest Pandemic in History*, Penguin Books, London, 2005

Barton, Brian, *From Behind a Closed Door: Secret Court Martial Records of the 1916 Easter Rising*, Blackstaff Press, Belfast, 2002

Bean, CEW, *Anzac to Amiens*, Australian War Memorial, Canberra, 1983

Beaumont, Joan, *Australia's War 1914–18*, Allen & Unwin, Sydney, 1995

Blainey, Geoffrey, *Jumping over the Wheel*, Allen & Unwin, Sydney, 1993

Blair, Dale, *Dinkum Diggers: An Australian Battalion at War*, Melbourne University Press, Melbourne, 2001

Boland, TP, *Thomas Carr: Archbishop of Melbourne*, University of Queensland Press, St Lucia, 1997

Bourke, Joanna, *An Intimate History of Killing: Face to Face Killing in Twentieth Century Warfare*, Granta Books, London, 2000

Bowman, Timothy, *Irish Regiments in the Great War: Discipline and Morale*, Manchester University Press, Manchester, 2003

Braddon, Russell, *The Siege*, Jonathan Cape, London, 1969

Brearton, Fran, *The Great War in Irish Poetry: WB Yeats to Michael Longley*, OUP, Oxford, 2003

Brenchley, Fred and Elizabeth, *Stoker's Submarine*, HarperCollins, Sydney, 2001

Bridgland, Tony, *Sea Killers in Disguise: The Story of the Q-ships and Decoy Ships in the First World War*, Leo Cooper, South Yorkshire, 1999

Brugger, Suzanne, *Australians and Egypt, 1914–1919*, Melbourne University Press, Carlton, 1980

Cain, Frank, *The Origins of Political Surveillance in Australia*, Angus & Robertson, Sydney, 1983

Campbell, Gordon, *My Mystery Ships*, Hodder and Stoughton, London [1928]

Carlyon, Les, *Gallipoli*, Macmillan, Sydney, 2001

Caulfield, Max, *The Easter Rebellion*, Gill & Macmillan, Dublin, 1995 (2nd edition; original edition 1963)

Chatterton, E Keble, *Q-ships and Their Story*, Sidgwick and Jackson, London, 1922

Coffey, Thomas M, *Agony at Easter: The 1916 Irish Uprising*, Penguin, Harmondsworth, 1971

Coogan, Tim Pat, *Michael Collins: A Biography*, Arrow Books, London, 1991

—— *Wherever Green is Worn: The Story of the Irish Diaspora*, Hutchinson, London, 2001

Corns, Cathryn, and Hughes-Wilson, John, *Blindfold and Alone: British Military Executions in the Great War*, Cassell, London, 2001

de Rosa, Peter, *Rebels: The Irish Rising of 1916*, Ballantine Books, New York, 1992

Denman, Terence, *Ireland's Unknown Soldiers: The 16th (Irish) Division in the Great War, 1914–1918*, Irish Academic Press, Dublin, 1992

Doherty, Richard and Truesdale, David, *Irish Winners of the Victoria Cross*, Four Courts Press, Dublin, 2000

Dudley Edwards, Owen, and Pyle, Fergus (eds), *1916: the Easter Rising*, MacGibbon & Kee, London, 1968

Duff, Charles, *Six Days to Shake an Empire*, JM Dent & Sons, London, 1966

Dungan, Myles, *Irish Voices from the Great War*, Irish Academic Press, Dublin, 1995

—— *They Shall Grow Not Old: Irish Soldiers and the Great War*, Four Courts Press, Dublin, 1997

Ellis, John, *Eye-deep in Hell: The Western Front 1914–18*, Penguin Books, London, 2002

Fewster, Kevin, et al., *A Turkish View of Gallipoli*, Hodja Educational Resources Cooperative, Melbourne, 1985

Fitzpatrick, David, *The Two Irelands 1912–1939*, Oxford University Press, Oxford, 1998

Foster, RF, *Modern Ireland 1600–1972*, Penguin, 1988

Foy, Michael, and Barton, Brian, *The Easter Rising*, Sutton Publishing, 1999 (paperback edition 2000)

Fussell, Paul, *The Great War and Modern Memory*, Oxford University Press, Oxford, 1977

Gammage, Bill, *The Broken Years: Australian Soldiers in the Great War*, Penguin, Ringwood, 1975

Gerster, Robin, and Pierce, Peter (eds), *On the Warpath: An Anthology of Australian Military Travel*, Melbourne University Press, Carlton, 2004.

Gilbert, Martin, *First World War*, HarperCollins, London, 1995

Guinn, Paul, *British Strategy and Politics 1914 to 1918*, Clarendon Press, Oxford, 1965

Harvey, Norman K, *From Anzac to the Hindenburg Line: the History of the 9th Battalion, AIF*, 9th Battalion AIF Association, Brisbane, 1941

Haughey, Jim, *The First World War in Irish Poetry*, Bucknell University Press, Lewisburg, 2002

Haverty, Anne, *Constance Markievicz: Irish Revolutionary*, Pandora, London, 1988

Hennessey, Thomas, *Dividing Ireland: World War I and Partition*, Routledge, London, 1998

Inglis, KS, *Sacred Places: War Memorials in the Australian Landscape*, Melbourne University Press, Carlton, 2001

Jeffery, Keith, *Ireland and the Great War*, Cambridge University Press, Cambridge, 2000

Johnson, Nuala C, *Ireland, the Great War and the Geography of Remembrance*, Cambridge University Press, Cambridge, 2003

Johnstone, Tom, *Orange, Green and Khaki: The Story of the Irish Regiments in the Great War, 1914–18*, Gill and Macmillan, Dublin, 1992

—— *The Cross of Anzac: Australian Catholic Service Chaplains*, Church Archivists Press, Virginia, Qld, 2000

Jupp, James, *The Australian People: An Encyclopedia of the Nation, Its People and Their Origins*, Cambridge University Press, Cambridge, 2001

Kiernan, Colm, *Daniel Mannix and Ireland*, Alella Books, Morwell, 1984

Kildea, Jeff, *Tearing the Fabric: Sectarianism in Australia 1910–1925*, Citadel Books, Sydney, 2002

King, Jonathon, *Gallipoli: Our Last Man Standing: The Extraordinary Life of Alec Campbell*, John Wiley & Sons, Brisbane, 2003

Laffin, John, *World War I in Postcards*, Alan Sutton, Gloucester, 1988

—— *We Will Remember Them: AIF Epitaphs of World War I*, Kangaroo Press, Sydney, 1995

Lecane, Philip, *Torpedoed!: The RMS Leinster Disaster*, Periscope Publishing, Cornwall, 2005

Lee, JJ, *Ireland 1912–1985: Politics and Society*, Cambridge University Press, Cambridge, 1989

Levine, Philippa, *Prostitution, Race, and Politics: Policing Venereal Disease in the British Empire*, Routledge, New York, 2003

Linder, Robert D, *The Long Tragedy: Australian Evangelical Christians and the Great War, 1914–1918*, Openbook Publishers, Adelaide, 2000

Macintyre, Stuart, *The Reds*, Allen & Unwin, Sydney, 1998

Marreco, Anne, *The Rebel Countess: The Life and Times of Constance Markievicz*, Phoenix Press, London, 2000

McCarthy, Mark (ed.), *Ireland's Heritages: Critical Perspectives on Memory and Identity*, Ashgate Publishing Ltd, Aldershot, 2005

McKernan, Michael, *Australian Churches at War: Attitudes and Activities of the Major Churches 1914–1918*, Catholic Theological Faculty, Sydney and AWM, Canberra, 1980

—— *The Australian People and the Great War*, Nelson, Melbourne, 1980

—— *Padre: Australian Chaplains in Gallipoli and France*, Allen & Unwin, Sydney, 1986

Middlebrook, Martin, *Your Country Needs You: From Six to Sixty-Five Divisions*, Pen & Sword, Barnsley, 2000

Moffett, Colin, *Newry's War Dead*, Newry and Mourne District Council, Newry, 2002

Morris, Ewan, *Our Own Devices: National Symbols and Political Conflict in Twentieth-Century Ireland*, Irish Academic Press, Dublin, 2005

Novick, Ben, *Conceiving Revolution: Irish Nationalist Propaganda during the First World War*, Four Courts Press, Dublin, 2001

Nowlan, Kevin B (ed.), *The Making of 1916: Studies in the History of the Rising*, Stationery Office, Dublin, 1969

Ó Broin, Léon, *Dublin Castle and the 1916 Rising*, Helicon, Dublin, 1966

Ó Dubhghaill, M, *Insurrection Fires at Eastertide: a Golden Jubilee Anthology of the Easter Rising*, Mercier Press, Cork, 1966

O'Farrell, Patrick, *The Irish in Australia*, New South Wales University Press, Sydney, 1993

Orr, Philip, *Field of Bones: An Irish Division at Gallipoli*, Lilliput Press, Dublin, 2006

Pugsley, Chris, *Gallipoli: The New Zealand Story*, Reed Books, Auckland, 1998

Rhodes James, Robert, *Gallipoli*, Pimlico, London, 1999

Rutherford, Anna, and Wieland, James, *War: Australia's Creative Response*, Allen & Unwin, Sydney, 1997

Scates, Bruce, *Return to Gallipoli: Walking the Battlefields of the Great War*, Cambridge University Press, Cambridge, 2006

Seal, Graham, *Inventing Anzac: The Digger and National Mythology*, University of Queensland Press, St Lucia, Qld, 2004

Sheehan, William, *British Voices from the Irish War of Independence 1918–1921*, Collins Press, Cork, 2005

Stanley, Peter, *Quinn's Post, Anzac, Gallipoli*, Allen & Unwin, Sydney, 2005

Stearns, Patrick, *Q ships, Commerce Raiders and Convoys*, Spellmount, Staplehurst, 2004

Steel, Nigel, and Hart, Peter, *Defeat at Gallipoli*, Papermac, London, 1995

Stephens, Alan, *The Australian Centenary History of Defence, Vol. 2: The Royal Australian Air Force*, Oxford University Press, Oxford, 2001

Stevens, David, *The Australian Centenary History of Defence, Vol. 3: The Royal Australian Navy*, Oxford University Press, Oxford, 2001

Sternbeck, Michael, *The Catholic Church in Singleton: An Historical Look at its People and Progress*, privately published, 1981

Stokes, Roy, *Death in the Irish Sea: The Sinking of the RMS Leinster*, Collins Press, Cork, 1998

Thompson, Robert, *Ballymoney Heroes 1914–1918*, self-published, Bushmills, 1999

—— *Portrush Heroes 1914–1918*, self-published, Bushmills, 2001

—— *Coleraine Heroes 1914–1918*, self-published, Bushmills, 2004

Thomson, Alistair, *Anzac Memories: Living with the Legend*, Oxford University Press, Oxford, 1995

Travers, Tim, *Gallipoli 1915*, Tempus, Stroud, 2002

Tyquin, Michael, *Madness and the Military: Australia's Experience of the Great War*, Australian Military History Publications, Sydney, 2006

Vamplew, Wray (ed.), *Australians: Historical Statistics*, Fairfax, Syme & Weldon Associates, Sydney, 1987

Wigmore, Lionel, *They Dared Mightily*, Australian War Memorial, Canberra, 1986

Winter, Denis, *25 April 1915: The Inevitable Tragedy*, University of Queensland Press, St Lucia, Qld, 1994

Winter, Jay, and Sivan, Emmanuel (eds), *War and Remembrance in the Twentieth Century*, Cambridge University Press, Cambridge, 2000

Wray, Christopher, *Sir James Whiteside McCay: A Turbulent Life*, Oxford University Press, Melbourne, 2002

Wrench, CM, *Campaigning with the Fighting 9th (In and Out of the Line with the 9BN AIF) 1914–1919*, Boolarong Publications for 9th Battalions Association, Brisbane, 1985

Articles, papers and theses

Anon., 'Blockading German East Africa, 1915–16', *Semaphore*, Issue 12, July 2005

Bartlett, Thomas, and Jeffery, Keith, 'An Irish military tradition?' in Thomas Bartlett and Keith Jeffery, *A Military History of Ireland*, Cambridge University Press, Cambridge, 1996

Beaumont, Joan, 'The Politics of a Divided Society' in Joan Beaumont, *Australia's War 1914–18*, Allen & Unwin, Sydney, 1995

Bourke, Joanna, 'Shell Shock and Australian Soldiers in the Great War', *Sabretache*, Vol. 36, No. 3, 1995, pp. 3–10

Boyce, DG, '"That Party Politics Should Divide Our Tents": Nationalism, Unionism and the First World War', in Adrian Gregory and Senia Paseta (eds), *Ireland and the Great War: 'A War to Unite Us All'?*, Manchester University Press, Manchester, 2002

Cochrane, Peter, 'Sergeant Donald E MacDonald and the Soldier-Photographers of World War One', *ozhistorybytes*, Issue 4, 2004, online journal: <http://www.hyperhistory.org/index.php?option=displaypage&Itemid=681&op=page>.

Connor, John, 'Irish Soldiers in the 1st Australian Imperial Force' in Rebecca Pelan (ed.), *Papers Delivered at the Seventh Irish-Australian Conference July 1993*, Crossing Press, Sydney, 1993

—— 'Some Examples of Irish Enlistment in the Australian Imperial Force, 1914', *Irish Sword*, Vol. 21, No. 83, pp. 85–94

Curran, James, '"Bonjoor Paree!" the First AIF in Paris, 1916–1918', *Journal of*

Australian Studies, No. 60, 1999

Ellis, John S, 'The Degenerate and the Martyr: Nationalist Propaganda and the Contestation of Irishness, 1914–1918', *Éire-Ireland*, Volume 35, Fall/Winter 2000–2002

Fitzpatrick, David, 'Commemoration in the Irish Free State: A Chronicle of Embarrassment' in Ian McBride, *History and Memory in Modern Ireland*, Cambridge University Press, Cambridge, 2001, pp. 184–203

—— 'Irish Immigrants in Australia: Patterns of Settlement and Paths of Mobility', *Australia 1888*, Bulletin No. 2, 1979

Fitzpatrick, Georgina, 'A Sideshow in Dublin' *Wartime*, Issue 14, Winter 2001, pp. 48–49

French, Maurice, 'The Ambiguity of Empire Day in New South Wales 1901–1921: Imperial Consensus or National Division', *Australian Journal of Politics and History*, Vol. 24, No. 1, 1978, pp. 61–74

Hally, PJ, 'The Easter 1916 Rising in Dublin: The Military Aspects', *The Irish Sword*, Volume 7, pp. 312–26

Hyslop, Anthea, 'A Question of Identity: JHL Cumpston and Spanish Influenza, 1918–1919', *Australian Cultural History*, Vol. 16, 1997–98, pp. 60–76

Jeffery, Keith, 'Gallipoli and Ireland', a paper delivered at a symposium 'Ireland, Australia and the Imperial War Effort, 1914–18' held at the National University of Ireland, Galway, 12 March 2004

Johnson, Niall, and Mueller, Juergen, 'Updating the Accounts: Global Mortality of the 1918–1920 "Spanish" Influenza Pandemic', *Bulletin of the History of Medicine*, Vol. 76, No. 1, 2002, pp. 105–15

Johnson, Nuala C, 'The Spectacle of Memory: Ireland's Remembrance of the Great War, 1919', *Journal of Historical Geography*, Vol. 25, No. 1, 1999, pp. 36–56

Johnstone, Tom, 'The Court Martial of an AIF Catholic Chaplain', *Australian Catholic Historical Society Journal*, Vol. 22, 2001, pp. 71–80

Kildea, Jeff, '1916 and All That: The Irish Struggle for Independence and Australian Nationalism' in Peter Gray (ed.), *Passing the Torch*, The Aisling Society of Sydney, Sydney, 2005

—— 'Called to Arms: Australians in the Irish Easter Rising 1916', *Journal of the Australian War Memorial*, No. 39 (October 2003).

Loughlin, James, 'Mobilising the Sacred Dead: Ulster Unionism, the Great War and the Politics of Remembrance' in Adrian Gregory and Senia Paseta (eds), *Ireland and the Great War: 'A War to Unite Us All'?*, Manchester University Press, Manchester, 2002, pp. 133–54

Leonard, Jane, 'Lest We Forget' in David Fitzpatrick, *Ireland and the First World War*, Trinity History Workshop Publications, Dublin, 1986

Luttrell, John, 'Cardinal Gilroy's Anzac Day Problem', *Journal of the Royal Australian Historical Society*, Vol. 85, June 1999, pp. 1–19

MacDonagh, Oliver, 'The Irish in Australia: A General View', in Oliver MacDonagh and WF Mandle, *Ireland and Irish-Australia: Studies in Cultural and Political History*, Croom Helm, London, 1986

Macleod, Jenny, 'The Fall and Rise of Anzac Day: 1965 and 1990 Compared', *War and Society*, Vol. 20, May 2002

McQueen, Humphrey, 'The "Spanish" Influenza Pandemic in Australia 1918–1919', in Jill Roe (ed.), *Social Policy in Australia: Some Perspectives 1901–1975*, Cassell, Stanmore, 1976, p. 131–47

McQuilton, John, 'Enlistment for the First World War in Rural Australia: The Case of North-eastern Victoria, 1914–1918', *Journal of the Australian War Memorial*, Issue 33, 2000

Martin, FX, '1916 – Myth, Fact and Mystery', *Studia Hibernica*, No. 7, 1967, pp. 1–124

Mosse, G, 'Shell-shock as Social Disease', *Journal of Contemporary History*, Vol. 35, No. 1, 2000, pp. 101–108

Newbury, George, 'Ex-AIF Members of the Royal Flying Corps', *Sabretache*, Vol. 37, No. 4, 1996, pp. 12–13.

Noymer, Andrew, 'Testing the Influenza-Tuberculosis Selective Mortality Hypothesis in Australia', Population Association of America Extended Abstract, 2005, p. 2 <http://paa2006.princeton.edu/download.aspx?submissionId=61313>

O'Brien, John, 'The Irish Revolutionary Movement and WM Hughes, 1916–1922' in Anne E O'Brien, *Studies in Irish, British and Australian Relations 1916–1963: Trade, Diplomacy and Politics*, Four Courts Press, Dublin, 2005

Officer, David, '"For God and for Ulster": The Ulsterman on the Somme', in Ian McBride, *History and Memory in Modern Ireland*, Cambridge University Press, Cambridge, 2001, pp. 160–83

Patterson, K David, and Pyle, Gerald F, 'The Geography and Mortality of the 1918 Influenza Pandemic', *Bulletin of the History of Medicine*, Vol. 65, No. 1, 1991, pp. 4–21

Perry, Nicholas, 'Nationality in the Irish Infantry Regiments in the First World War', *War & Society*, Vol. 12, No. 1, May 1994, pp. 65–95

Rae, Ruth, 'Jessie Tomlins: An Australian Army Nurse – World War One', unpublished PhD thesis, Department of Clinical Nursing, University of Sydney, 2000

—— 'Reading Between Unwritten Lines: Australian Army Nurses in India, 1916–19', *Journal of the Australian War Memorial*, May 2002

Regan, PM, 'Neglected Australians: Prisoners of War from the Western Front, 1916 to 1918', MA (Hons) thesis, ADFA, UNSW, 2005

Rice, Geoffrey W, and Palmer, Edwina, 'Pandemic Influenza in Japan, 1918–19: Mortality Patterns and Official Responses', *Journal of Japanese Studies*, Vol. 19, No. 2, 1993, pp. 389–420

Robson, LL, 'The Origin and Character of the First AIF, 1914–1918: Some Statistical Evidence', *Historical Studies*, Vol. 15, No. 61, 1973, pp. 737–49

—— '"Mad Ireland Made Me": The Arrest and General Court-martial of Captain the Reverend Father TJ O'Donnell, AIF 1919', *Tasmanian Historical Research Association Papers and Proceedings*, Vol. 34, No. 4, 1987, pp. 100–17

Spiers, EM, 'Army Organisation and Society in the Nineteenth Century', in Thomas Bartlett and Keith Jeffery, *A Military History of Ireland*, Cambridge University Press, Cambridge, 1996

Stevens, Anne, 'The Hughes Family and the Great War', a paper delivered to the Australian Catholic Historical Society, 10 September 2006

Taksa, Lucy, 'The Masked Disease: Oral History, Memory and the Influenza Pandemic 1918–19' in Kate Darien-Smith and Paula Hamilton, *Memory and History in Twentieth-Century Australia*, Oxford University Press, Oxford, 1994

Tobin, GM, 'The Sea-Divided Gael: A Study of the Irish Home Rule Movement in Victoria and New South Wales, 1880–1916', Australian National University, MA thesis, 1969

Townshend, Charles, 'Religion, War, and Identity in Ireland', *The Journal of Modern History*, Vol. 76, No. 4, Dec 2004, pp. 882–902

White, Richard, 'Motives for Joining Up: Self-sacrifice, Self-interest and Social class', *Journal of the Australian War Memorial*, Vol. 9, 1986, pp. 3–16

—— 'The Soldier as Tourist: The Australian Experience of the Great War', *War & Society*, Vol. 5, No. 1, 1987, pp. 63–77

—— 'Sun, Sand and Syphilis: Australian Soldiers and the Orient, Egypt 1914', *Australian Cultural History*, No. 9, 1990

—— 'Europe and the Six-bob-a-day Tourist: the Great War as a Grand Tour, or Getting Civilised', *Australian Studies*, No. 5, April 1991, pp. 122–39

Wieland, James, 'There and Back with the Anzacs: More Than Touring', *Journal of the Australian War Memorial*, No. 18, April 1991, pp. 49–56

—— '"What Do You Think of this Card?" Postcards to and from Australia during the First World War' in Anna Rutherford and James Wieland, *War: Australia's Creative Response*, Allen & Unwin, Sydney, 1997

Wilson, Graham, 'The Relevance of Miscellany Administrative, Support and Logistic Units of the AIF', *Sabretache*, Vol. 44, March 2003, pp. 53–72

INDEX